Mr Ma and Son

Lao She was born in 1899 to a poor Manchu family in Beijing. He left China in his mid-twenties to teach Chinese at the University of London, where he stayed for the next five years. *Mr Ma and Son*, serialized in 1929, was his third and final novel written during his London years. Lao She continued to teach and write upon his return to China, and became an established and respected author renowned for his humourist style. He committed suicide in Beijing in 1966, a few years after being labelled an anti-Maoist and counter-revolutionary by the Red Guards

William Dolby (1936–2015) was a translator from Chinese and Professor of Chinese at Edinburgh University.

Julia Lovell is the author of *Maoism: A Global History* and *The Opium War*, and the translator of *The Real Story of Ah Q and Other Tales of China: The Complete Fiction of Lu Xun* and *Monkey King: Journey to the West* (both published by Penguin Classics). She is professor of modern China at Birkbeck College, University of London, and writes about China for *The Guardian*, *Financial Times*, *The New York Times* and *The Economist*.

LAO SHE

Mr Ma and Son

Translated by William Dolby
With an Introduction by Julia Lovell

PENGUIN BOOKS

PENGUIN CLASSICS

UK | USA | Canada | Ireland | Australia
India | New Zealand | South Africa

Penguin Books is part of the Penguin Random House group of companies
whose addresses can be found at global.penguinrandomhouse.com.

First published in Chinese as *Er Ma* by *Fiction Monthly (Hsiao-shuo Yüeh-pao)* 1929
This edition first published by Penguin Group (Australia) in association
with Penguin (Beijing) Ltd 2013
Published in Penguin Classics 2022
001

Printed and bound in Great Britain by Clays Ltd, Elcograf S.p.A.

The authorized representative in the EEA is Penguin Random House Ireland,
Morrison Chambers, 32 Nassau Street, Dublin D02 YH68

A CIP catalogue record for this book is available from the British Library

ISBN: 978-0-241-57955-8

www.greenpenguin.co.uk

MIX
Paper from
responsible sources
FSC® C018179

Penguin Random House is committed to a
sustainable future for our business, our readers
and our planet. This book is made from Forest
Stewardship Council® certified paper.

CONTENTS

A NOTE ON

CHINESE USAGE

IN RECENT years the international community has increasingly used Pinyin as the standard Romanization method for Chinese characters. However, in this edition, the translator's original usage of the Wade-Giles Romanization system and other earlier systems has been retained.

INTRODUCTION

BETWEEN 1924 and 1929, a young, bespectacled Chinese man called Lao She made his way in London. Almost invariably dressed in a khaki suit and cardigan, he spent his days in the east of the city, around Finsbury Circus, teaching Chinese in the School of Oriental Studies to classes of missionaries, housewives and City boys (an ability to pay fees being the only test of admission), or studying in the school's library. In the evenings he dined on tough chops and stodgy puddings in his lower-middle-class lodgings before retiring to his room to nurse dyspepsia and work on his novels.

The average Briton of the 1920s – his brain fevered by the excoriations of Chinese villainy commonplace in popular culture – would have found Lao She's sedate lifestyle a grave disappointment. For at least a hundred years before Lao She's arrival in London, the British had eagerly consumed assassinations of the Chinese character in travelogues, pamphlets, newspapers, plays and (later) film.

Distrust of China and the Chinese had its origins at the end of the eighteenth century, when George III's requests for 'free trade' had been rebuffed by the patrician emperor Ch'ien-lung. In a fit of pique, the king's envoy – Lord Macartney – had denounced China as 'an old crazy first-rate man-of-war' fated to be 'dashed to pieces on the shore'. After Britain fought and won the Opium Wars in the nineteenth century to protect the contraband drugs trade between India and China, it came to regard China with contempt (for its military weakness) and then with guilty fear.

London's small but growing Chinese migrant community, it was assumed, must be plotting revenge for Britain's past misdeeds.

By the early 1900s, the Chinese master criminal (with his 'crafty yellow face twisted by a thin lipped grin', dreaming of world domination) had become a staple of children's publications. In 1911, 'The Chinese in England: A Growing National Problem' (a hack article distributed liberally around the Home Office) warned of 'a vast and convulsive Armageddon to determine who is to be the master of the world, the white or yellow man'. After World War One, cinemas, theatres, novels and tabloids chorused hysterical visions of the 'Yellow Peril' scheming to destroy respectable white society. The British 'knew all about Chinamen', one young traveller to China in the 1920s pronounced: 'They were cruel, wicked people.' In March 1929 alone, the chargé d'affaires at London's Chinese legation complained, five plays showing in the West End depicted Chinese people in 'a vicious and objectionable form'.

Lao She was a living refutation of the cartoon Chinaman that the British imperial imagination had created. Yet in other respects – in his cosmopolitan nationalism – he was typical of his generation; brutal childhood experiences had schooled him in the anti-imperialism rife among Chinese youth of the 1920s. In 1900, when Lao She was one, his father was burned to death while fighting Allied soldiers during their invasion of Beijing at the height of the Boxer Rebellion. Lao She narrowly escaped death himself when Western soldiers ransacked his parents' house. It is likely that he would have been killed had he not been asleep beneath an upturned trunk. The plunderers left, having contented themselves with bayoneting the family's elderly dog. His father's death at the hands of imperialist aggression condemned Lao She to a childhood of penury, as his mother struggled alone to feed, clothe and educate three children.

As he reached his early twenties, Lao She – again, like many educated young people of his age – participated in a broad national movement for cultural reform that drew on Western philosophy and literature in its quest to remake China. He worked at a school teaching an American-inspired curriculum ambitious to modernise China and its people. He converted to Christianity and learned English; he became devoted to foreign writers, including Shakespeare, Swift, Dickens and Conrad. He was appalled not only by rapacious imperialists, but also by China's own 'reactionary forces': the corrupt warlords ('hobgoblins and devils') who had carved the country up between themselves after the collapse of the last dynasty in 1912, blocking the creation of a functioning republic. In 1924, Lao She resolved to see England for himself, taking up a five-year teaching post in London's School of Oriental Studies. And it was there that he began his career as a writer of patriotic but complex fictions about contemporary China.

Mr Ma and Son – his third novel, completed in 1929 – was probably the first Chinese novel to confront directly British racism towards China. The tragicomedy of a father and son, whose attempts to settle in London are met by prejudice and chicanery, expresses the paradoxes of being an educated Chinese patriot in the early twentieth century. Within its pages, resentment of imperialist bigotry mixes with curiosity about the West and self-disgust for China's failure to stand up for itself in the world.

The novel is above all a passionate denunciation of the British sinophobia that Lao She knew well. 'All because,' the narrator tells us early on,

China's a weak nation, every crime under the sun is attributed to this community of hard-working Chinese, who are simply seeking their living in a strange and foreign land. If there were no more than twenty Chinese people dwelling in Chinatown, the accounts of the sensation-seekers would without fail magnify their number to five thousand. And every one of those five thousand yellow-faced demons will smoke opium, smuggle arms, commit murder – hiding the corpses under their bed – rape women – regardless of age – and commit an endless amount of crimes, all deserving, at the very least, gradual dismemberment and death by ten thousand slices of the sword. Authors, playwrights and screenwriters are prompt to base their pictures of the Chinese upon such rumours and reports. Then all who see the play, watch the film or read the novel – the young girls, the old ladies, the little children and the King of England – firmly imprint these quite unfounded pictures upon their memories.

Thus are the Chinese transformed into the most sinister, most foul, most loathsome and most degraded two-legged beasts on earth. In this twentieth century, people are judged according to their nation. The people of a powerful nation are people; the people of a weak nation are dogs.

The casual contempt that Mr Ma and his son, Ma Wei, experience in London was part of a much bigger phenomenon. The historian Gregor Benton suggests that anti-Chinese feeling in Europe, the US and other white settler societies, at its peak in the early twentieth century, 'was greater than that aimed at any other racial group' – perhaps even including Jewish communities. The Chinese remain a troublingly easy target in Britain today. After the 2004 Morecambe Bay tragedy, in which twenty-three Chinese immigrant labourers drowned when they were trapped by a rising tide, a Conservative MP called Ann Winterton told a 'joke' in a speech about a shark tired of eating tuna that decided instead to 'go to Morecambe Bay for a Chinese'. The right-wing television personality Jeremy Clarkson, expressing his scorn for synchronised swimming in early 2012, described it as 'Chinese women in hats, upside down, in a bit of water . . . You can see that sort of thing on Morecambe Beach. For free'.

In the hands of a less talented comic writer, *Mr Ma and Son*'s frequent attacks on British sinophobia – however justifiable – might become repetitive. But Lao She's pitch-perfect satire (testament, perhaps, to his reading of Dickens) keeps the novel sharp. The bigotry of the Mas' landlady, Mrs Wedderburn, is exposed with masterful archness: waiting to meet her Chinese tenants for the first time, 'she went and seated herself quietly in the drawing room, taking out a copy of De Quincey's *Confessions of an English Opium-Eater* to read, so that when her Chinese guests arrived, she'd have a suitable topic of conversation ready.' The Reverend Ely – the Mas' former pastor in Beijing and representative of the worst sort of ignorant missionary condescension towards China – is lampooned in a few well-chosen sentences.

> Leaving aside the fact that he spoke Chinese very poorly, he was a walking Chinese encyclopedia. And yes, he truly loved the Chinese. At midnight, if lying awake unable to sleep, he would invariably pray to God to hurry up and make China a British dominion. Eyes filled with hot tears, he would point out to God that if the Chinese were not taken in hand by the British, that vast mass of yellow-faced black-haired creatures would never achieve their rightful ascent to the pearly gates.

Lao She is harsher still on the reverend's terrifying wife, 'whose whole being was a command . . . On no account would Mrs Ely permit her children to play with Chinese children, and she only allowed them to speak the absolute minimum of indispensable Chinese words, such as those for "Bring tea!", "Go!", "One chicken!"' Finally, Lao She turns his attention to Mrs Ely's dreadful brother, Alexander, a bellowing former doyen of the China trade. As a young man, we learn, 'Alexander had possessed flawless manners and etiquette. But when he went to China, he felt that being polite to the Chinese wasn't worth the bother, and was forever bawling and glaring at the Chinese working under him, with the result that he was now past changing even if he'd wanted to.' Lao She's gruesome family portrait summarises the smug boorishness of the Western presence in China in the early twentieth century: the bumptious missionary, his barking memsahib and the crude, profiteering merchant.

The novel excels also in its crafting of dialogue (in his later career, Lao She would be celebrated for his plays as well as for his fiction). The Reverend Ely's first conversation with Mrs Wedderburn, trying to persuade her to take in the two Mas, is a study in hypocrisy, '"You and I are both Christians,"' Reverend Ely enjoins her, '"and we must fortify ourselves with the true spirit of

Christian humility in our efforts to provide some succour for this Chinaman and his son." Mrs Wedderburn stroked the long hair under the little dog's neck, and said nothing for a long while. In her mind she was feverishly working out exactly how much rent she could charge.'

A remarkable scene at the cemetery, when an old woman feigns tears in order to overcharge the elder Ma for flowers for his brother's grave, is rich in Dickensian humbug.

'The money,' she said suddenly, at the hysteric height of her lamentations, stretching out her hand. 'The money.'
 Without a word, Mr Ma fished out a ten-shilling note and handed it to her. At the sight of the note, she lifted her head and peered closely at Mr Ma.
 'Thank you. Oh, thank you. Yes, the first Chinaman buried here. Oh, yes. Oh, thank you. I do hope a few more Chinamen die and get buried here.'

Although understandably bitter at the treatment of the Chinese in London, Lao She is also disillusioned by the behaviour of these Chinese themselves. The elder Mr Ma is a comfort-loving buffoon fantasising about becoming an imperial official (a decade and a half after the empire collapsed in 1912). Not content with eating and sleeping away the capital he has inherited from his brother, Mr Ma is delighted to confirm the English in all their anti-Chinese prejudices, merely for the sake of ingratiating himself socially – even to the point of taking a part in a film demonising the Chinese as yobbish fiends. The younger Ma, although intelligent and idealistic, is paralysed by infatuation with his landlady's vulgar daughter, Mary, and Mao, the student campaigner, turns out to be a loud-mouthed chauvinist. The novel echoes with a disconsolate mockery: Lao She wants to find a utopian solution to the problems that face his beloved country, but is let down by his compatriots' lack of backbone. His abhorrence of British racism is shadowed by disappointment at the insufficiencies of his countrymen.

*

A curious thing happened to Lao She after the founding of the People's Republic of China in 1949. This independent-minded patriot tried to reinvent himself as a true believer in Communism. He approved the use of mob violence, shouting at public trials for class enemies to be beaten. He jived to the baroque twists and turns of policy, denouncing the Party's targets and cheering its favourites. He churned out essays on demand about the wonders of the Communist leadership and the need to subject literature to political ends. He attacked America as a fascist state in which capitalist magnates oppressed the people like serfs. A man well versed in the glories of classical Chinese poetry, he praised, perhaps sarcastically, propagandistic doggerel ('The east is red/ The sun rises/ China has produced a Mao') as 'exquisite . . . always exquisite'.

Yet his efforts to shed his old cosmopolitan scepticism were only partly successful. Despite the panegyrics that he wrote to the dictatorship of the proletariat after 1949, the satirist in him was not yet dead. He wrote plays that exposed the corruption of the Socialist bureaucracy, or implicitly compared censorship under the Communists with repression under their predecessors, the Nationalist government. And try as he might, he could not lose his internationalism. In May 1966 he received his last foreign visitors, a British couple called Roma and Stuart Gelder, in Beijing. At the very heart of Mao's brave new world, nostalgia for imperfect England welled up in him. He asked them to tell him about 'Piccadilly and Leicester Square and Hyde Park and St James, and the Green Park . . . Beijing is beautiful, but I shall always think of London in spring as one of the most attractive cities in the world. And the people – I received great kindness in England.'

In the summer of 1966, Mao began his last purge: the Great Proletarian Cultural Revolution. Originally devised as a means of removing Mao's enemies in the Party, the campaign rapidly expanded into a witch-hunt against anyone vaguely suspected of deviation from Mao's anti-Western, ultra-modernising dogmas.

Lao She, a writer steeped in the sights and sounds of old Beijing, and also associated with foreign places and books, was an early victim. One day in late August, Red Guards – Mao's teenage shock troops – dragged Lao She to their headquarters at the Confucian temple and there forced him to stand for hours in the dusty heat while they harangued him for his 'criminal, counter-revolutionary' past. Eventually they told him to return home: 'We will carry on with you tomorrow. That evening, Lao She left his courtyard house, made his way to the Lake of Great Peace north of the Forbidden City and drowned himself. (Some dispute the verdict of suicide, alleging instead that Red Guards beat Lao She to death then threw his body into the lake.)

Lao She's life and death share the melancholy ambivalence of *Mr Ma and Son*. Despite the titles and honours that the Communist government showered upon him – People's Artist, Vice-Chairman of the Writers' Union – and despite his professions of loyalty to the regime (it was rumoured that a copy of Mao's writings in the chairman's own calligraphy was found on Lao She's corpse), Lao She was incapable of allying himself simplistically with any single cause. But Mao's China was not a place in which a Chinese citizen could harbour doubts. Perhaps it was the realisation that his country would not tolerate his non-alignment – expressed some four decades earlier in *Mr Ma and Son* – that guided his final steps to the Lake of Great Peace.

— JULIA LOVELL

PART ONE

HEAD BOWED low, Ma Wei made towards Marble Arch. After a few paces, he found himself coming to a halt and standing dazedly, glancing from side to side. What at? Nothing. He was looking at nothing, and nothing was what he saw. Like runny fish-glue, his thoughts had gummed up his mind completely, leaving not even a crack for matters of the outside world to creep in, and depriving him of all mental control over his physical movements. His glance shot out and came straight back in, bringing nothing with it. He'd long since forgotten the world, and fiercely wished for it to be destroyed, and himself along with it. Right now! So why bother looking at anything any more?

He stood rooted there. It was a good two or three minutes before the scenes in front of him registered. 'Oh, yes,' he murmured to himself, 'it's Sunday today.'

On Sunday afternoons, there's always a bustle and stir around Marble Arch. All over the green lawns and gravel paths stand bunches of people. Workmen with red flags crane their necks, wave their big, rough, brown, hairy hands, and bellow at the top of their voices, like minor bursts of thunder, 'Down with the capitalists!', blaming the latter for all the ills of the world. Even last night's bad sleep was the capitalists' fault.

Right next to the red flag stands the Conservative Party with a Union Jack. The men there hold their heads very high, because they're wearing two-inch stiff collars and their necks have no chance whatsoever of slumping, and as they wave their big, fine,

3

lily-white, hairy hands, they're shouting with might and main, 'Down with the socialists!', 'Down with the unpatriotic traitors!', heaping blame for all the world's wickednesses on the heads of the workers. Even the fact that it rained this morning, and that the egg boiled for breakfast turned out to be a bad one, was all a consequence of the workers' troublemaking.

Right next to that group stands the Salvation Army flying a blue and red flag, bashing tambourines, blowing little pipes and singing hymns nonstop. The more ecstatically they praise the Lord, the more powerful grow the bellows of the workmen beneath the red flag. Sometimes, however, when they're filled with the Holy Spirit, they shudder all heaven and earth so much with their singing that our red-flag friends yonder are forced to resort to swearing, with words not found in any dictionary. Just next to the Salvation Army is a Catholic preacher, and, beyond him, any number of other groups with various causes to promote: independence for India, rapid elimination of China, the revival of the Liberal Party . . . and some groups not really promoting anything at all – just a crowd surrounding a wizened old man with a red beard, looking at one another and laughing.

Almost without exception, the men standing under the red flag have small clay pipes dangling from their mouths, and their hands stuck in their pockets, and they nod their heads in approval of whatever is uttered by their leader. The listeners who stand beneath the Union Jack mostly wear little black bowler hats. They nod their heads, smack their lips appreciatively and murmur, 'Hear, hear!', 'Absolutely!' Sometimes, when two of them simultaneously come out with the words 'Hear, hear!', they give each other a wink, and squeeze a tenth of a grin from one side of their mouths.

The smaller gatherings aren't as well ordered and spiritually united as these big ones. For the most part their primary raison d'être is discussion and disputation. Heads press together, like those of huddled sheep, as principles are bandied to and fro in subdued tones. In addition, there's a flock of fierce-browed fiery-eyed youths, caps rakishly askew, who circle round these little groups, cracking clever jokes and scattering quips, all for no other motive than to make everyone laugh and to show off their own smartness. Round the outside of the groups there are bands of three or four policemen, uniformly tall and each with the same big hands and feet, as if London policemen were all brothers.

Among these crowds of people, none stand out as much or excite as much admiration as the guardsmen in their red uniforms. Their backs are straighter than a drawing board, and the creases of their trousers are as stiff and straight as if held in place by a rod of iron. Every man jack of them is spick and span, with a perpetual smile on his face to display his snow-white incisors, and with his hair cut close to reveal a blue scalp. None are listening to anything – they're just standing outside the groups, placing themselves where they attract the most attention, and letting their gazes rove all around. After one's been standing there a few minutes, suddenly some girl's pale wrist will curl around his arm, and the pair will spin sharply on their heels and go off onto the grass for a cosy private chat together.

On the lawns, the various couples sit tête-à-tête, while others are lying with their arms around one another's necks. Beside them are isolated men, sitting with an evening paper in their hands. These men's eyes are not on the newspapers but on the girls' legs. Masses of fat dogs are gallivanting about in wild ecstasy for no apparent reason. The little children present, some clad in suits of white velvet and others dressed from chin to toe in red-velvet rompers, are haring to and fro over the grass, their chubby legs waddling and tottering about. Their nurses, sporting white bonnets, chase after these little gods, grumbling and complaining all the while.

Ma Wei stood there for an age. He lacked any enthusiasm for listening to the speeches, but couldn't think where else to go. He was twenty-one or twenty-two years old, fairly tall but very thin, with a sallow complexion and a narrow face that showed a resolute willpower. His long eyebrows swept slightly upwards, and the corners of his eyes turned up a bit too. These eyes were extraordinarily black and extraordinarily bright, and that combination rendered the whites of his eyeballs paler by contrast, so that his eyes avoided the dull, lifeless-looking monochrome that

5

paper dolls in funerary shops have. Apart from these eyes, with their constant hint of a smile, his face would have looked quite fearsome. His nose wasn't very prominent, but it seemed to stick out just the right distance because his cheeks weren't plump. And his lips curled upwards a bit, serving in conjunction with his twinkly, smiling eyes to create an overall geniality.

He wore a grey woollen suit under his black woollen overcoat. The suit was very elegantly tailored, but it had, like his face, become drab, lost a lot of its original glow. From his looks and from his age, you'd imagine he oughtn't really to be so miserable. But with his forehead screwed up in a frown and his back slightly bent, he was missing much of youth's sprightliness. Compare him with those red-uniformed young men arm in arm with the girls, and he'd certainly seem to come off rather the worse.

He absent-mindedly fished out a handkerchief and wiped it across his face. Then he stood there in a dumb blur, just as before.

The sun was setting. Red clouds turned the green-flannel grass a purplish colour. The workmen's red flag slowly transformed into a patch of congealed scarlet blood. And each minute the speakers' audiences grew smaller.

Ma Wei buried his hands in his overcoat pockets, walked on a few steps then came to a stop, leaning against the iron railing that bordered the grass. The red clouds to the west slowly dispelled the last lingering light of the sun. In the dying rays, the sky was covered layer by layer in a pale grape colour, like the frost-blue under the grey of a wood pigeon's plumage. The grey steadily deepened and imperceptibly merged with the wisps of ground mist, and swallowed all the colours into the dark. The workmen's flag, too, became a patch of black. And the trees in the distance quietly embraced the dusky shadows and slipped off into the night with them.

The people departed in ones and twos, until they'd almost all dispersed. The gas lamps all around were lit. Big red and green buses going round Marble Arch flashed past one after the other, looking like some long, moving rainbow. There was no one on the grass now. Only one black shadow leaning by the iron railing.

Li Tzu-jung had wriggled down into his bedclothes. As he stretched out a leg to the left, and shifted an arm to the right, in the half-asleep stage, he was dimly conscious of the doorbell ringing. His eyes got to the verge of opening, but then, in spite of himself, he let his head slip back onto the pillow. He could still recall hazily that something had been making a noise just now, but . . .

DRRRRR!

The doorbell rang again. He cracked open his only just-closed eyes, then once more lowered his ear back onto the pillow.

DRRRRRR!

'Who the hell can it be, calling here at midnight! Who is it?'

He propped himself up with one arm into a sitting position, and with the other hand pulled open the curtain a bit to look outside. Although there was a gas lamp in the street, the mist hung very thick, and it was so dark he couldn't see a thing.

DRRRRRRRRRR!

This time the bell rang a little longer and louder than the previous rings. Li Tzu-jung got up, felt around for his shoes and groped them on in the gloom. The ice-cold innersoles gave him a shock as they met the hot perspiration of his feet. He felt goosepimples all over. It was April, but the nights were still chilly. He fingered for the light and switched it on. Then, wrapping his overcoat around him, and holding his breath so as to make no sound, he tiptoed downstairs. The old lady on the ground floor had gone to bed, and if he was careless enough to wake her, he could bank on a good telling-off. He gently eased open the front door.

'Who is it?' he asked. His voice was as quiet as if he were frightened of scaring off the thick mist.

'Me.'

'Ma, old chap! What were you doing, banging away at the door-bell like that?'

Without a word, Ma Wei walked in and went upstairs. Li Tzu-jung softly pushed the front door to, and silently followed Ma Wei upstairs. Nearly at his room, he came to a halt and listened. There was no sound from downstairs.

That's all right, anyhow, he mused to himself. *The old lady hasn't*

7

woken up. Else I'd be getting a mixture of toast and curses for break-fast tomorrow.

The two of them went into Li's room. Ma Wei pulled off his overcoat, and laid it over the back of a chair. He still hadn't ut-tered a word.

'What's up, Ma, old lad?' asked Li Tzu-jung. 'Been having a row with the old man again?'

Ma Wei shook his head. In the light, his face looked more sombre and sallow than ever, and his brow was knit so tightly that it looked as if he were trying to squeeze drops of water from it. There was a faint blue round the rims of his eyes, and beads of sweat hung from the tip of his nose.

'What's up?' Li Tzu-jung asked again.

After what seemed an endless pause, Ma Wei gave a sigh. Then he licked his lips, and at last spoke. 'I'm done in, old Li. Can I stay here for the night?'

'Only one bed here, though,' said Li Tzu-jung with a grin, point-ing at it.

'This settee'll do me,' said Ma Wei. 'Just so I can get through the night. I'll be fit to sort things out for tomorrow then.'

'What's happening tomorrow?' asked Li Tzu-jung.

Ma Wei shook his head again. Li Tzu-jung knew old Ma's nature – if he wasn't of a mind to tell you something, there was nothing to be gained by asking him.

'Right then,' said Li Tzu-jung, scratching his head, still smiling. 'You go off to sleep in the bed, and I'll take care of this settee.' With these words, he spread a blanket over the seat. 'There's one thing, though,' he added. 'You'll have to clear out at the crack of dawn, so the old lady downstairs doesn't catch sight of you. Right then, off to sleep!'

'No, you sleep in the bed, Li, old chap. I'll stick it out on the settee for a while. That'll do me fine.' There was a speck of a smile on Ma Wei's face. 'I'll be off at dawn. Don't you worry.'

'Where will you be going?' Noticing Ma Wei's smile, Li Tzu-jung tried again to get him to speak. 'Tell me. Otherwise you can forget any hopes you've got of a good night's sleep. You've had a row with the old man, haven't you?'

'Need you ask?' Ma Wei yawned. 'I didn't mean to come around knocking; I'd intended to leave this evening but didn't, so I had to come and bother you.'

'Where is it you're going?' Seeing that Ma Wei was determined not to sleep in the bed, Li Tzu-jung was considerately wrapping both his own overcoat and his blanket round Ma Wei as he spoke. Then he switched off the light, and climbed back into bed.

'Germany, France . . . Can't say for sure.'

'On business for the old man?'

'My father's finished with me now.'

'Oh,' said Li Tzu-jung, and left it at that.

Neither of them said any more. It was extremely quiet out in the town, with nothing but the sound of trains and steamers whistling and hooting occasionally. The clock of the church in the next street chimed two o'clock.

'You're not cold, are you?'

'No, I'm not cold . . .'

As Li Tzu-jung drifted off to sleep, he was making resolutions: *Get up very early so as not to let Ma just run off. Get up, wash your face in cold water, and write a note telling the old lady downstairs you've got some urgent business, and won't be around for breakfast. Then go out with him. See him back home. That's what I'll do. Be best to go round to their shop, though. If he meets his father there, the two of them won't have a dust-up – too embarrassing in public. Common enough, rows between a father and son . . . He's a youngster, old Ma . . . Takes things too seriously . . .*

He went rambling on and on in his dreams with thoughts like these. The rumble-trundle of the little milk carts started up, and there was a growing noise of cars on the main road. Li Tzu-jung opened his eyes with a start. The sun was already beaming a thread of gold silk into the room through a crack in the curtain.

'Ma, old chap!'

Li's blanket and overcoat were both draped over the back of the settee. There was no sign of Ma Wei.

Li got up, opened the curtain, threw on his overcoat and stood vacantly by the window. Through it he could see the River Thames. There was nobody walking along the banks of the river yet, but all the small riverboats were astir. The saplings on the banks had newly popped their light-green leaves, and an airy mist hung around the treetops. Through the thinner patches of mist, the sun's rays shone on the tender leaves, making them sparkle faintly, like little pale-green pearls freshly fished from the water. Only a few of the smaller boats on the river had hoisted their sails, which fluttered like large butterflies in quest of flowers to settle on.

The early tide was rising, the ever-rolling crests of its waves inlaid with gold scales by the sunlight. The waves surged up, hustling each other on and on, rank upon rank, crowding the shining gold to pieces. And as the shattered stars of gilded light fell back again, the next wave stirred up a heap of small white flowers, white as the soft juice new-pressed from a dandelion stem.

The furthest of the boats drifted slowly off, the waves of the river ever surging on in pursuit, writhing and rolling as if some shining dragon were chasing the little butterfly away.

Li Tzu-jung stood staring dumbly at the small boats until they turned the bend in the river, then he finally pulled himself together, walked over to the other window, which faced onto the street, and opened it. Then he got a notion to tidy up the things on his writing table. There was a small bauble on the desk, flashing and sparkling, and under the little object there was a short note. He picked up both at the same time, with a chill feeling inside him. Walking slowly over to the settee, he sat down and carefully scrutinised the note. It was only a few words, written in pencil, the strokes all haywire, showing signs of its having been fumblingly written in the dark,

> *My dear friend Tzu-jung, I thank you. Please hand*
> *this little diamond ring to Miss Wedderburn.*

> *See you, Wei*

PART TWO

I

FOR OUR present story, we must now go back a year from the day when Ma Wei slipped away from Li Tzu-jung's place. The Reverend Ely was an old missionary who'd spread the Word for twenty years in China. He knew everything there was to know about China, from the ancient sage ruler and demigod Fu-hsi, who invented the divination hexagrams and Chinese characters, right up to President Yüan Shih-k'ai, who'd tried to set himself up as emperor in 1915. The latter endeavour the Reverend Ely greatly approved of.

Leaving aside the fact that he spoke Chinese very poorly, he was a walking Chinese encyclopedia. And yes, he truly loved the Chinese. At midnight, if lying awake unable to sleep, he would invariably pray to God to hurry up and make China a British dominion. Eyes filled with hot tears, he would point out to God that if the Chinese were not taken in hand by the British, that vast mass of yellow-faced black-haired creatures would never achieve their rightful ascent to the pearly gates.

Dawn till midnight, Oxford Street is always packed with women. Nearly all the shops along this central thoroughfare, apart from a few tobacconists, sell things for women, and no matter what urgent business women may have, they never manage to proceed along this street quicker than two steps per minute. On display in the shops are gaudy hats, leather shoes, little gloves, dainty handbags . . . all of which exert a peculiar fascination on the eyes, bodies and souls of women.

In Oxford Street the Reverend Ely's clerical composure and religious dignity would never fail to suffer a spectacular reduction. With each big stride of his feet onwards, his prominent nose would unerringly clash with some old lady's umbrella. As he retreated, stepping sharply backwards, his large leather shoes – which for some reason he always refused to sole with rubber – would almost always land squarely on the delicate little toes of some young miss. Then, as his hands clutched for his handkerchief, you can bet your life he'd jam an elbow into some lady's shopping basket. Every time he made the journey along this street, he'd need to change his shirt and replace a couple of sweat-soaked handkerchiefs when he got home. And during the journey, he'd inevitably utter the words 'Sorry!' and 'How careless of me!' at least one hundred times.

On this particular occasion, he succeeded at last in squeezing his way into Oxford Circus. There he drew a deep breath, and let out a pious 'Thank God!' His pace increased, and he forged ahead in an easterly direction, beads of perspiration drifting down like snowflakes through the white hair at his temples.

Although he was over sixty, the Reverend Ely's back was as straight as a writing brush. He possessed little hair but what he had was pure white. His cheeks were shaven to a glazed sheen, with no whiskers at all. Indeed, but for the wrinkles, his face would have resembled nothing more than a piece of china. His eyes were large, with a pair of tiny yellowy-brown eyeballs lolling in them, and above them hung two wedges of flesh, where twenty or thirty years earlier eyebrows must once have grown. Under the eyes dangled a little pair of spectacles. Because of his large nose, there was a full two inches between his eyes and the spectacles, which meant he generally looked at things over the top of the frames, rather than through the lenses. His lips were very thin, and dropped slightly at the ends. When he preached, with his eyes aimed unwaveringly across the rims of his glasses and his mouth yanked firmly down, he set the congregation's hearts trembling without a single word. In general, though, he was exceedingly affable; a missionary who can't be friendly will never get anywhere in this world. Reaching Museum Street, he veered left, cut across Torrington Square and entered Gordon Street.

There were quite a few Chinese people living in this street. The Chinese living in London can be divided into two classes: workmen and students. The workmen mostly live in East London, in the Chinatown that brings so much ignominy to the name of China. Those Germans, French and Americans who lack the money for a journey to the Orient always nose around Chinatown in quest of material for novels, travelogues or news articles. Chinatown has no outstanding tourist spots; nor is there anything of note to be observed in the behaviour of the workmen living there. The mere fact that Chinese people inhabit the place is enough to draw the voyeurs. And all because China's a weak nation, every crime under the sun is attributed to this community of hard-working Chinese, who are simply seeking their living in a strange and foreign land. If there were no more than twenty Chinese people dwelling in Chinatown, the accounts of the sensation-seekers would without fail magnify their number to five thousand. And every one of those five thousand yellow-faced demons will smoke opium, smuggle arms, commit murder – hiding the corpses under their bed – rape women – regardless of age – and commit an endless amount of crimes, all deserving, at the very least, gradual dismemberment and death by ten thousand slices of the sword. Authors, playwrights and screenwriters are prompt to base their pictures of the Chinese upon such rumours and reports. Then all who see the play, watch the film or read the novel – the young girls, the old ladies, the little children and the King of England – firmly imprint these quite unfounded pictures upon their memories.

Thus are the Chinese transformed into the most sinister, most foul, most loathsome and most degraded two-legged beasts on earth. In this twentieth century, people are judged according to their nation. The people of a powerful nation are people; the people of a weak nation are dogs.

People of China, open your eyes and take a look around. Yes, it's time you opened your eyes and straightened your backs. Unless, that is, you wish to be dogs forever.

The fine reputation enjoyed by Chinatown is quite naturally not very beneficial to the Chinese students in London. The bigger hotels, let alone respectable individual householders, just won't let rooms to Chinese people. Only the homes and small boarding houses behind the British Museum are prepared to. It's not that the people there have uncommonly kind hearts, I don't think. Rather, they realise there's money to be made, and so bring themselves to put on a good face and make the best of dealing with a bunch of yellow-faced monsters. A poultry merchant doesn't have to be a lover of chickens; when did English people ever let rooms to Chinese people out of a love for the Chinese?

Number 35, Gordon Street was the widowed Mrs Wedderburn's house. It wasn't very big, just a small three-storied building with a row of green railings at the front. Three white stone steps were scrubbed spotless, and the brass knocker on the red-painted door was polished sparkling-bright. On entering the house, you came first to the drawing room, behind which was a small dining room. If you passed through the dining room, took a turn, and descended some stairs, you'd come to a further three small rooms. Upstairs there were just another three rooms: one facing onto the street, and two at the back.

While still a good way off from the little red door, the Reverend Ely removed his hat. He wiped the perspiration from his face, adjusted his tie, and assured himself that he was all in order, before at last gingerly mounting the steps. He stood for a few moments at the top, then finally, with the delicate touch of a musical maestro playing a note on the piano, gave two or three raps on the door with the knocker.

A series of sharp, pattering footsteps fussed down hurriedly from upstairs, then the door opened a little gap, and half of Mrs Wedderburn's face revealed itself.

'Oh, Reverend Ely! How are you?'

She opened the door a little wider, and stretched out one of her small white hands to lightly brush the minister's arm. He allowed her to lead him in, hung his hat and overcoat on the hatstand in the hall, and followed her into the drawing room.

This room was kept very spick and span. Even the little brass nails on which the pictures hung seemed to wear a smile. A green carpet was spread across the centre of the room, bearing two rather narrow armchairs. By the window stood a small table, crowned with a Chinese porcelain vase containing two small white roses. Two oak chairs flanked the table, each set with a green velvet cushion. An oil painting hung on the wall, with a pair of matching plates on either side. Underneath the painting there was a small bookcase holding a few anthologies of poetry, a few novels and the like. Against the opposite wall there was a small piano with two or three photographs on its lid, and on its varnished stool lay a fat white Pekingese dog. As the dog saw the Reverend Ely come in, it swiftly leapt from its perch, and, shaking its head and wagging its tail, bounded wildly around in between the old clergyman's legs.

Mrs Wedderburn seated herself on the piano stool, and the little white dog jumped up into her lap. From there, head cocked to one side, it challenged the Reverend Ely to play. He sat down in an armchair, pushed his glasses higher, and launched into praises of the dog. This went on for some time before he at last dared broach the subject of his visit.

'Mrs Wedderburn,' he began diffidently, 'are the rooms upstairs still vacant?'

'Yes, indeed,' she said, one hand securing the dog, and the other passing an ashtray to her visitor.

'Are you still of a mind to rent them out?' he asked, filling his pipe.

'Well, yes. But only to the right kind of person,' she replied in a measured tone.

'I have two friends who urgently require accommodation. I can vouch for their absolute respectability.' He peered at her over the top of his spectacles, and pronounced the word 'absolute' with great clarity and vehemence. Then he paused a while, lowered his voice, and allowed himself a small smile. 'Two Chinese fellows.'

As he said 'Chinese', his voice was barely audible. 'Two extremely nice Chinese fellows.'

'Chinese?' said Mrs Wedderburn, her expression suddenly stiffening.

'Extremely nice Chinese,' he repeated, stealing a glance at her. 'I'm sorr—'

'I vouch for them! If anything goes amiss concerning them, you can refer it directly to me.' He didn't give Mrs Wedderburn time to finish, but continued quickly. 'I simply must find them some rooms, and there's no one else I can turn to. You must help me, Mrs Wedderburn. It's a young boy and his father. And the father, you will be glad to know, is a Christian. For the sake of our dear Lord, you must . . .' He deliberately let his words trail short, waiting to see whether the mention of our dear Lord would have any effect.

'But —' Mrs Wedderburn didn't seem overly concerned about the Lord, and her face showed signs of impatience.

Again he granted her no leeway to expand upon her protests. 'You see, there's nothing to stop you asking them for a somewhat higher rent. And should you find that they don't fit in, you can turn them out to look for lodgings elsewhere, and I won't give a —' Feeling that he was on the point of adding something not quite in accord with the spirit of the Holy Scripture, he took a puff of his pipe, and swallowed his words along with his smoke.

'My dear Reverend Ely,' said Mrs Wedderburn, rising to her feet, 'You know my feelings. There are quite a number of people in this street who make their fortunes by renting to foreigners, and I am almost the only one left who would rather earn less than do such a thing. I think I may justifiably feel proud of myself in that respect. Don't you think you could find a room elsewhere for them?'

'Don't you think I haven't looked?' said the Reverend Ely, looking most distressed. 'I have asked from door to door in Torrington Square and Gower Street, but none of the accommodation offered was suitable. I feel that your three nice little rooms would be ideal, most adequate for their purposes. Two of the rooms could serve as bedrooms, and the other as their study. It would be an excellent arrangement.'

She pulled out a dainty handkerchief from her pocket, and, quite unnecessarily, dabbed her lips. 'You can't imagine that I would allow two Chinese men to cook rats in my house?'

'The Chinese do not —' He was on the point of averring that the Chinese don't eat rats, but realised that to argue the toss would only further upset her, and might well jeopardise his chances of getting the rooms at all. So he hastily changed tack.

'Of course I shall enjoin them not to eat rats. Well, Mrs Wedderburn, I shan't waste any more of your time. Let us settle the matter like this: rent the rooms to them for a week, and if you don't approve of the way they conduct themselves, have them out. As for the rent, you charge whatever you deem fit. They couldn't go to a hotel. You never know with hotel people – most unreliable. You and I are both Christians, and we must fortify ourselves with the true spirit of Christian humility in our efforts to provide some succour for this Chinaman and his son.'

Mrs Wedderburn stroked the long hair under the little dog's neck, and said nothing for a long while. In her mind she was feverishly working out exactly how much rent she could charge, or whether she should put her foot down and refuse to accommodate two murderous, fire-raising, rat-eating Chinamen. Anxious not to leave the Reverend Ely just hanging there frozen in silence, she could only prevaricate, 'And they don't smoke opium?'

'No, no,' the Reverend Ely assured her.

She proceeded to pose countless questions based on the Chinese things she'd learnt from novels, films, plays and missionaries. She left no stone unturned. But when she'd exhausted all her questions, she suddenly regretted ever having asked them. Didn't her questions show quite clearly that she already intended letting the rooms to them?

'Thank you, Mrs Wedderburn,' said the Reverend Ely with a smile. 'We'll leave it at that then. Four pounds five shillings a week, and you'll see to their breakfast.'

'I can't allow them to use my bath.'

'No, of course not. I'll tell them they must go out for their baths.'

With these words, and without any further effort to entertain

LAO SHE

the little dog, the Reverend Ely snatched up his hat and coat, and hastened off. He rushed along the street, and when he found himself in a secluded spot, exclaimed in pent-up tones, 'Bloody hell! All for two Chinese chaps!'

II

MR MA and his son boarded a steamer at Shanghai, and sailed all the way to London in a vague daze. During the forty days they spent at sea, the elder Mr Ma struggled up on deck but once. The moment he stepped out of the cabin door, the ship lurched and he was thrown head over heels. Without a murmur, he steadied himself against the door and went back inside. The second time he came up, the ship was already in London, and completely motionless. Young Mr Ma did much better than his father, and only felt a little seasick as the boat passed Taiwan, experiencing no trouble at all after Hong Kong.

We've already observed young Mr Ma's appearance. There was a difference on board ship, though: he wasn't so thin then, and his brow wasn't so tightly furrowed. It was, moreover, his first trip abroad, and the first on an ocean liner, and everything struck him as fresh and exciting. As he leant on the ship's rail, with the sea breezes whisking up spray and blowing his face bright red, he felt almost as free as the waters of the ocean.

The elder Mr Ma was no more than fifty, at the most. But he deliberately conveyed an air of decrepitude, as if he felt that on attaining a certain age one should no longer lift a finger, but should pass the day in sleeping and eating, and eating and sleeping, without taking one more step than was necessary. He was shorter in stature than his son, but his face was much fuller. He had very bushy eyebrows and very rounded cheeks, and on his upper lip there was a little crescent-moon of a moustache, which in the last couple of years had acquired its first strands of white. His eyes were the same as Ma Wei's: big, bright and pleasant-looking. He always wore large tortoiseshell spectacles, but since he was neither short-sighted nor long-sighted, the sole purpose of the spectacles was to make him appear more dignified and venerable.

When he was young, Ma Tse-jen – such being the elder Ma's name – had studied at the Methodist Congregational Mission school. He managed to commit to memory quite a few English words and learn the grammatical rules off pat, but in exams he'd never get a mark of more than thirty-five per cent. Sometimes he would collar a fellow student who'd obtained a hundred per cent and drag him off to some quiet spot, saying, 'Come on! Let's do some swotting! You ask me fifty words, and I'll ask you fifty, so I can learn to be a genius like you, and get a hundred out of a hundred.'

Then he would proceed to wipe the floor with the hundred-per-cent hero, and leave him glaring helplessly. With the dictionary tucked under his arm, the hero muttered, 'A noun is . . .' and Ma would at one fell swoop obliterate all the humiliation of his thirty-five per cent.

Mr Ma was a Cantonese, but had lived in Peking since childhood. He would always tell people he was a native of Peking, until Mr Sun Yat-sen's Three Principles of the People rose in market value and the power of the National government in Canton expanded, whereupon he arranged for the words 'hailing from Canton' to be printed upon his visiting card.

After graduating from the Methodist school, he scrambled around trying to find himself a wife, and succeeded. With a bit of inherited property and Ma's elder brother helping them out, the couple were able to live a jolly little life in complete harmony together. Ma Tse-jen sat the exam for the Board Of Education several times, but his papers failed to shine, and he was obliged to forgo all hope of a position there. Through a connection, he tried to find work with foreign interests, but his English wasn't up to it. Someone recommended him for an English-teaching post in a school, but he wasn't going to pick up the cane and turn himself into a teacher – not him!

Out of work and at leisure, he would discreetly visit the singsong houses, returning home late, and sometimes the cosy couple would have a minor squabble. But fortunately, as it was night-time, no one else knew of it. On other occasions, he'd take his wife's gold ring, and slip off to pawn it. But he'd always cheerfully promise to buy her a new one once his elder brother sent some money. Half vexed and half smiling, she would give him a good telling-off. This only put him in even better spirits, and he would narrate the detailed saga of how he'd come to pawn the ring.

Three years after the marriage, Ma Wei was born. Ma Tse-jen wrote to his elder brother, asking for some money so that he might provide for the customary ceremony when the child reached the age of one month. The elder brother's money duly arrived, and thus it came about that on the thirtieth day after Ma Wei's entry into the world, all the family's relatives and friends partook of a gargantuan feast. Even the neighbour's pregnant dog came round for a gnaw of some pig's trotters and fish bones.

Now the young couple had taken a step up in society, having made the transition from 'man and wife' into 'parents'. Although they had no exact notion of parental duties, they were amply aware of their moral obligation to display their parental status and dignity. So Ma Tse-jen stopped shaving his upper lip, and in two or three months he had duly grown a small black moustache. As for Mrs Ma, to match her husband's dapper black moustache she took some of the rouge off her cheeks, leaving them only half as red.

A most tragic event occurred when Ma Wei was eight years old. Mrs Ma, possibly through overeating or catching a chill, suddenly departed this life. Ma Tse-jen was utterly grief-stricken. To be left with a child of eight and nobody to look after him didn't matter so much; what was worse was that Ma Tse-jen had been married to his wife all those years and never acquired her any noble titles through his own achievements. He'd let her down, and he felt thoroughly ashamed. He found huge teardrops coursing in one continuous stream down his cheeks, and he wept until his little moustache resembled the tiny sugar brush of the honey-twist vendors.

23

All the cost of the funeral was borne by his elder brother. What did it matter whose money it was? You have to give the deceased a decent send-off, after all. The Buddhist rituals of the reception, third requiem and the release of the flame-mouth, and the burial were held, with even more jolly revelry than had accompanied the first-month ceremony for Ma Wei.

Little by little, Mr Ma's grief lessened, and his relatives and friends all took it upon themselves to fix him up with another wife. He was himself already well disposed towards the idea, but it was certainly no easy matter to choose the girl. A second marriage isn't as easy to tackle as the first, and one had to take into account that he was by now somewhat of a connoisseur of women. Pretty ones had to be provided with an upkeep; then again, so did not so pretty ones, so why not have a pretty one? But there are so many pretty girls in this world! This remarrying really was a knotty problem.

On one occasion it nearly came off, but someone was an interfering gossip and said that Ma Tse-jen was a gluttonous idler without any prospects, and the girl's side beat a hasty retreat. On another occasion, when Ma was again on the verge of concluding the matter, somebody told him that the girl had three spots on her nose, like the 'long three' on a domino. That broke it up again – how could a man marry a girl with a long three on her nose!

There was another reason to be choosy. The only way in which Ma Tse-jen felt he could cast lustre upon his ancestors was by becoming a government official. He had an earnest devotion to the notion of being a mandarin, and would not lightly pass up any chance of becoming one. Remarriage offered one such opportunity, so it went without saying that you shouldn't rush it. Supposing he married the daughter of some senior government bigwig? Surely he'd be bound to obtain some post on the strength of his father-in-law? Or supposing . . . He did a lot of supposing, but, all said and done, supposing is mere supposition, and none of it transformed into reality.

'If I could marry the daughter of a government department head,' he would often say to others, 'I'd be able to bank on an assistant secretaryship at the very least.'

'If a department head's got a daughter, do you imagine she would ever marry you?' the others would reply.

It was soon pretty clear that there were no hopes of either marriage or a government career for Ma Tse-jen.

By the time Ma Wei had read three novels and completed his studies of the Four Books of the basic Confucian canon, Mr Ma sent him to a church school in the west end of the city, because Ma Wei could board there, which would save his father a lot of bother. When he'd nothing else to do, Mr Ma would often go to church to visit his son. There, the Reverend Ely's words gradually enlightened his heart, and he was in due course baptised into the Christian Church. In any case, he didn't have anything else to do, and taking a leisurely trip to the church not only proclaimed his piety but also cost him no money. After he'd been baptised, he stopped playing cards and drinking wine for a whole week, and bought an English-language bible bound in red leather for his son.

The year the Great War ended, Ma Tse-jen's elder brother had gone to London and opened a business selling curios. Every four or five months he would send his younger brother some money, and sometimes he would also entrust him with the task of searching for goods in Peking. Ma Tse-jen despised traders and merchants, but now and again he would bring himself to buy a few old vases and teacups and so on for his brother. Every time he went to Liu-li-ch'ang, where all the china potteries were, to purchase a few such things, he would pop round to a place by the Ch'ien-men Gate and drink a few cups of Shao-hsing wine, and eat some fried triangles.

And then Mr Ma's elder brother died in England. In his will he directed his brother to come to London to carry on the business.

By this time, the Reverend Ely had already been back in England for two or three years, and Mr Ma took up his English dictionary, and wrote him a long letter, asking him whether he should in fact come to England or not. The Reverend Ely was naturally tickled by the idea of a Chinese member of his church coming to England; he could show his parishioners that missionaries in China really did do more than eat food and collect money. He sent a reply to Mr Ma, telling him that he and his son absolutely must come to England.

So Mr Ma took his son to Shanghai and bought two first-class boat tickets, two Western-style suits, a few canisters of tea and a few other odds and ends. As the ship left port, the elder Mr Ma got the sense that his innards were all surging in unison. He took off his spectacles and lay down in his cabin, and barely moved an inch.

III

ALTHOUGH THE officials of the English Customs vary in appearance, you would never mistake them for those of any other profession. One of their eyes is always looking at you while the other is consulting some dog-eared book of regulations. A pencil, which is always a half-pencil, is stuck behind an ear. There are invariably a few wrinkles on their noses, contributing to the overall animation of their faces. Towards their fellow countrymen they are most affable, jesting and joking as they examine passports, and when it's a lady they encounter, they're particularly chatty. Towards foreigners, however, they have a different attitude. They straighten their shoulders, set their mouths and bring their imperial superiority to the fore. Sometimes, it's true, they go so far as to give the ghost of a smile. Which is certain to be followed by refusal to permit you to land. When they've examined the passports, they disembark with everyone else, and, rubbing their hands together, they inform you, 'Very cold weather.' They might even praise your English, assuring you that it's 'quite good'.

Mr Ma and son went through the passport examination. The elder Ma had several of his brother's documents at the ready, and young Mr Ma had an overseas-study certificate issued by the Chinese Board of Education, so they both passed through peacefully and uneventfully, without the slightest fuss. They proceeded to the medical examination. Neither of them had any internal complaints – no afflictions of the heart, liver, spleen, lungs or kidneys – so they passed yet another barrier without hindrance.

The doctor even smilingly gave them some advice, 'Eat a bit more beef while you're in England. Make you fitter still. England beat Germany in the last war, and we won because English soldiers eat beef every day.'

The medical examination concluded, father and son opened their suitcases for the contents to undergo inspection. Fortunately, as it happened, they'd brought neither opium nor weapons with them, and the only duty that they had to pay was fifteen pounds or so on a few silk gowns of the elder Ma's and a few canisters of tea. Mr Ma had no idea why he'd brought these treasures with him, nor why they should be dutiable. He puckered up his scrap of a moustache and quickly handed over the money, so as to be done with the matter. When he'd got through all the formalities, he was on the verge of fainting.

If I'd known it'd be so tiresome, he told himself, *I'd never for the life of me have let anything persuade me to go abroad!*

After leaving the dock, the pair boarded a train, where the elder Mr Ma plonked himself in a corner of a compartment, closed his eyes, and, without a word, went to sleep. Ma Wei sat by the window, looking out. The landscape was all ups and downs, no flatness anywhere. The high ridges of the land were green, and so were the dips, but the train was speeding along at such a pace that he couldn't pick out any details. All that he could see was the bumpy green fields, green wherever he looked. The train went faster and faster, and gradually the green land became one verdant undulation. The few cows and sheep in the distance seemed like coloured flowers floating on springtime waves.

The elder Mr Ma was still sleeping like a little Buddha. Suddenly his lips parted. Probably he was talking in his dreams.

And then the train began to slow, and presently arrived in London. There was a huge crowd on the platform.

'Hello, over there!' called the porters to the passengers as they pushed their trolleys. 'Hello there!' called a husband, flapping his hat, to his wife. On another platform a train was setting off, and the passengers were waving to the people waiting, some with handkerchiefs. Then, in a puff of black smoke, the train disappeared.

Newspaper vendors, flower vendors and cigarette vendors glided their trolleys about in solemn silence: English people approach buying and selling with the same air as they approach funerals.

Ma Wei gave his father a nudge to wake him up. Mr Ma gave a yawn, and was just about to drop off again when a young woman carrying a handbag walked out of the compartment. As she flung the door open, the corner of her handbag caught him bang on the nose. 'Sorry,' said the young woman, and Mr Ma rubbed his face, now thoroughly awake. Ma Wei scuffled wildly around to try to move their cases and other belongings. Just as they were about to step off the train, the Reverend Ely leapt on board. Forgoing the bother of shaking hands, he picked up the biggest of the cases and carried it out for them.

'You're here very promptly! Did you have any awkwardness at sea?' the Reverend Ely asked, turning to the Mas as he deposited the big case on the platform.

Bearing a small valise, Mr Ma sauntered off the train, with the grand air of a Ch'ing dynasty circuit intendant alighting from his great palanquin.

'How are you, Reverend Ely?' he said, placing his tiny box on the platform. 'How is Mrs Ely? How is Miss Ely? How —'

Without waiting for Mr Ma to complete his solicitous enquiries, the Reverend Ely snatched up the big case. 'Ma Wei! Move all the cases over here. Except for the valise. You can carry that. Bring all the rest this way.'

Ma Wei went with the Reverend Ely to move all the cases into the left-luggage room. The elder Mr Ma, carrying not a single thing, slowly swaggered over to join them.

The Reverend Ely filled in the left-luggage form at the counter, inquired as to the charge and turned to Mr Ma.

'Give the attendant the money,' he said, 'and the cases and other stuff will all be delivered to you this evening. That'll save you a lot of trouble, eh?'

Mr Ma handed over the money, but felt rather uneasy. 'The cases won't go astray, will they?'

'Of course not!' The Reverend Ely's little brown eyeballs rolled, and he gave Mr Ma a sharp glance. Then he asked Ma Wei, 'Are you hungry?'

'No, we're not,' the elder Ma hastily answered. It would be most unseemly for them to be clamouring for food the moment they arrived in England, and on top of that, it would make him feel guilty to have the Reverend Ely treat them to a meal.

'Come on, now!' the reverend said, 'Just a little something or other to eat. Not hungry? I don't believe it!'

Feeling that any further polite refusals might be out of place, Mr Ma said in an undertone in Chinese to Ma Wei: 'If he wishes to treat us, don't embarrass him by arguing.'

Father and son followed the Reverend Ely through the crowds and away from the platforms. Ma Wei stomped on ahead, with his back stiff as a coffin and his head held high, while Mr Ma, both arms swinging, and coat collar turned up a little at the back, swayed and swaggered behind him with a lordly gait. Outside the station, under a large glass-covered awning, there were two or three small cafes, into one of which the Reverend Ely led them. He selected a little table, and the three of them sat round it. Then he asked them what they'd like to eat. Mr Ma still insisted that he wasn't hungry, although his stomach was rumbling. Ma Wei lacked his father's politeness, but, having only just arrived, didn't know what to ask for.

The Reverend Ely perceived that it was no use asking them, so he put forward his own suggestion: 'How about this? A glass of beer and two ham sandwiches each.'

He stood up and marched over to the counter to place their order. Ma Wei got to his feet, and helped him bring the beer and sandwiches across. The elder Ma didn't lift a finger.

You spend money for food, he was saying to himself, *and you bloody well have to serve yourself? Pah!*

'I don't normally drink,' the Reverend Ely told them, picking up his glass, 'but when I'm meeting friends, I like to have a glass or two – join them in a spot of good cheer.'

When he'd drunk alcohol in China, he'd always done so in secret, to escape the notice of his parishioners, and thus he felt obliged to offer some excuse. He downed half the glass in one gulp, and began to laud the cleanliness of the cafe to Ma Wei, going on from there to extol the orderliness of England in general. 'There's good old England for you! Notice it, Ma Wei? Aha!' He chewed a mouthful of sandwich, grinding it meticulously between his false teeth before swallowing. 'Were you seasick, Ma Wei?'

'No, I didn't feel bad at all,' replied Ma Wei, 'but my father didn't surface the whole voyage.'

'What did I say! And you said you weren't hungry, Mr Ma! Ma Wei, go and ask for another glass of beer for your father. Oh, and bring me another glass, too. I like to have a drink, just for a spot of good cheer. Ah, Mr Ma, I've already found rooms for you, and I'll take you to them presently. You must have a proper rest.'

Ma Wei brought their beers over and the Reverend Ely gulped his down in one draught, for 'a spot of good cheer'. When all three had finished their meals, the Reverend Ely told Ma Wei to return the glasses and plates. Then he said to Mr Ma, 'A shilling each. No, that's not right – we two had an extra glass of beer, so it's a shilling for Ma Wei, and one and sixpence for you. Got any change?'

Never for the life of him had the elder Mr Ma foreseen such a sly blow. *A paltry matter of a few shillings,* he said to himself, *And you a clergyman! Some clergyman you are!* Trying to be funny, he made to pay the Reverend Ely's bill as well as their own.

'No, no! When in England, do as England does. Each pays our own way. No insisting, now!' said the clergyman.

As the three of them were walking out of the cafe, the reverend fished out six pennies, which he handed to Ma Wei. 'Off you go, and buy three tickets over there. Twopence each. British Museum. Three tickets. Can you manage it?'

Ma Wei took only two of the proffered pennies, produced a further four from his own pocket and went to buy the tickets at the little window indicated by the Reverend Ely. As he returned with the tickets, the Reverend Ely guffawed. 'Good lad! So now you've learnt how to buy tickets, eh?' he said, pulling out a little map. 'You, Ma Wei, I'll give you one of these. Look, here we are at Liverpool Street. D'you see this red line? Go four stops, then we'll be at Museum. This is the London Underground Central Line. Fix that in your mind, and don't forget it.'

And with that, the Reverend Ely led the two Mas down into the Tube.

IV

MR WEDDERBURN had been dead for ten years or more. All that he'd left Mrs Wedderburn was the small house and a few shares.

Mrs Wedderburn could never recall her husband without soaking two or three dainty handkerchiefs with her weeping. Apart from his not dying in battlefield glory or leaving her a fortune, she had no cause to complain of her late husband. But every time she wept over him, those two things would somehow always pop into her thoughts. Had he died in battle for his country, not only would he have been called a hero, but she herself would at least have obtained some financial compensation – not in the realm of millions, but enough for her to buy a few more hats and a few more pairs of silk stockings each year. And on Sundays, when she wasn't in the mood for going to church, she could buy a bottle of beer or something to drink.

It wasn't long after her husband's death that the Great War had broken out in Europe. She went to work, typing for a petrol company. She was patriotic but also pragmatic: they were short of staff everywhere, and she was able to earn some three pounds a week. As she typed, sudden memories of her husband would reawaken her bitter regrets. If only he'd lived long enough to do his utmost bit for the nation! And her tears would patter down in rhythm with her typewriter keys.

Had he still been living, he would have undoubtedly killed at least eight hundred German soldiers. And if he'd actually managed to capture the German Kaiser alive, they'd have promoted him to Field Marshal, wouldn't they? And then of course she'd be well appointed, wouldn't she? The more she pursued this train of thought, the more she detested the Germans. It was as though the Germans had purposely waited until her husband had died before starting the war, quite deliberately preventing Mr Wedderburn from earning his rightful heroic status. Kill the Germans! Wipe them out, every one of them!

As she mused along these lines, she bashed her typewriter with extra force, and when she'd finished the typing and took a look through it, she'd sometimes discover she'd punched several holes in the paper . . . and would have to retype the lot.

Young Miss Wedderburn was half her mother's age. On leaving school, she'd gone to a trade school for six months and learnt how to sell hats, how to display hats in shop windows, and how to put hats on the heads of ladies young and old. On leaving the trade school, she'd found a job in a milliner's shop in the City, where she earnt sixteen shillings a week.

During the war, Widow Wedderburn saved up a bit of money, and after the war she would only work when the petrol company was short of staff, so more often than not she was at home. While Miss Wedderburn was still at school, mother and daughter got on very well, and the daughter always did what her mother told her. But once Miss Wedderburn went to work in the milliner's shop, feelings between mother and daughter took a turn for the worse. Often they would argue hammer and tongs with each other.

'Botheration! Let her do what she likes! The mousy-haired wretch!' With tears in her eyes, Mrs Wedderburn would confide to her little dog, and, so saying, plant a kiss on the dog's small pointed ears. And the dog would sometimes spill a tear too, to keep her company.

The problem of mealtimes was the major source of their rows. For the mother, everything had to have its proper order and set time. But for the daughter, in her first job, the City was an exciting place. On the way home she'd look for a few minutes in the sweet-shop window, then stand looking for a few minutes in the dress-shop window, and then into the jeweller's window for another few minutes.

Just wait! she'd tell herself as she looked. *Some day I'll get a pay rise, and then I'll buy that box of crystallised fruit, and that green satin gown with the embroidered hem.*

The more she looked, the more she enjoyed looking and felt disinclined to move on, and she would completely forget about getting home. It wasn't just that she came back late, either: no sooner had she finished her tea than she'd pop on her hat, and fly out again like some little bird. Her mother knew full well that the girl was off for some fun with her boyfriend. Nothing remarkable about that. What riled her, though, was that when the young lady returned – well into the night – she would launch into an endless account of all that had happened while she'd been out with the boy. Then she'd discuss at length various problems concerning marriage and divorce, without the slightest inhibition.

Once when the Reverend Ely was paying a visit, Miss Wedderburn selected several long passages from a letter that her boyfriend had sent her and read them out to the old clergyman. He had in fact dropped by with the intention of persuading Miss Wedderburn to come to church on Sunday, but as soon as he heard the letter, he departed in haste.

In her youth, Mrs Wedderburn too had had boyfriends. But her ideals were vastly different from her daughter's. The hero she pictured was a man who could slay a tiger with one punch, and knock a wild elephant flat with a couple of kicks, but who, the moment he encountered a woman, would turn infinitely tender, suave and flatteringly attentive. The heroine, for her part, would always have a very slender waist and tiny hands, and be ever ready to swoon, at which time she'd unerringly fall into the hero's arms. Such a man was only permitted to utter a few fond words beneath the moonlight amid blossomy gardens, or to discreetly request a kiss in some private grove.

Miss Wedderburn's romantic ideals and experiences had nothing in common with such literary notions. The moment she opened her mouth, it was to tell her mother how, after she was married, she'd go driving with her husband at eighty miles an hour; how, if they didn't hit it off with one another, they'd go to court and get a divorce; and how she'd like to marry an Italian chef so she could go to Italy and find out for sure whether Mussolini had a moustache or not. Or else she'd marry a Russian, and go to have a look round Moscow, just to see whether Russian women's skirts went down past their knees, or whether they went bare-legged and didn't wear skirts at all.

Since Mrs Wedderburn's husband had died, she had occasionally thought of marrying again. But the greatest obstacle to remarriage was the economic problem. She'd never involve herself with any man who lacked a secure and steady income. She'd never mentioned this to anyone, however, as the notion of love was a private one, to be mused over in secrecy. And even if she thought about the economics of it all, she still wanted to believe in true love.

'Go on, then! Be off with you and marry your Russian blighter!' would say Mrs Wedderburn to her daughter, losing patience.

'Yes, that's what I'll do! Furs are bound to be cheap in Moscow. I'll get him to buy me a dozen fur coats, and I'll wear a different one each day. Wouldn't I look beautiful, eh? Eh, Mum?'

Mrs Wedderburn, without a word, would pick up her little dog and go off to bed.

It wasn't only in the matter of love that Miss Wedderburn's opinions differed from her mother's, for the same rift existed with regard to clothes, hats and jewellery. The daughter's aesthetic viewpoint held that, whatever it was, the newer the better, and that as long as a thing was new, it was good. Any further enquiries as to whether it was beautiful were unnecessary. The shorter the skirt, the more fashionable the hat, the better it was. In her view, at least a foot should be cut off all her mother's skirts, and not only were the brims of her mother's hats absurdly broad, but the long-petalled flowers on them were utterly ludicrous. Her mother always talked about the quality of the material, while the daughter was more interested in the latest style that had come out in Paris. They would go at it till they talked themselves to a standstill.

'If you buy another of those little eggshell hats,' the mother would say, 'you needn't eat at the same table as me any more!'

'And if you go on wearing that green country-bumpkin coat,' the daughter would say, 'I'm not going shopping with you any more!'

Mother and daughter differed in looks as well. Mrs Wedderburn's face was very long, slipping away as it descended to leave only a tiny triangle when it reached the chin. Her light-brown wavy hair, which already bore a few streaks of white, was curled up into two buns and secured on the top of her head. She had brown eyes, a small pointed nose and a small thin-lipped mouth, which revealed something of the prettiness of her younger days when she smiled. She wasn't very tall, and when she wore broad-brimmed hats, she looked even shorter.

When Miss Wedderburn stood next to her mother, you could see that she was the taller by a head. And if you compared her large feet with the slim, tapering ones of her mother, you'd think they were unrelated. Because the young lady wanted to make her feet look dainty, she'd always buy shoes that were a size too small, and when she laced them up, two dumplings of flesh would bulge out. The mother walked like a bantam cock pecking at grains of rice, tripping prettily about, whereas the daughter pounded along with a mountainous, booming tread, making even the flesh of her cheeks quiver. Glancing upwards from her feet, you saw a pair of long legs. Her skirt just made it to the top of her knees, so her stockings were on show all year round. As she always wore narrow skirts and walked fast, her gait was invariably a cross between a run and a wriggle. And while her left hand clasped her umbrella and handbag, her right arm was obliged to swing rather stiffly, with the wrist brushing against her hip in little semicircles, to and fro. To make her hat look nice she had to tuck her head in a bit (otherwise her neck would seem too long). The cumulative effect was that she resembled a little round jug with a short neck and a lid on top.

As for her face, her cheeks were plump, with two dimples in them, and even when she wasn't smiling the dimples were there, like two bubbles about to burst. Her mousy-brown hair was cut like a man's, and her blue eyes sparkled merrily, the mischievousness and candour of her whole being radiating from those orbs of blue. With her flushed cheeks and bright eyes, she was a tender, rosy apple new-picked from the tree. Her lips were curled upwards a little at the corners, and forever in motion.

Mrs Wedderburn considered her daughter both lovable and irritating. 'Look at your legs!' she'd often say. 'Just how short are your skirts going to get?'

Her daughter's dimples would crease as she smoothed her short hair. 'But Mum,' she'd say, 'everyone's got them like this!'

V

MRS WEDDERBURN was busy all morning, tidying the three upstairs rooms so that everything would be in order. She had a piece of green silk cloth round her head to keep her hair from running wild, and her sleeves were rolled up to above her elbows, revealing the fine blue veins of her arms, like the mountain ranges on old-style Chinese maps. With an apron tied around her waist over her housecoat, she washed all the tables, moved the carpets down into the back garden and gave them a thorough beating, polished the floors, and, after wiping the bulbs of the lights, changed the lampshades for two new, green satin ones.

When she'd finished she stood clasping her hands, and surveyed the scene around her. The pink curtains in the study, she realised, didn't quite match the blue-patterned wallpaper, so she hurried downstairs to her own room, took down the curtains there, which had fine white patterns on a light-blue background, and put them up in the study instead of the pink ones. The curtains changed, she sat on a chair, placed her hands on her knees and breathed a gentle sigh. Then she called Napoleon – that chubby little white dog – took him on her lap, and rested her delicate pointed nose on Napoleon's head.

'Just look!' she said. 'Isn't the floor shiny now I've polished it? And don't the curtains look pretty?'

Napoleon shook his head, from which Mrs Wedderburn immediately deduced that even dogs had an aversion to Chinese people, and she rather regretted what she'd agreed to. Grumbling away to herself, she gathered the little dog in her arms and went downstairs for her lunch.

After eating, Mrs Wedderburn feverishly set about making herself look presentable as she prepared to welcome her guests. She combed her hair again, rubbed some powder into her cheeks and put on her favourite blue crepe-silk jacket with the fox-fur collar – English women wear furs regardless of the season. She despised Chinamen from the depths of her heart, but having consented to rent them her rooms, she had to go through the proper procedures. At last, when she'd finished getting ready, she went and seated herself quietly in the drawing room, taking out a copy of De Quincey's *Confessions of an English Opium-Eater* to read, so that when her Chinese guests arrived, she'd have a suitable topic of conversation ready.

When they were almost at Mrs Wedderburn's door, the Reverend Ely said to the elder Mr Ma, 'When you meet the landlady, if she extends her hand to you, you may shake hands. Otherwise it will be quite sufficient to just nod to her. That's our etiquette. Don't mind me telling you, eh?'

Mr Ma not only didn't object to the Reverend Ely's briefing, but even voiced a 'thank you'.

Mrs Wedderburn had already seen the trio by the time they came to a halt outside the door. She hastily brought out her little mirror once more and took a look at herself, before gently pressing the hair behind her ears into place with her fingers. Then, after waiting till she heard a knock, she came to the door holding Napoleon, and opened it. Napoleon pricked up his ears at the sight of the visitors and let out two yaps.

'Naughty! You mustn't!' Mrs Wedderburn said, and the little dog rolled its eyes, drooped its ears and fell silent.

Holding the dog in one arm, she used her free arm to shake hands with the Reverend Ely. He introduced the Mas to her, and, head held stiffly erect, she merely let her eyebrows and chin dip by way of greeting. The elder Mr Ma gave her a profound bow, but before he'd straightened up, she'd already marched into the drawing room. Ma Wei, carrying the valise, glared at her from behind the Reverend Ely's back. The three visitors put their hats and things in the hall, then together entered the drawing room. With her little finger, Mrs Wedderburn indicated the two arm-chairs, inviting the Reverend Ely and Mr Ma to sit down. Then she told Ma Wei to sit on the chair next to the small table, while she herself sat on the stool in front of the piano.

Not waiting for anyone else to open the conversation, the Reverend Ely launched into praises of Napoleon. Mrs Wedderburn began to narrate the dog's life story. The clergyman greeted with approval every sentence that she uttered, although he'd heard the story more than twenty times before.

While she was telling the dog's history, Mrs Wedderburn was watching father and son from the corners of her eyes. *These two Chinamen don't look as ugly as they do in the films,* she thought. And she couldn't help feeling rather suspicious; perhaps they weren't real Chinese? If they weren't Chinese, then what . . . ?

The elder Mr Ma was sitting with all the formal correctness of a minor government official in the presence of his superior man-darin. His back formed a right angle with the cushion of his chair, and his two hands were placed firmly upon his knees. Young Ma, in imitation of the Reverend Ely, had his legs crossed, and his left hand stuck in his trouser pocket. Already Ma Wei had taken in all the objects around him in the room. And when the Reverend Ely smiled, he likewise pursed his lips in the motions of a smile.

'Shall we go and have a look upstairs, Reverend Ely?' asked Mrs Wedderburn, having at last come to a point of conclusion in her dog story. 'Mr Ma?'

Seeing the Reverend Ely stand up, the elder Ma rose stiffly to his feet. Young Mr Ma, not waiting for any social awkwardness, quickly got up and opened the door for Mrs Wedderburn.

When they arrived upstairs, Mrs Wedderburn showed them each room and where they might put their things. After everything she said, the Reverend Ely exclaimed 'Splendid!' All the elder Mr Ma wanted to do was lie down and have a rest. He nodded at the landlady every time the Reverend Ely said 'Splendid!', but in actual fact took in not a word of what she said. Nor did he spare a glance for any of the rooms, just telling himself, *Anyway, all that matter's is there's somewhere for us to sleep. Why bother about anything else?*

One thing rather disturbed him: there seemed to be too few blankets on the beds. He went over and felt them. There were only two. *Surely that'll be too cold!* he said to himself. When in Peking he always had two thick quilts, and wore a fur jacket and cotton-wadded trousers on top of that.

After they'd looked at all the rooms, the Reverend Ely, realising that Mr Ma hadn't said a thing, hurriedly told Mrs Wedderburn, 'Splendid! I was telling them on the way here, "You'll see that you couldn't have found rooms to match Mrs Wedderburn's in the whole of London, take my word!" Eh, Mr Ma?' His fawny-brown eyes riveted themselves on Mr Ma. 'Now d'you believe me?'

Mr Ma gave a smile and said nothing. Ma Wei got the Reverend Ely's message, and hastily assured Mrs Wedderburn, 'The rooms are excellent. Thank you.'

They all went downstairs, and seated themselves in the drawing room once more. While she still had the Reverend Ely present, Mrs Wedderburn clarified all matters concerning rent, mealtimes, when the door was locked in the evening and all the other rules, stipulating everything very precisely. Whenever she paused or took a breath, and whether he'd heard what she'd been saying or not, the Reverend Ely would chime in with a 'Splendid!', like the drummer in a band coming in with a roll on his snare when the trumpets pause. The elder Mr Ma uttered not a peep, and was saying to himself, *What a mass of rules! Marry a foreign woman and I bet she'd be on your tail all the time, like a cat after a mouse.*

When Mrs Wedderburn had finished, the Reverend Ely stood up. 'Mrs Wedderburn,' he said, 'we can't thank you enough. You must come round to my house some day for tea, and have a good long chat with Mrs Ely. Can you manage it?'

Something clicked in Mr Ma's mind as he heard the clergyman mention tea. 'What about our tea?' he asked Ma Wei in an undertone. Ma Wei replied that there were only two canisters in the valise, and that the rest were all in the big trunks.

'Well, you've got the valise with you, haven't you?' asked Mr Ma.

Ma Wei assured him it was in the hallway.

'Go and fetch it!' said Mr Ma softly. Excusing himself, Ma Wei stepped into the hall, returning quickly with the valise. He opened it and handed the two canisters of tea to his father. Mr Ma, a canister in each hand, addressed the rest of the company. 'Some tea we've brought with us from Peking. One canister for the Reverend Ely, and one for Mrs Wedderburn, as small tokens of our respect.'

He handed one canister to the Reverend Ely, and placed the other on the piano. The Confucian philosopher Mencius says that 'Men and women should not touch when giving or receiving', so there was no question of his personally placing it in Mrs Wedderburn's hands.

The Reverend Ely, having been in China for many years, knew the ways of the Chinese, so as he took the canister he said to Mrs Wedderburn, 'Here's some good tea, I'll be bound!'

Mrs Wedderburn hurriedly deposited Napoleon on the stool, and picked up her own canister. Her dainty mouth opening slightly, she peered closely at the tiny Chinese letters on the canister, with its trademark phrase, 'The Moon Fairy Flees to the Moon'.

'How quaint! How quaint!' she said, for the first time looking directly at Mr Ma and not from the corners of her eyes. 'Can I take something so nice without paying you anything for it? Is it really for me, Mr Ma?'

'Of course it is!' said Mr Ma, twitching his scrap of moustache.

'Oh, thank you, Mr Ma!'

The Reverend Ely asked her for a piece of paper to wrap his canister of tea in. 'Mrs Wedderburn's frightfully fond of China tea,' he said as he wrapped it. 'After drinking your tea, Mr Ma, I feel sure that she will include you in her prayers to our Lord.'

As he finished wrapping, he suddenly froze, his fawny-brown eyes slowly widening. To accept the tea, he thought to himself, and not take the Mas out for a spot of sightseeing . . . Well, it didn't seem very nice. He really ought to put on a good show in front of Mrs Wedderburn, let her see what a uniquely virtuous lot missionaries are. Nonetheless, he didn't relish the idea of walking around town with two Chinamen.

'Mr Ma,' said the Reverend Ely, 'I shall see you tomorrow. I'll take you to have a look at London. Get up early in the morning.'

With those words, he left the room, sticking the canister inside his coat and holding it wedged under his arm. If he walked along carrying a round, wrapped object in his hand, people might suspect it to be a bottle of beer. In every aspect of his conduct, a clergyman had to live up to the Lord's expectations.

Mr Ma wanted to see him off, but the Reverend Ely shook his head at him over Mrs Wedderburn's shoulder.

Mrs Wedderburn saw the Reverend Ely out, and the two of them remained standing an age, talking outside the door. Now Mr Ma realised what the Reverend Ely had meant by shaking his head.

These foreign devils are subtle, and no mistake! he said to himself. *You have to watch for their tricks.*

'What do you think of the two Chinamen then?' asked the Reverend Ely at the door.

'Quite all right, really,' replied Mrs Wedderburn. 'The elder one's very presentable. And to think of it, all that tea!'

Meanwhile, indoors, Ma Wei was saying to his father, 'Just now when the Reverend Ely was praising the rooms, why didn't you say a thing? Haven't you noticed that with foreigners, especially with women, you have to flatter them? If you don't say nice things about them, they don't take it at all well.'

'If one knows inside one's heart whether something is good or not, that's quite sufficient! What's the point of mentioning it?' The elder Ma put Ma Wei sharply in his place, then pulled out a Szechwan-silk handkerchief, and, with the air of one dusting a mandarin's green leather boots, gave his shoes a polish.

VI

IT WAS typical April weather: bright one moment, dull the next, then suddenly there'd be a shower of rain, and, while the raindrops were still falling, the sun would come out again. Tiny pearls of water hung in a string across the window frame of the house at Gordon Street, and as soon as the sun hit them they would slowly disappear in wisps of white vapour. Outside the house there were tall poplar trees that had just thrown forth their spring leaves. After the rain, their trunks were as moist and sleek as the legs of a freshly bathed elephant: slippery, shiny and very grey.

Although the elder Mr Ma had already had forty days' sleep at sea, he was still extremely tired. When he lay down in his bed that first night, he could feel the bedding rise up and down, and seemed, too, to hear the shush-shushing of the sea. He woke up a good few times during the night. It was lacquer-black in the room, and in his soporific state he couldn't remember where he was. On the ship? In Peking? Shanghai? He felt utterly lost and helpless, and when he'd properly woken up, and recalled that he was in London, he experienced quite another feeling, that of inexpressible gloom and melancholy. His friends in Peking, the meat dumplings of the Great Beauty Restaurant, the K'un-ch'ü opera of the Extending Virtue Theatre, his late wife, his elder brother . . . Shanghai . . . He recalled them all, and the next moment forgot them all again, but from the corners of his eyes two big teardrops escaped.

Parting's sorrows and meeting's delights. Such is life. Make the best of things wherever you are, the elder Ma comforted himself. *When Ma Wei's finished his studies, I'll be able to enjoy a few more days' happiness, live as a gentleman for a bit.*

The very thought of it made him feel cheerful. He stretched out his sweaty palm and brought it up over the blanket to smooth his minute moustache. Then he lifted his head from the pillow a bit, to hear if there was any sound from next door. There was nothing.

'Young and strong, you can eat like a hog and sleep like a log! He'll do well, that boy of mine,' he mumbled to himself, and slowly closed his eyes once more.

He kept on waking up and dozing off, and it wasn't until the sun had risen that he at last shifted into a steady sleep. He seemed to hear Ma Wei getting up, and half heard the sounds of traffic in the street, but didn't open his eyes. It was probably about half past seven when there came two gentle taps on the door, followed by Mrs Wedderburn's voice: 'Hot water, Mr Ma!'

'Thank you, er . . . ugh . . .' He went off to sleep again.

Ma Wei was up before seven o'clock. He was set on taking a look round London, and was so impatient to do so that nothing could have induced him to carry on sleeping. What's more, he'd met Miss Wedderburn yesterday, but he couldn't very well chat to her while his father was around. Breakfast this morning would give him his chance, as his father was bound to sleep in.

He rose, and gently drew open the curtains. The rain had just stopped, and the rays of the sun were like yellow bees bearing the sweet honey of springtime, crawling along Ma Wei's hand as they came through the window. He donned the Western-style patterned dressing-gown that he'd bought in Shanghai, and silently waited for Mrs Wedderburn to bring the hot water so that he could shave.

He'd acquired the habit of shaving only while on board ship. Before embarking, he'd bought a safety razor in the Sincere Department Store in Shanghai. On the ship each morning, before anyone else had risen, he'd hurry to the bathroom for a careful shave. There was a grand total of ten or so moderately thick whiskers on his face, but after Ma Wei had been shaving for a week, the stubble was terribly prickly if he skipped a day. Looking at himself in the mirror after shaving, he felt that his face looked extraordinarily virile and vital, with a certain intrepid air to it. Film heroes would often get involved in a fight in the middle of shaving, with soap lathered all over their faces, and no sooner have finished the fight than they were back shaving, with nary a tremble. Or sometimes when they'd won the fight, they'd take a nearby young lady in their arms and kiss her, leaving soap-lather all over her cheek. Shaving, viewed in such a light, wasn't a mere habit but in fact the embodiment of a variety of subtle emotional implications.

At long last the hot water arrived, and he hastily rinsed his mouth and shaved. After combing his hair and washing, he gave his suit a meticulous brushing-down. Once fully dressed, he thought to go downstairs, but was afraid to head down too early in case it incurred him the landlady's displeasure. He eased open the door and peeped out. A little steam was still curling up from the white enamel bowl outside his father's door. From downstairs he could hear very clearly the voices of Mrs Wedderburn and her daughter. The daughter's voice sounded especially clear, with an exciting note to it, and every word he heard set his heart trembling like a rain-pattered petal.

The bell rang downstairs. He guessed it must mean that breakfast was ready. He took another look at himself in the mirror: his eyebrows didn't shoot up at the tips, they curved down now, almost down past his eyes. Adjusting his tie again, he pulled his lapels straight, and finally clomped downstairs.

Mrs Wedderburn and her daughter usually ate breakfast in the kitchen, but because of Mr Ma and son's arrival, they now ate in the dining room. As Ma Wei entered the room, Mrs Wedderburn was still in the kitchen, and only Miss Wedderburn was there, sitting at the table with a newspaper in her hands, studying the latest fashion illustrations. Seeing Ma Wei come in, she gave a 'Hello', without raising her head, and carried on reading her newspaper.

She wore just a sleeveless green dress, which left her neck and arms on display. Her well-fleshed white arms were like a pair of elephant tusks, an ivory of mysterious composition: silk-floss soft, supple and lustrous, and emanating some fragrant scent.

Ma Wei straightened his shoulders. 'Quite nice weather, isn't it?' he said.

'Cold.' She squeezed the word from her deep-red lips, still not looking at him. Mrs Wedderburn came in bearing a tea tray.

'What about your father?' she asked Ma Wei.

'I'm afraid he isn't up yet,' said Ma Wei in a subdued voice.

She said nothing, but her face dropped like a blind. She sat down opposite her daughter, and poured tea for them. She'd made a special point of using the tea leaves that Mr Ma had given her, and but for the sake of the tea, she would have exploded. All the same, as she poured the tea, she did remark in a quiet voice, 'I really can't make breakfast twice.'

'Whose fault is it if you let the rooms to Chinamen!' said Miss Wedderburn, flinging the newspaper away and cocking her head to one side.

Ma Wei blushed deeply, and he thought of getting up and marching out. He frowned, but didn't get to his feet.

Miss Wedderburn looked at him with a smile, as if to say, 'Cringing cowards, the Chinese. They can't even get properly angry.'

Mrs Wedderburn gave her daughter a look, and hastily passed Ma Wei a cup of tea. 'Lovely tea. The Chinese are great tea drinkers, aren't they?' she said.

'Yes, they are.' Ma Wei nodded.

Mrs Wedderburn took a mouthful of toast, and was just about to drink her cup of tea, when Miss Wedderburn tugged at her and exclaimed, 'Watch out, there might be poison in it!'

She pronounced these words so earnestly, as if Ma Wei weren't present, as if it were an absolute, unshakable truth, beyond all shadow of doubt, that the Chinese were poisoners. Her lips shuddered spontaneously and her reaction was utterly natural, with no thought of offending anyone nor any attempt to be smart. It didn't seem to occur to her that she could be insulting Ma Wei. In every play in which a Chinese person appeared, he was sure to poison someone. It was the same in all films and novels as well.

Miss Wedderburn's anxiety was drawn from a long creative history, and had something about it that was akin to religious faith. Muslims don't eat pork, and, as everyone knows, the Chinese poison people. Yes, a kind of faith.

Ma Wei smiled. He picked up his cup of tea, and took a sip without saying a word. He knew what she meant, because he'd read English novels about the Chinese murdering people with poison.

Mrs Wedderburn, embarrassed, sipped some tea through her delicate lips, and then peppered Ma Wei with questions: How many different kinds of China tea were there, whereabouts in China was it produced, what was the name of the tea that they were now drinking, and how was it manufactured?

Swallowing his indignation, Ma Wei gave her the first answers that came into his head, telling her that what they were now drinking was called Hsiang P'ien, or 'fragrant flakes'.

Mrs Wedderburn asked him to say it again, then mumbled 'Hang Ben', and asked Ma Wei whether she'd got it right.

Meanwhile, Miss Wedderburn was thinking of a film she'd seen a few days earlier. An English hero had fought and killed some fifteen yellow-faced, noseless Chinese men in a marvellous fight. She'd clapped her plump hands so hard they'd looked like a couple of beetroots plunged in boiling water. As she drifted off into such reminiscences, she clenched one hand under the table, waving her fist in Ma Wei's direction, and saying to herself, *It's not only English men who can beat you cringing cowards – even our heroines could knock you head over heels!*

At the same time, she thought of her boyfriend, John, who was now in China. What a fine figure John would cut in Shanghai. With those two big fists of his, he could surely thump dead a few dozen Chinese with one punch. Her blue eyes shone ever more radiantly. John was the hero of her heart. In his letter he'd written: *I've joined up as a volunteer. Yesterday with one burst of gunfire I shot dead five of the yellow devils, one of them a girl . . .*

Miss Wedderburn felt that killing a girl wasn't very humane, but then, it had been a Chinese girl. In awe of John's heroism, she was

49

oblivious to anything else. But it had said in the newspaper that the Chinese had massacred some English people – surely John couldn't have been boasting and telling lies? At which juncture in her thoughts, she heard her mother saying 'Hang Ben'.

'What, Mum?' she asked, turning her head.

Her mother told her that the tea was called Hang Ben. Miss Wedderburn tried to pronounce it too. The English always have to show off. She temporarily forgot how loathsome Ma Wei was.

'Hang Ben. Hang Ben. Is that right?' she asked Ma Wei.

Naturally Ma Wei said, 'Yes, that's right.'

Breakfast over, Ma Wei was about to go upstairs and see how his father was. Miss Wedderburn came running downstairs, wearing a new hat she'd bought the previous day and on which was displayed a mouse's tail, as though she had stuck a strip of buckwheat vermicelli there. Mousetails were the latest fashion, and so she was wearing one, too.

'Cheerio!' she said, giving Ma Wei a sideways glance. And off she dashed like a puff of smoke.

VII

WHILE MISS Wedderburn went off to work, Mrs Wedderburn wove in and out of the rooms, doing the housework with Napoleon in tow, leaping wildly all around her. Ma Wei sat alone in the drawing room, waiting for the Reverend Ely to arrive.

Since his mother's death, when he was eight years old, Ma Wei had had virtually no experience of female love or concern. At primary school, he went round all day in a pack of little ragamuffin boys, and at high school he mixed with slightly bigger ragamuffins. It was only on Sundays, when he went to church, that he had been able to see a few women. During prayers, with his head lowered, he would secretly peep at them out of the corner of his eye. But many a time he was caught at it by Mrs Ely, who would report it to the Reverend Ely. And the reverend would give him a thorough telling-off, partly in English, partly in Chinese.

'Little boy! Mustn't look at young ladies during prayers! Understand?' he'd say in Chinese. 'See?' he'd add in English.

As Mrs Ely prayed, she'd always have one eye closed, looking up to God in heaven, and the other eye open to watch the crowd of hell-worthy pupils. Ma Wei's 'girl-spotting' couldn't escape her.

Eighty or ninety per cent of the girls in the church were even uglier than Mrs Ely, and, as Ma Wei's roving glance encountered them, he would sometimes instinctively shut his eyes, musing to himself that when God made humans, He sometimes went a bit wrong. Occasionally, though, he did spy a pretty girl. But her prettiness was only skin-deep, and even if her face was really beautiful, he couldn't help being reminded of the paper effigy-dolls in the funeral parlours. That, inevitably, was somewhat off-putting. But never mind if she was a paper doll – she was still a pretty girl, and it was no small thing to catch a glimpse of one. Chatting with her, or holding her hand, however, was beyond the realm of possibility – a foolish fantasy.

Just once he had actually been around a girl for a good few days. It happened the year before he came to England. Things were hotting up in the student world. Headmasters were striking, teachers were striking, and students were striking. Not many knew what it was all about, but everyone jumped on the bandwagon. Even the church school downed bibles and joined the strikers. Ma Wei had always been a capable speaker and looked present-able enough, and thus he was elected a representative, thanks to his natural eloquence and the fact his father didn't keep too close an eye on him.

On the representative committee, there were of course female delegates, and during the campaign, Ma Wei had numerous oppor-tunities to speak to them, and even once physically joined hands with them. But periods of unrest are so unreliable: they might last three days, they might be five months. Although everybody might feel that the longer the better, all good things must come to an end. It just so happened that this particular period of unrest was unfortunately brief, which meant that Ma Wei in his social contact with women was fated to resemble some minor acrobat: no sooner has he turned one somersault than he crawls under the stage-curtain and disappears into the wings.

Did fate play a hand in determining that Ma Wei and Miss Wedderburn should come together? Had Yüeh Lao, the old man in the moonlight, tied their big toes together across the Indian Ocean and the Mediterranean with a strand of invisible thread? She was one of countless Western girls, and she just happened to be the first one that Ma Wei met. The moment he set eyes on her, with her playful manner and kittenish skipping about, his feelings sped from surprise to admiration, and from admiration to infatuation, like someone drinking wine for the first time, face flushing headily after just one cup. Her expression and way of speaking cooled him off considerably, it was true; yet she had smiled when she'd said 'Cheerio!' to him, and her eyes had glanced his way, however fleetingly . . . Surely she wasn't deadset against him then. If only she could just come to like Chinese people. Wait and see – sooner or later he'd make her understand what the Chinese were really like . . . No need, no absolute necessity, to get on affectionate terms with her, was there? Especially not with so many other girls around.

Such thoughts churned around in Ma Wei's mind, presenting a host of problems but no other solution than 'wait and see'. He felt his face. On his cheekbones were two particularly hot spots, as if a stub of incense were burning there. 'Wait and see. Don't be in a hurry. Don't be impatient,' he murmured away to himself, his mouth slightly agape as if he were about to smile – though he didn't – or as if he were almost annoyed . . . Annoyed about her? That'd never do! He shot looks at himself in the drawing room mirror, glancing at his white teeth, while pacing back and forth with his hands in his trouser pockets. 'Don't be impatient. Just wait and see.'

'Ma Wei! Ma Wei!' shouted the elder Mr Ma from upstairs, with a frog in his throat. Then he coughed, and his voice rang out a little sharper and smoother: 'Ma Wei!'

Pulling himself together, Ma Wei raced upstairs two or three steps at a time. With one hand, Mr Ma was holding open the door, and in the other he held the enamel bowl. There were red creases on his face from where he'd been sleeping, and his scrap of moustache was all twisted.

'Go and get some hot water.' He handed the enamel basin to Ma Wei.

'I daren't go into the kitchen,' said Ma Wei. 'Didn't you hear what the landlady said yesterday? We're not to go into the kitchen. You didn't turn up at breakfast, and she's already been going on about that. What do you think —'

'All right, all right,' said Mr Ma, rubbing his eyes, 'Does it matter if I don't shave?'

'The Reverend Ely's coming round in a bit to take us out, isn't he?'

'Would it matter if I didn't go?'

Ma Wei said nothing, just poured some water into a glass and handed it to his father.

While Mr Ma gargled to rinse his throat and mouth, Ma Wei opened up their cases, which had been delivered the previous evening, and asked his father whether he wanted to wear a different suit. Feeling irritable, Mr Ma ignored him. Ma Wei thought first of telling his father that when in England you had to do as the English did, but seeing the expression on his father's face, he crept out without saying a word.

The more Mr Ma thought about it, the angrier he grew: *So this is what it's like when you go abroad! And what have I done to deserve such treatment? Yes, what have I done? Can't get up late, or there's no hot water! No hot water!*

He brooded for quite some time.

Ah! I know. We'll go and live in a hotel. Blow the cost – just as long as I don't have to put up with such foul insults!

But then, as he glanced at the cases and their other belongings, his ardent resolve cooled off somewhat. *We've got too many things. Be too much bother to move them.*

A moment later, and his angry determination had wilted yet further.

Let's give it a try here first. Stick it out. And then, if we come across a suitable place, we'll move.

His wrath thus dispelled, he put on his big spectacles, picked up his pipe and marched into the study.

Thoughts are the cheapest thing in life. You think something, and you feel there's some truth to it. You have another ponder, and you realise your first thought wasn't so enlightened and ingenious after all. And when you give it yet more thought, it sends you into a proper muddle, and the more you think, the more fuddled you get, so that all you've thought up till then can be viewed as a sheer waste of effort. In Mr Ma's case, however, this effort was considerably less than had he decided to up sticks and leave.

Downstairs, Mrs Wedderburn was specially waiting for Mr Ma to get up and ask her for some breakfast, so that she could give him a piece of her mind. If he was pulled up sharply and painfully the first time, you could bet he wouldn't try it on again. Hearing him get up, and calculating when he'd have finished his morning ablutions, she walked upstairs grumbling to herself. When she reached Mr Ma's door it was half open, and there was no sound from inside. Suddenly she heard two coughs, and, turning her head, noticed that the study door was also half open . . . and that Mr Ma was sitting on a chair in the study, with a pipe in his mouth.

No wonder the Reverend Ely says there's something spooky and supernatural about the Chinese, she said to herself. *Leave him without his breakfast, and – what do you know! – he doesn't even turn a hair. Doesn't even ask for any. All right, you can go hungry!*

Mr Ma sat there quite immobile, just sucking away on his pipe, puffing ring upon ring of blue smoke above his head.

The Reverend Ely didn't arrive till eleven o'clock and didn't come inside, but just stood at the front door and asked Ma Wei, 'What about your father? Is he coming out or not?'

Ma Wei ran upstairs to ask his father. Mr Ma gave a slight shake of his head, dispersing the rings of blue smoke around his head. Ma Wei hurried downstairs and told the Reverend Ely that his father still wasn't sufficiently rested, and didn't intend going out. So he went off with the Reverend Ely by himself.

VIII

IF A nation is old, then its people are old from the moment they're born: myopic, deaf, coughing and wheezing. If the nation's got four hundred million of these ancient neophytes, that nation will keep on getting older and older, until it's too old even to crawl, and then it'll kick the bucket without a sound. 'Our civilisation's much older than yours, sir!' say the haughty Chinese students who come to Europe, addressing the foreign devils. (All Chinese people who come to Europe to study are mainly concerned with promoting Chinese culture. Studying the foreign devils' books is a mere excuse: as if their books were worthy of study.) 'Moreover, there are four hundred million of us,' they continue. 'A great nation. A great nation!'

Note the vigorous emphasis they give to the words 'old' and 'great'.

'If "old" is equal to "good", then why is it that your esteemed country is old yet not apparently good?' the tricky foreign devils reply with a smile. 'If all four hundred million of you are useless layabouts, what good would another four million do?'

When they hear such words, the students can do nothing but creep off to that sole overseas enterprise of the Chinese, the Chinese restaurant, and eat a meal of roast pork to try to crowd out all the disgruntled humours that fill their bellies.

Mr Ma Tse-jen was, beyond all shadow of doubt, an 'old' element of the 'old' nation. Having established his credentials, you may take it for granted that he'd never put his brain to any use,

56

nor had he ever fixed his eyes on anything for more than three minutes. What was life for? So that one could become a government mandarin! How did one set about becoming a mandarin? Invite some people round to dinner and try to get them to pull some strings for you. Why get married? Because one was the right age to do so. How should one acquire a wife? Consult a professional matchmaker. If one already had a wife, why should one still want a concubine? One wasn't enough . . .

Such preoccupations provide a lifetime's pleasures for the people of the old nation. And true to form, the elder Mr Ma's aspirations went no further than such things.

Coming to England was like some hazy dream for him; he knew nothing about business, and in addition had always despised businessmen. The honourable way of making one's fortune was by becoming a mandarin – nothing good would come of trade and earning one's money by one's own sweat and blood. That was ignoble! Vulgar! He sat there in the study, without aim or plan, smoking away at his pipe.

He grew fed up of just sitting there. *We're in England now,* he suddenly thought, *and Ma Wei's got a chance to study. Some day he'll go back and take up a government post . . . And then what about me? I'll sit back and live in clover. Ha ha!*

Such was the sum of his activity. He didn't even open the curtains to take a look at what London streets were really like. He was in London – why be bothered looking at it? Wasn't it bad enough just being there? Even Peking was by now a vague recollection, even though he'd only been away from it for forty or fifty days. Was there in fact a cake shop just south of the Four Archway Gates? He couldn't remember for certain. Oh dear: he wouldn't be able to eat Peking po-po cakes any more now. Perish the thought! In this way he got more and more caught up in his homesickness for Peking, forgetting all else. *Oh dear . . . those Peking cakes!*

By the time it was almost one o'clock, and his stomach was emitting a few mild rumbles. He forced himself to carry on smoking, and as he did so, his belly started feeling frantically empty. *Looks like I'll just have to have a bite of something or other,* he thought.

It occurred to him quite a number of times to go downstairs and mention the fact to the landlady. But each time he thought better of tackling her. He stood up, and took a few paces. That was no good – activity increases hunger. He sat down again and filled his pipe once more, but then put it down, unsmoked. Minutes passed, by which time his stomach was aching as well as thundering.

I'll go downstairs and have a try. He stood up and slowly walked downstairs.

'Did you have a good sleep last night, Mr Ma?' asked Mrs Wedderburn with a trace of sarcasm.

'Excellent! Excellent!' replied Mr Ma. 'And how are you, Mrs Wedderburn? Has Miss Wedderburn gone out then?'

Mrs Wedderburn mumbled a sniffy reply.

The words, 'I'd like to have something to eat' came a good few times to Mr Ma's lips, but each time were swallowed. In fact the questions he asked strayed ever further from the topic of food.

'The weather's very cold, isn't it? Er, Miss Wedderburn has gone out then? Oh, I've already asked you that. My apologies. And how is Napoleon?'

Mrs Wedderburn called Napoleon over, and Mr Ma picked him up. Napoleon was delighted, and licked Mr Ma's ear incessantly.

'This little fellow's a very intelligent dog.' Mr Ma began singing Napoleon's praises.

Mrs Wedderburn at once grew chatty, and nattered on about various things. 'Are the Chinese fond of dogs, too?' she asked.

'Oh yes, we love dogs. When my wife was alive, she used to keep three Pekingeses and a baby rabbit, and the four little pets would all take their meals together, without ever fighting,' he replied.

'How fascinating! How simply fascinating!'

He told her a few more stories about Chinese dogs, and she listening with growing interest. Mr Ma had ample experience in idle chatting with Aunty Changs and Granny Lees, so was well furnished with colourful replies for her questions. It was his view that women were the same the world over. The only difference was that Western women's noses were pointier than Chinese women's.

When he'd been through all his doggy tales, Mr Ma had still

neglected to mention that he felt like a bite to eat. Mrs Wedderburn could never for a moment have imagined that he was hungry. The English think in black and white, and as long as the rules are followed, all's fine and dandy, and nothing else is of any concern. Mr Ma hadn't had any breakfast because he'd got up late. It stood to reason that when you got up late, you didn't get any breakfast. As for lunch, Mrs Wedderburn had made it quite clear when she rented the rooms that she wasn't going to cater for that. Under the terms of the agreement, she was under no obligation to make lunch, so what did she care whether he was hungry or not?

Seeing that there was no hope and resigning himself boldly to hunger, Mr Ma put Napoleon down and went upstairs. Napoleon, seemingly very taken with Mr Ma, pursued him, tail wagging, and, as Mr Ma reinstalled himself on his chair, came up barking and clawing, intent on having some fun with him, one moment hiding behind the chair and tugging at his coat, the next moment coming round to gnaw on his shoes.

'I say! Don't carry things too far. Don't get too excited!' said Mr Ma. 'All right, you've got a nice full tummy, so here you come leaping and bounding. You just don't care whether anyone else is hungry or not!'

Anxious about Napoleon, Mrs Wedderburn had come upstairs. The door of the study was open as she reached it, and purely by chance she overheard Mr Ma's complaint to Napoleon.

'Oh, Mr Ma! I never realised you wanted something to eat! I thought you'd be going out for your meals.'

'Never mind, I'm not too —'

'If you'd like a meal, I can make up a little something for you, one shilling a time.'

'Let's say two shillings, and give me a little extra.'

After what seemed an eternity, she brought him up a pot of tea, a plate of cold veal, a few slices of bread and a bit of lettuce. When he saw that the food, apart from the tea, was all cold, Mr Ma frowned. But being famished, he had no choice but to eat it. He slowly drank all the tea and ate only half the meat, but polished off the bread and lettuce. Then, having eaten and drunk his fill,

LAO SHE

he returned to the armchair, gave several sonorous belches, then broke off a matchstick-end to make himself a toothpick, and with great relish cleaned between his teeth.

Napoleon was still there, glancing sideways at Mr Ma, and waiting for him to play. But Mr Ma wasn't inclined to, and, feeling hard done by, the dog lay down beside the chair.

Mrs Wedderburn came in to collect the dishes. Seeing Napoleon, she knelt on the carpet and picked the dog up, asking him what games he'd been playing with Mr Ma.

Not since he'd first come into the house, not until this very moment, had Mr Ma ventured to look directly at Mrs Wedderburn. A gentleman can't go round taking casual looks at women! But now, with the scent of her hair in his nostrils, he felt himself suddenly go hot inside, then give a shiver, and was at a loss as to what to do next.

Mrs Wedderburn asked him how many dog shows were held each year in China, what protection the laws of China afforded dogs, and whether Pekingeses did in fact originally come from China. Mr Ma's knowledge of doggology was as sparse as his knowledge of natural sciences, so he was obliged to fob her off with made-up answers. Anyway, so long as he told her what she wanted to hear, he couldn't go wrong. As he spoke, he plucked up the courage to look at her more closely. She looked to be thirty-six or thirty-seven, but with no signs of age on her face. And the smart, elegant clothes she wore served to heighten the impression of her youth.

Rousing himself, he tentatively stretched out his hand to play with Napoleon. Mrs Wedderburn didn't move out of his way, and even came forwards to push the dog towards him. Mr Ma's hand almost brushed her bosom. His nerves leapt to attention. Then suddenly, in a flash of inspiration, he stood up and gave Mrs Wedderburn his chair, moving a stool over for himself. Their conversation turned to business, of which she also seemed to have had some experience.

'The most important thing in business nowadays is advertising,' she said.

'I sell antiques, so surely advertising is no use to me,' he replied.

'Even with antiques, you have to advertise! It's essential.'

'Yes, of course one must.' He switched from argument to agreement so quickly that she got quite a shock. She stood up.

'I'll leave Napoleon here, shall I?' she said.

Aware that Napoleon was not to be regarded lightly, he hastened to take the little dog from her. She cleared the crockery onto her tray, and as she was going, said to the dog: 'Behave yourself now. Mustn't be naughty!'

When she'd gone, Mr Ma deposited the dog on the floor, lay back in the chair and went to sleep.

IX

MA WEI didn't get back until after six o'clock, and he was so tired that the veins in his temples were bulging, and there were streaks of red across the whites of his eyes. The Reverend Ely had taken him to see the Tower of London, looking at London Bridge in passing, St Paul's Cathedral and the House of Commons. You couldn't see all the sights of London in one day, any more than you could understand it in one day. The Reverend Ely had left the museums, art galleries, zoos and so on for Ma Wei to explore by himself later on, when he'd got used to finding his way about London. On the way to St Paul's, he'd pointed out to Ma Wei his uncle's antiques shop, which was in a little street just to the east of the cathedral.

The Reverend Ely's beanstalk legs had pounded along at a tremendous pace, and Ma Wei had been hard put to keep up with him. But he'd refused to be beaten, and for a good part of the day had been desperately haring around after the clergyman.

As he came home, Miss Wedderburn was just arriving home too. She was very hot from walking, and her cheeks were a prettier red than ever. On some clumsy pretext, he tried to tell her about what he'd just seen, but she hurried off into the kitchen.

He went upstairs to see his father. Mr Ma was still sitting in the study smoking his pipe. Ma Wei told him about each sight in turn. Mr Ma listened none too attentively until his son mentioned the antiques shop, when an idea suddenly occurred to him. 'Ma Wei! Tomorrow we'll go to visit your uncle's grave, and then we'll go and have a look at the shop. Don't forget!'

The bell rang, and they both went down to the dining room for their evening meal, after which, as Mrs Wedderburn busied herself with the washing-up, Mr Ma returned to the study for a smoke once more. Ma Wei was sitting alone in the drawing room when Miss Wedderburn suddenly ran in.

'Have you seen my handbag?'

Ma Wei was on the point of replying when out she ran again.

'I know,' she called as she went, 'it's in the kitchen.'

Ma Wei stood at the drawing-room door and watched her. She found the handbag in the kitchen and rushed his way again, jamming her hat on her head in a great fluster.

'Are you going out?' he asked.

'Can't you tell? To see a film!'

Looking out through the drawing room window, he saw her walk off with a boy, the two of them side by side, close together, talking and laughing as they moved away.

Mr Ma was thinking of his brother. That night he dreamt several times of him, and in one dream they wept a few commiserative tears together. As he recalled his brother's kindness, he felt somewhat ashamed. He'd spent so much of his brother's money. And it was money his brother had come by through hard graft. It wasn't merely that Mr Ma had spent all that money from his brother, either – every time he'd received some, he'd gone and got himself drunk as a lord, so sozzled he'd needed a couple of policemen to help him home. Imagine taking money from his brother just to booze it away! And getting drunk in public like that!

But the past is past, like it or lump it. What was the good of dwelling on it? He was here in London now, and the manager of a shop. Not as glorious as being a mandarin, but still, you had to admit that his horoscope hadn't been such a bad one, and that his guiding star was on the up and up . . . Now why hadn't he brought a fortune-telling almanac with him? How could he tell whether it'd be a good day tomorrow for going to the cemetery? But Christians should fear nothing. The power of the Lord was much greater than that of any other gods. What about the astrological gods? Not a chance! An astrological god would never be impertinent enough to compete with the Lord God . . . But still . . . Questions of every kind assailed him thick and fast, preventing him from getting any proper sleep at all.

The following morning, the sky hung dull and heavy and the east wind blew very chilly. The elder Mr Ma donned his camel-hair coat, his flannel shirt and his thick blue woollen suit. Still afraid that he might catch cold when he went out, he tried to put on his cotton-padded jacket over the shirt, but it was too bulky, and if he wore it he wouldn't be able to fasten his trousers. Cursing the Western devils' attire, he took the padded jacket off again. Didn't that just go to show how the cultures of East and West could never blend? You can't even wear a little Chinese quilted jacket together with Western trousers.

After breakfast, he took a few puffs of his pipe before making a move. Eventually Ma Wei took him down Gordon Street, across Torrington Square and straight towards Oxford Street. As they walked, Ma Wei asked whether they should take the Tube or a bus. He'd already made certain where the cemetery was from the Reverend Ely the previous day.

'We'll just see when we get into town,' was all Mr Ma said, having no notion either way.

On reaching Oxford Street, they discovered a steady two-way stream of traffic, with cars jammed nose to tail. There were little vehicles squeezed between big ones, and motorbikes tagging along behind the little cars, the whole like a flock of ostrich chicks being taken for a jolly walk by their mother. They all seemed about to crash into each other, and in fact it wouldn't have taken much for them to do so. They seemed on the verge of butting the vehicle in front of them before somersaulting into the distance.

Puffs of blue smoke came from each car; the wheels swish-swished along; the horns blared wildly. There were vehicles on every side, far and near, all chugging out blue smoke and whoosh-ing along, and all honking mightily. The whole of this huge street had become an ocean of traffic. On each side of the mass, people – men, women, young and old – were all hurrying along with their heads craned forwards, as if they were looking for something they'd lost. Glancing down, all you could see were packs of legs, and glancing up, one endless bobbing stretch of heads, as if waves from the sea of traffic were dashing against the pebbles on either footpath, shifting them up and down, up and down.

Mr Ma raised his head and looked up at the sky. It was a sullen, grumpy grey. He thought of telling Ma Wei that they should cancel the trip, but then felt that wouldn't do. He stood in a quandary for a moment, then caught sight of a rank of cars parked in the middle of the street.

'Ma Wei, are those taxis?'

'The fare would be very expensive,' said Ma Wei.

'No matter. We must hire one.' The sight of the big buses was making him dizzy.

'How about going by Underground?' asked Ma Wei.

'I can't breathe in the Underground!' Mr Ma recalled his experience of the Tube on his first day in London.

'We mustn't waste too much money,' said Ma Wei with a smile.

'What are you on about? We're going to hire a taxi. And that's not all – we'll have to get the taxi driver to find some quiet way to the place. I tell you, I'm feeling dizzy!'

Ma Wei was left with no option but to hail a taxi, and tell the driver to take a less busy route, no matter how circuitous. In the taxi, Mr Ma still felt uneasy; you never knew when you might have a crash and get your head smashed in.

'Why didn't we bring a fortune-telling almanac with us?' he muttered under his breath, 'If it happens to be a "black day", it's suicide careering round in one of these things.'

'What do you want an almanac for?' asked Ma Wei.

'Just talking to myself. Don't butt in so much!' Mr Ma glared at Ma Wei.

As requested, the driver took the backstreets, dodging alternately eastwards and westwards, round a green, into a narrow alley. . . they were driving for forty or fifty minutes before they reached an open area, bounded by a high iron railing and lined with bushes. The grass was covered with stone monuments and slabs, both tall and short, and the silence was profound. London's a funny place like that: the noisy parts are really noisy, but the quiet spots are as quiet as can be.

The taxi circled the iron railing until it came to a small gate, at which it stopped. Father and son alighted. Ma Wei wanted to send the taxi away, but Mr Ma insisted on its waiting. Beyond the small iron gate there was a little red house, standing in isolation before the sea of stone. Its little chimney was sending out a curving, curling plume of smoke.

They knocked on the gate, and the door of the red house opened a crack. The crack widened, and slowly a round, plump face peeped out, mouth moving as though chewing something. The door opened wider still, and the plump face became a short, fat, little old woman.

The old woman's face looked featureless, as if it were just one shiny globe of soft flesh. And arms and legs aside, her body was one little round wheel. It wasn't until she'd walked right up to them that they realised all parts of her face were intact, and that her eyes were twinkling away merrily. Wiping her mouth with her apron, she asked whose grave they were looking for. As she spoke, it became clear that she had only one tooth, which, being deprived of any company, looked exceptionally large, as if it had made itself sole tyrant of the area by brute force.

'We're looking for the grave of a Mr Ma, a Chinese man,' Ma Wei told the woman. She'd finished wiping her mouth, and now vigorously scrubbed her face, seemingly to wipe her eyes.

'I know, I remember him. He died last autumn. Such a tragedy!' She made to raise her apron again. 'There were three wreaths on the coffin . . . In the autumn, it was. October the seventh. The first Chinaman buried here. Yet, that's it, he was the first. Oh, poor man.'

As she spoke, tears flowed sideways down her face, as her cheeks were too chubby to let the tears flow straight. 'Come with me. Of course I remember him.'

The old lady set off, waddling on her stumpy legs like a newborn duckling. And as she walked, her cheeks trembled like the jellyfish eaten in winter.

The Mas followed her, and after going a few hundred yards, she indicated a small stone pillar.

'There it is,' she said.

The Mas hastened over to it. The name on the stone pillar wasn't that of a Chinese person.

'No,' she said, as they were about to mention their doubts, 'that's not it. We'll have to go a bit further. Of course . . . I remember him . . . Over there. The first Chinaman, he was.'

They proceeded another few hundred yards, then Ma Wei, with his sharp eyes, noticed a small square pillar to their left that bore an inscription in Chinese characters. He tugged at Mr Ma, and the two of them walked towards it.

'Yes, that's right, there it is. I remember. Of course!' said the old woman from behind them, her plump finger pointing to the stone pillar that they'd already discovered themselves.

The pillar was a mere three feet high. On it was inscribed the name of Ma Wei's uncle: Ma Wei-jen. Beneath his name were inscribed the year and month of his death. The stone itself was light grey, streaked with greyish-purple lines. The wreaths in front of it had by now lost their colour, washed by the rain, and the notes attached to them had long since been blown away by the wind. On the grass at the foot of the stone grew a few light-yellow flowers in pale bloom, their petals hung with drops of dew like teardrops. The black clouds in the sky, the stone pillar and the tattered wreaths combined to produce an atmosphere of forlorn desolation. A feeling of distress welled up inside Mr Ma, and he found himself shedding tears. And although Ma Wei had never met his uncle, his eyes grew red-rimmed too.

Ignoring Ma Wei and the old lady, Mr Ma knelt down before the slab, and with great reverence performed three kowtows. 'Elder brother,' he said in a quiet voice, 'protect your younger brother so that he may make his fortune and carry your coffin back to China.'

As he uttered these words, his voice broke, and he couldn't say anything more.

At his father's side, Ma Wei bowed three times towards the stone slab. The old woman behind him was crying so brokenly that her face was awash with tears. Rendered powerless to even lift up her apron, she was reduced to rubbing her face with her fists.

In the midst of her nonstop weeping, she asked, 'Do you want any fresh-cut flowers? I've got some.'

'How much?' asked Ma Wei.

'Bring some,' said Mr Ma as he knelt before the grave.

'All right, I'll go and get some. I'll go and get some.'

The old woman picked up her skirts, seemingly to run, but, as her ankles were rather bent, she merely stumped along, face to the sky, tottering unsteadily. She was away for an age, and when at last she slowly waddled back, her face and neck were as red as the bricks of her little red house. With one hand she clutched her skirts, and in the other held a bunch of apricot-yellow tulips.

'Here's the flowers, sir. Nice and fresh. Oh, yes . . .' she rambled on as she handed the flowers to Mr Ma.

He picked up one of the wreaths and stuck all the flowers in it. Then he placed it back at the foot of the slab. He stepped back two paces, contemplated it, and wept once more. As he wept, the old woman accompanied him with her sobs.

'The money,' she said suddenly, at the hysteric height of her lamentations, stretching out her hand. 'The money.'

Without a word, Mr Ma fished out a ten-shilling note and handed it to her. At the sight of the note, she lifted her head and peered closely at Mr Ma.

'Thank you. Oh, thank you. Yes, the first Chinaman buried here. Oh, yes. Oh, thank you. I do hope a few more Chinamen die and get buried here.'

This last sentence was addressed to herself, but was quite distinctly overheard by the Mas.

All at once, the sun shot a ray of light through a broken cloud and cast their shadows on the stone pillar, rendering that melancholy spot unique in its gloom and misery. Mr Ma gave a sigh, wiped his eyes and turned round to his son. 'Ma Wei, let's go.'

Slowly, father and son made their way out of the cemetery. The old lady ran after them to ask whether they wanted any more flowers as she'd got other kinds, too. Ma Wei shot her a look, and

Mr Ma shook his head. By the time the two of them reached the iron gate, they'd left her far behind them, but they could still hear her saying, 'The first Chinaman...'

They both got into the taxi again. Mr Ma closed his eyes, and wondered how he would manage to carry his elder brother's coffin back to China. Then he remembered that his elder brother had been younger than sixty when he died. How would he fare himself? He was already heading for fifty! *Life's but a dream with no meaning. Yes, a dream...*

Ma Wei was also ruminating on his impressions of the cemetery. As he sat leaning back in the corner of the taxi, his eyes staring fixedly at the broad back of the taxi driver, he thought to himself, *What a hero my uncle was, setting up business in a foreign land. A hero.* True, selling antiques wasn't necessarily a particularly magnificent enterprise, but, all the same, he'd at least shown it was possible to earn foreign money. *My father's useless.* He glanced at Mr Ma; if his father wasn't banging on about becoming a mandarin, he was juggling a wine cup and playing the poverty-stricken gentleman-scholar. A would-be mandarin, a famous gentleman-scholar. Ha! Real ability was being able to apply genuine knowledge to earn an honest penny.

X

THE MAS' antiques shop was in a little side street to the east of St Paul's. If you stood outside the shop, you could see part of the church's dome, looking like a slice of watermelon. The shopfront was as long as a single room, with a small door on the left and a full-length glass window on the right. In the window were displayed some porcelain, bronzes, old fans, little images of Buddha and various other odds and ends. Past the window stood another door, which was the entrance for the umbrella and suitcase repairer upstairs, and past that lay a clothing storage depot, which had two horse-drawn carts in front of its door, with people going in and out moving goods onto the carts. To the left of the shop there were three other small shops in a row, the one immediately next door to the Mas' being another antiques shop. Opposite there was nothing except a continuous stretch of wall.

As father and son stood surveying the shop, Li Tzu-jung stepped out of the door.

'Mr Ma?' he said, smiling. 'Please come in.'

Mr Ma took a look at Li Tzu-jung. There was nothing particularly objectionable about his face but he was smiling too extravagantly. What's more, he was in his shirt sleeves, with dust on his hands, having just been cleaning and rearranging the display cabinets. Intuitively, Mr Ma summed him up in two syllables: vulgar.

'Mr Li?' Ma Wei hastened over to shake hands with Li Tzu-jung.

'Don't shake hands, I've got muck on them.' Li Tzu-jung hastily searched in his trouser pockets for a handkerchief, but finding none, had to give Ma Wei his wrist to shake. It was a thick, powerful wrist, of handsomely defined muscle and bone. As Ma Wei shook that warm wrist, he became rather taken with Li Tzu-jung. From Li's shirt, his rolled-up sleeves and his soiled hands, you could tell he was a man of action, and you needed to tackle things with real vigour and capability to compete with the English.

As foreigners would see it, Li Tzu-jung was more Chinese than Ma Wei. The Chinese man, to the foreign mind, is short of stature and wears a pigtail. He has a flat face with swollen cheekbones, no nose, eyes that are two slits each an inch or so long, a thin-lipped mouth, a stringy moustache dangling in the breeze from his upper lip and waddling Pekingese-dog legs. And that's only his appearance; as for his hidden devilry and deceit, his habit of keeping poisonous snakes up his sleeves and concealing arsenic in his ears, how, when he exhales, he turns into a chlorine-gas gun, and how, just by winking his eye, he can send you to kingdom come . . . all such things serve yet further to make foreign men and women, young and old, shudder to the very depths of their hearts.

Li Tzu-jung's face almost exactly fitted the image. If he'd been slightly taller, the foreigners might have accorded him more honour by calling him Japanese. (Yellow-faced people with the slightest points of merit are all Japanese.) Unfortunately, he was only about five feet tall, and his short legs did indeed bend outwards at the knees as he walked. His hair was thick and copious, and what with that untidy mass and the lowness of his forehead, there wasn't much space between his eyebrows and his hair. His eyes, nose and mouth were not unattractive, but, alas, his cheekbones were rather too flat. He had a very fine physique, though, with a broad, straight back and a solid, erect neck, which, with his slightly bowed legs, made him look like a little howitzer gun.

Yes, Li Tzu-jung really got the foreigners in a muddle. They might think he was Japanese, but then his face was scarcely what you could call handsome. (The Japanese are all decent lookers.) But then, if they took him for Chinese, his yellow face was as clean and sparkling as a new pin, and no Chinese fellow can ever spare the cash for a bar of soap, can he now? Anyway, just look at those upright shoulders of his! The Chinese always keep their backs bent, ready for a beating, so he couldn't be Chinese. And although his legs were somewhat bandy, he walked briskly, fairly pounding along. He not only failed to waddle, he even walked at tremendous speed . . . Foreign gentlemen were truly nonplussed as to precisely which inferior race he belonged.

'Ah,' Li Tzu-jung's landlady had concluded, 'the fellow's half Chinese, half Japanese.' And in private she'd confide to others, 'Oh, he's definitely not proper Chinese. What, a Japanese? Not likely! Not his sort!'

Before Ma Wei had even finished shaking hands, the elder Ma had already drawn back his shoulders and made his entrance into the shop. Li Tzu-jung hurried in after him, cleared up the things on the floor and ushered him to a seat in the back room.

The shop had two rooms in total, one where the business was conducted and another that served as the accounts office. Hard against the back wall of the latter stood the safe, in front of which there was just enough space for three or four chairs and a table. Next to the safe stood a small table bearing a telephone and a telephone directory. There was a rather dank smell about the room, which, combined with the acrid smell of metal polish, produced an atmosphere very much like that of one of those tiny foreign-goods shops in Peking.

'Shop assistant Li.' Mr Ma had reflected for some time before hitting upon 'shop assistant' as his chosen form of address. 'Before we begin, make us a pot of tea.'

Li Tzu-jung raked at the unkempt hair on his head, glanced at Mr Ma, then turned to Ma Wei with a smile.

'We haven't got a teapot or any cups here,' he said. 'If the old gentleman's set on having a cup of tea, I'll have to go out and buy some. Got any money on you?'

Ma Wei was about to pull out some money when Mr Ma, his face darkening, again addressed Li Tzu-jung.

'Shop assistant!' (This time he even omitted the 'Li'.) 'Do you mean to tell me that if the manager of a shop wishes to drink a cup of tea, he is required to pull out his own money? And there are numerous teapots and cups on the shelves, yet without any thought you declare that we have none!'

Mr Ma drew up a chair, seated himself next to the small table, and, leaning back, almost knocked the telephone over.

Slowly and leisurely, Li Tzu-jung rolled the sleeves of his shirt down and turned round to survey Mr Ma.

'Mr Ma,' he said. 'While your brother was alive, I helped him here for a year or more. When he died, he put the business in my hands. Every decision I make is for the good of the business. Drinking tea's a private matter, which can't be put down on the expense account. It's not like in China. Business accounts have to be signed by a lawyer, to assist the government in collecting taxes. We can't cut loose and put any old costs down on them. As for those teapots and cups, they're for sale, not for our use.'

Then he turned to Ma Wei. 'I expect you've got the gist of what I mean?' he asked. 'You may feel I'm a bit direct, but we're in England now. The English way is that business is business, and nothing personal. We've got to do things the same way.'

'Yes,' said Ma Wei in a small voice, not daring to look at his father.

'Very well,' said Mr Ma, with lowered head, looking a bit afraid of Li Tzu-jung. 'Very well, I won't have any then. I won't have any. Will that suit you?'

Li Tzu-jung said nothing, but went into the other room and fetched the keys to the safe. He came back and opened it, took out several account books and other documents, and placed them on a chair right under Mr Ma's nose.

'Here are the account books and so on, Mr Ma. Take a look at them, please, and when you've done so, I've got something else I want to say.'

'Why should I look at them? That's just a routine matter. Surely you haven't been cheating me, have you?' said Mr Ma.

Li Tzu-jung laughed. 'Mr Ma, I take it you've never been in business before.'

'Been in business? Huh!' Mr Ma exclaimed.

'Right. Well, whether you've been in business or not's beside the point. It boils down to the same thing: business is strictly business, and the personal is neither here nor there. That's a matter of procedure, and whether you suspect me of cheating or not just doesn't come into it.'

Li Tzu-jung was in a quandary, not sure whether to smile or not. He was well aware that it was the Chinese way to maintain politeness and to bring personal feelings to play on things. But he also knew that to do business in England, one must do so like the English – everything above board and straightforward (except in their foreign diplomacy), and no beating about the bush or approaching things in a roundabout fashion. In the throes of this dilemma, he couldn't think what to do. He was reduced to raking at his hair, then twirling the long forelock around and around into a small curl.

'My father's just got back from my uncle's grave,' said Ma Wei with a smile, not waiting for his father to speak, 'and he's still feeling rather upset. We'll look at the accounts tomorrow, shall we?'

Mr Ma nodded his head. *That's how things should be,* he thought to himself. *The son sticking up for his dad! This Li Tzu-jung fellow's deliberately trying to make matters awkward for me.*

Li Tzu-jung looked at Mr Ma, looked at Ma Wei, spluttered a laugh, and, gathering up all the books and documents, put them back. When he'd stowed them all away, he felt gently around in the depths of the safe, and, after a moment, brought out a small lilac brocade-covered box. Mr Ma felt like laughing as he watched him.

The young fellow thinks he's a magician, he said to himself. What will his next trick be?

Li Tzu-jung handed the brocade box to Ma Wei. Ma Wei looked at his father, then slowly opened it. It was filled with cotton wool. Lifting that up, he discovered a diamond ring.

Placing the ring on his palm, he scrutinised it. It was a lady's ring, a fine gold one, with a twisted hemp-flower design. The back of it broadened out a little, and the front had a diamond set in it, which sparkled and shone.

'It's a keepsake your uncle left you,' said Li Tzu-jung, locking up the safe.

'Let me have a look at it,' said Mr Ma.

Ma Wei at once passed him the ring, and Mr Ma, anxious to show off his know-how in front of Li Tzu-jung, turned it over to inspect it. He looked at the design, then peered closer, and with half-shut eyes examined the characters engraved on the inside of the ring. Then with a finger he rubbed some spit on the diamond, and gave it a few wipes.

'A diamond. Not bad. A woman's ring,' said Mr Ma, nodding his head and smacking his lips in a sign of appreciation. As he spoke, he thrust the ring into his pocket.

Li Tzu-jung opened his mouth, but a glance from Ma Wei made him bite back his words.

There was a short pause. Then Li Tzu-jung brought out the safe keys and a string of other little keys, and handed them to Mr Ma. 'These are the keys of the shop. You look after them, Mr Ma.'

'Tcha! You look after them. It'll be simpler,' said Mr Ma, still fingering the ring in his pocket.

'Mr Ma, we ought to get matters straight. Are you going to keep me on?' asked Li Tzu-jung, still holding the keys.

Ma Wei nodded to prompt his father.

'I've told you to take the keys,' said Mr Ma. 'So I must be employing you, mustn't I?'

'Right. Thank you. When your brother was alive, I used to come in at ten in the morning and leave at four in the afternoon, and he gave me two pounds a week. My job was to attend to the customers and arrange the wares. When he fell ill, I came in at ten as usual, but worked until six o'clock, so he gave me three pounds a week. Now, I'd be glad if you'd tell me my wages, the nature of my job and my hours of work. It doesn't matter if I work a bit less, as I have to keep some time for my studies.'

'Oh, you're a student, too?' Mr Ma had never for a moment pictured Li Tzu-jung as a studying person. *Such a vulgar chap studying!* he said to himself. *You'd never guess it from the looks of him. That's not how students look in China.*

'Yes, that's what I really am, a student,' said Li Tzu-jung. 'Do you —'

'Ma Wei!' Mr Ma, devoid of ideas, looked at Ma Wei, his eyes seeming to say, 'You suggest something.'

'I think the best thing would be if I talked it over with Mr Li, and then we can get everything fixed later on. How about that?' said Ma Wei.

'Let us do that then.' Mr Ma stood up. It was decidedly chilly in the room, and his knees felt a bit stiff. 'Take me home, then come back and discuss things with shop assistant Li. And you can look through the accounts while you're at it. Not that it matters whether you look through them or not.'

With these words, he slowly walked towards the front door. Reaching the display shelves in the outer room, he stopped and stood still again, looking at them for a long time. Then he turned to Li Tzu-jung and said, 'Shop assistant Li, pass me down that small white teapot.'

Li Tzu-jung gently brought down the teapot, and handed it to Mr Ma. Mr Ma pulled out his handkerchief, wrapped the teapot in it and handed it to Ma Wei to carry.

'Wait for me. We'll have a meal together,' said Ma Wei to Li Tzu-jung. 'See you in a bit.'

XI

FATHER AND son walked out of the antiques shop. After a few paces Mr Ma halted, and peered hard at the exterior of the shop once more. This time he noticed the long sign behind a sheet of glass above the window, with its gold lettering on a black background.

'What vulgar lack of taste,' he said, shaking his head, while leaning back and surveying the repair-shop sign on the next floor. Then he turned around and looked at the walls across the road.

'That chimney's right opposite our window. The feng shui of our shop doesn't seem very good.'

Paying no attention to what his father was saying, Ma Wei was looking up towards the dome of St Paul's. The more he looked the more beautiful he found it. 'There's a nice place for you to go and worship some day, Dad,' he said.

'Yes, the church isn't bad. But its spire's robbed us of all the geomantic advantages. We won't be able to get any.'

Mr Ma seemed quite oblivious to the fact that he was a Christian, and grumbled away about the poor feng shui. He was still shaking his head and grumbling as they left the little street. Ma Wei caught sight of a bus going to Oxford Street, and, as there was a stop right by St Paul's, didn't consult his father about boarding it, but pulled him along and jumped onto the bus with him. As Mr Ma registered his surroundings, the bus moved off again. Ma Wei bought their tickets.

'Don't call Li Tzu-jung "shop assistant",' he told his father. 'Just look how the people on this bus say thank you to the conductor, even though all they're doing is paying for their ticket. And Li's a proper godsend in the shop, we can't lose him. You'll upset him if you call him shop assistant. What's more —'

'What do you imagine I ought to call him then? I'm the shop manager. Are you trying to tell me that the shop manager should address the shop assistant as "boss"?'

As he spoke, Mr Ma shot out a hand, took the little teapot that Ma Wei was holding, removed the handkerchief and closely scrutinised the seal-script calligraphy on the bottom. To tell the truth, our good gentleman was decidedly limited in his ability to read seal script, and what with the bus swaying wildly about, the characters were all the more difficult for him to read. He inwardly reproved Ma Wei for having boarded a bus without consulting him.

'Call him "Mr Li". You won't be lowering yourself.' Ma Wei frowned, but had no intention of starting a row with his father.

The bus passed under an iron bridge, and the train rumbling across the bridge was so noisy overhead that Mr Ma heard nothing of Ma Wei's words at that point. The bus suddenly shot to the left and Mr Ma slipped violently forwards, almost letting go of the little teapot. He muttered several swearwords, but, in the confused hubbub of the traffic, Ma Wei didn't hear him either.

'Do you want to keep Li on or not then?' Ma Wei asked his father, seizing his chance while the bus was idling at a stop.

'What else? I have to employ him, don't I? He knows how to run a shop. I don't.' Mr Ma's cheeks reddened and he made to move, as if he would leap off the bus were Ma Wei to pursue his questioning. But he stuck his leg out too forcefully and almost trod on the dainty toes of the old lady sitting opposite. Hastily withdrawing his foot, he abandoned any notion of jumping off the bus.

Ma Wei knew there was nothing to be gained by questioning him. All it came back to, anyway, was, 'Are you going to keep him on?' – 'How could I do otherwise?', and 'Why not address him as "Mr"?' – 'I'm the manager. If I call him "Mr", what's he going to call me!' No point going round in circles. Ma Wei turned away, and concentrated on observing the street names, afraid they might go past their stop. Although the conductor was calling out the name of each stop as the bus arrived, his pronunciation of English was one that would take Ma Wei more than a couple of days to get used to.

Reaching Oxford Street, they both got off, and Ma Wei led his father homewards. They'd not gone far when Mr Ma stopped, snorted, and lifted up the little teapot to inspect it again. He was in the habit of coming to a sudden halt, forcing people behind him to hastily dodge to the right or left if they hoped to avoid bumping into him and piling up in an ever-mounting heap. He would stop whenever the mood took him. Ma Wei was helpless to do anything except slowly trail after him, following in his footsteps, making father and son look like loach fish in a bowl, the first moving steadily before abruptly stopping, sending the other fish darting in sudden confusion.

At long last, they arrived home. Mr Ma stood outside the door and wiped the little teapot all over with the cuff of his sleeve. Then, teapot in hand, he unlocked the door.

Mrs Wedderburn had long since finished her lunch and was resting in the drawing room. She saw them return, but didn't call out hello.

The moment Mr Ma stepped in through the front door, he exclaimed, 'Mrs Wedderburn!'

'Here, Mr Ma!' she said from the drawing room, 'Come in.'

Mr Ma went in, followed by Ma Wei. Napoleon, in the middle of his siesta, heard them arrive but didn't open his eyes, just snuffled two nasal grunts.

'Look, Mrs Wedderburn!' Mr Ma raised the teapot aloft, his face wreathed in smiles, and his voice unusually soft and tender, as if he felt an imminent return to youth.

Having just finished her meal, Mrs Wedderburn was finding herself hard put to stay awake. The powder had worn off her nose, leaving her petite nose-tip exposed like a half-ripe hawthorn berry. In Mr Ma's eyes, there was some inexpressible beauty about that nose.

She was on the point of getting up when Mr Ma forestalled her by placing the little teapot right before her eyes. He still remembered how, when he'd been playing with Napoleon, her hair had almost brushed against his jacket, and he was now beginning a concerted campaign to win her heart. Love was a step-by-step advance. Only by moving forwards could one hope to attain a kiss. And without a kiss, what chance for love?

In all other matters, Mr Ma retreated. Only with women did he advocate advancing. And his technique in this respect was not without its strong points. Indeed, we must admit that in this field Mr Ma was something of a genius.

Mrs Wedderburn leant forwards, took the little teapot from him, cocked her head to one side and examined the object closely. Mr Ma watched her, his face as bright as a little red balloon.

'How pretty! Oh, lovely! It's real china, isn't it?' said Mrs Wedderburn, pointing at the red cockscomb flowers and the two little chickens on the teapot.

Hearing her praise Chinese porcelain tickled Mr Ma pink. 'I bought it for you, Mrs Wedderburn.'

'For me? Really, Mr Ma?'

Her eyes shone big and round, her lips formed an O and what little of her décolletage was visible turned a gentle pink. 'How many pounds would this little teapot be worth?'

'Oh, it's nothing,' said Mr Ma, and pointed at the vase on the table. 'I knew you were fond of Chinese porcelain. That little vase is Chinese, isn't it?'

'Oh, what sharp eyes you've got. You do notice things! I bought that vase from a soldier. Napoleon, why don't you get up and thank Mr Ma!'

She picked Napoleon up, and pressed down the dog's head with one hand to make it perform two nods in Mr Ma's direction. Very sleepy, Napoleon never opened his eyes. Even when she'd made Napoleon thank Mr Ma, Mrs Wedderburn still felt guilty about taking the little teapot.

'Mr Ma, we'll do a swap. I do love your teapot. If you'll let me have it, you can take my vase and sell that. Though it probably isn't worth that much. I paid . . . How much did I pay for it now? I've forgotten.'

'A swap? Now then, don't make any fuss,' said Mr Ma with a smile.

Ma Wei was standing by the window, his eyes riveted on his father, his fingers crossed that his father's next move wouldn't be to give her that ring. Mr Ma was indeed fingering the ring in his pocket, but didn't bring it out.

'Tell me, Mr Ma: how much is this little teapot worth? Just so that I can tell people when they ask me.' Mrs Wedderburn clasped the teapot to her breast, like a little girl clutching a doll she's just been bought. 'How much is it worth?'

Mr Ma pushed his spectacles upwards and turned to Ma Wei. 'How much would you say it's worth?' he asked him.

'How should I know?' said Ma Wei. 'Take a look to see if there's a price inside the lid.'

'Ah yes. Here, give it to me and I'll have a look,' Mr Ma said melodiously.

'No, let me look,' said Mrs Wedderburn, anxious to show that she could do something, and gently removed the lid of the teapot. 'Goodness! Five pounds ten shillings! Five pounds ten shillings!'

Twisting his neck, Mr Ma leant closer so that he could see. 'Why, so it is. How much is that in Chinese money?' He paused. 'Sixty yuan. That's a bit steep! Paying sixty yuan *for a teapot!* Why, if you paid one yuan twenty at the Tung-an Market you'd get a bigger one!'

Listening to all this, Ma Wei found it less and less to his liking. He grabbed his hat. 'Dad,' he said, 'I have to head off to meet Li Tzu-jung. He's waiting for me to have lunch with him.'

'Oh yes, Mr Ma. You haven't eaten lunch yet, have you?' asked Mrs Wedderburn. 'I still have a slice of cold veal. It's very tasty. Would you like it?'

Ma Wei was already out in the street, and through the curtain he could see his father's lips in motion as he chatted away still.

XII

MA WEI went back to the antiques shop to see Li Tzu-jung. 'Sorry, Mr Li. You must be starving. Where shall we eat?' asked Ma Wei.

'Call me Li. Don't worry about the Mr,' said Li Tzu-jung, grinning. By now, he'd finished tidying and cleaning the display shelves. He'd also washed his face, which made his brown cheeks even shinier. 'There's a cafe round the corner where we can get a bite to eat.' As he said this, he locked up the shop and led Ma Wei off to lunch.

The cafe was across the way from St Paul's, and through the windows the front of the cathedral and the statues outside it were clearly in view. A crowd of old women and small children were standing round the statues, feeding the pigeons with grain and bread.

'What'll you have?' asked Li Tzu-jung. 'I usually have a cup of tea, with a couple of slices of bread and a piece of cake. This is about as basic a cafe as you can find in London, and if you want a posh meal, you won't get it here. I can't afford posh meals though.'

'Whatever you feel like, order the same for me.' Ma Wei had no idea what to ask for.

Li Tzu-jung ordered his usual tea and bread, but got some fried sausages extra for Ma Wei.

All the small cafe's tables had marble tops and iron legs, the surfaces polished to a gleaming sheen. Big mirrors hung on the walls, which gave the room a bright and cheery interior and a strong impression of being crowded and busy with custom. The cakes, bread and so forth were displayed in a cabinet just inside the door, and regardless of whether the food was tasty or not, it at least looked good. The waitresses were all young girls, and very pretty too. Each wore a trim short skirt and a white pleated mop-cap. They shot to and fro like shuttles as they served the tea and food, their cheeks as shiny and rosy as the red apples in the display cabinet.

The customers were practically all from nearby shops. Everyone held an evening paper in their hands – the London evening papers come onto the streets not long after nine o'clock in the morning – and was absorbed in the horseracing or dogracing news. All you could hear in the room was the swishing sound of the girls running back and forth and the rattle of knives and forks. Hardly anybody was talking. As long as the English have got a newspaper to read, they don't feel any need to converse. Ma Wei watched closely to see what everyone was eating. By and large, they took a cup of tea with some bread and butter, and there was hardly anyone eating a meal with any vegetables in it.

'So this is regarded as the lowest class of restaurant?' asked Ma Wei.

'Doesn't it look like it?' replied Li Tzu-jung, keeping his voice down.

'It's very clean,' mumbled Ma Wei, recalling to himself the lower grade of cafes in Peking, and the black muck of the long tables with the big bowls on them.

'Oh yes, the English spend more time on presenting their food than they do eating it. Anyone here with a sense of decency prefers eating a bit less to having to put up with a dirty restaurant. We Chinese are real eaters, and we don't bother about the state of the place where we're eating. Net result: the ones who eat a bit less in a clean place are healthy and strong, while those who eat smoked chicken and roast duck in a filthy hole get thinner and thinner the more they eat —'

Before he'd finished, a girl brought them their food. As they ate, they conversed in subdued tones.

'Li, old fellow, this morning my father spoke rather —' began Ma Wei very earnestly.

'Forget it,' interrupted Li Tzu-jung. 'Aren't all old people like that?'

'Are you still willing to help my father out?'

'Without me, you'd never manage. And from my point of view, I've got to earn some money. So don't worry – we've a long and fruitful partnership yet!'

Not thinking, Li Tzu-jung laughed rather loudly, and the old men eating opposite shot him a glare. He hastily lowered his head and chewed a mouthful of bread.

'Are you still studying, then?' Ma Wei asked.

'You can't get by without studying.' As he said this, Li Tzu-jung nearly laughed again. He was so convinced of his own wit that no matter what others thought he'd always beat them to the laugh. 'Look here; eat up quick, and we'll go back and have a talk in the shop. There's a lot to be said, and you can't enjoy yourself here. The old blokes are doing nothing but glaring at me.'

The two of them hurriedly finished their meal and drank up their tea, then Li Tzu-jung stood up and asked a girl for their bill. As he took it, he pointed to Ma Wei.

'Don't you think he's handsome?' he said. 'He just told me he thought you were a right looker!'

'Get away with you!' said the young girl with a smile. Then she glanced at Ma Wei, clearly flattered that someone had found her attractive.

Ma Wei smiled back. From the way Li Tzu-jung spoke to her, it seemed obvious that they knew each other quite well, probably because he was a regular customer. Li Tzu-jung fished out two pennies and carefully placed them under the plate as a tip. He settled the bill for their meal, but asked Ma Wei for ten pence for his share. Ma Wei paid on the spot.

'That's the English way. No standing on ceremony with one another,' said Li Tzu-jung, smiling and taking the money.

They both returned to the shop, where fortunately there were no customers waiting. As if the floodgates had suddenly been released, Li Tzu-jung's speech flowed forth in mighty rivers.

'Look here, I'll give you a tip: when you're drinking tea, keep the noise down. Just now when you were drinking, didn't you notice those old blokes glaring away at you? When the English blow their noses, they put all their force into it, but when they drink, they don't make a sound. It's just a custom of theirs – right and wrong doesn't come into it. But if you don't toe the line, you're a barbarian. And they look down on us Chinese enough even without that!

'Don't scratch your head or clean your nails or belch when in the presence of others. I know – so many rules of etiquette! Some of our famous gentlemen-scholars who study abroad just completely ignore these things. But since the foreigners already turn up their noses at us, I don't see the point of doing one's best to make them dislike us all the more.

'I didn't bother about such things myself at first, but I learnt my lesson fast. I went with a friend once to someone's house for a meal. After we'd finished, I was feeling nicely satisfied, so I raised my chin and let out a long, deep belch. Well, that did it – a young lady next to me at once turned her face away and said to my friend, "People without manners should do us all a favour and stay home!" The person who'd invited us to the meal was an old clergyman, an ex-missionary in China, and he immediately grabbed his chance. "Now you see why we have to go and teach in China," he told the girl. "They need us to teach them proper table manners." What could I do? Stay put? I was rigid with panic. Clear off? But I felt that'd be awkward too – it was mortifying! Of course there's nothing in a belch, but if you do it they really treat you like a savage. Just watch it, Ma, old lad. Don't mind me telling you, do you?'

'Oh no,' said Ma Wei, sitting down.

Li Tzu-jung took a seat too, and continued. 'Right, I ought to tell you my history. I started off as a student studying abroad on a scholarship from the Shantung provincial government. First I went to America and got a BA in Commerce. After I'd got my degree, I came to Europe – France first. But when I got to Paris, I found myself in a tight spot. There was fighting going on in China, which cut off any hopes of my getting any more money from the authorities there. I'm from a poor family, and it wasn't any use asking my folks for money. So I scraped around here and there, and got together enough cash to see me to England.

'Of course, I knew that the cost of living was higher in England than in France, but I also knew that if I got a job in England the wages would be higher. And England's a trading nation, so I thought I could probably learn something there. And I'll confess there was another reason. I really couldn't afford to go out with Parisian women. Here in London, nobody apart from prostitutes has any time for the Chinese, so I thought I might be less troubled by temptations!' At this point, Li Tzu-jung broke into a guffaw, and raked his hair vigorously.

'Li, old chap, didn't you just say you shouldn't scratch your head in company?' said Ma Wei jokingly.

'You're not a foreigner, though! I certainly wouldn't do it in the presence of a foreigner. Where was I? Ah, yes. When I got to London, there was still no money to be had from the government at home, and I was properly desperate. I lived in the East End of London for about a month, and apart from a few books and the clothes I stood in, I was really skint.

'Eventually the police took pity on me, and found me a job doing a bit of interpreting for Chinese people. The Chinese workmen here have got very limited English, and the police pull them in for questioning at the drop of a hat. And even the best Chinese person is forever bent on lawsuits. Must be why they say "Never get reincarnated as a Chinaman", eh? So I did the rounds as an interpreter. My Cantonese isn't actually that good, but I could get by with it – better than the English police, anyway. If I hadn't been scared I'd die of starvation, I'd never have taken on a job like that, but when hunger stares you in the face, you don't have much choice. And when I saw all my fellow countrymen getting mucked around and made fun of by the English police, well, I wanted to do it. I was in the same boat as those workmen – helpless. All I managed from the job was three or four pounds a month, but that was enough to see me through.

'Later, I gradually got into doing translations into Chinese, for ads and that sort of stuff. That was quite a good wicket. The firms that sell goods in China aren't small ones, of course, so I'd always make a decent pound or two from translating an ad. Combining my two incomes I managed to get by, but I still couldn't afford to study. Luckily, your uncle was looking for a shop assistant, one who knew something about business and could speak English. I went to see him, and clinched the job straight away.

'Ask yourself: how many of our young gentlemen studying abroad would stoop to working in a shop, earning themselves a couple of pounds a week as an errand boy and odd-job man? But when I got my hands on that extra two pounds, it was like I'd gone to heaven. So things were all right then – I could study. I do the interpreting and work in the shop during the day, and attend my university lectures in the evenings. What do you think of that, Ma, my old lad?'

'Can't have been easy. You're a good sort, old Li.'

'Not easy? Nothing comes easy in this world.' Li Tzu-jung plonked his feet heavily as he stood up, wearing a decided look of self-satisfaction.

'What's the least one person could get by on per month in London?' asked Ma Wei.

'Twenty pounds, minimum. But I'm an exception. All the time I've been here, I've never once eaten a Chinese meal. It's not that I couldn't afford one, but I'm afraid that once I had one, I'd never be able to stop.'

'Are there some Chinese restaurants here then?'

'Oh yes! Cooking food and washing laundry, those are the two great Chinese overseas enterprises.' Li Tzu-jung sat down again. 'Wherever the Japanese go, there are Japanese brothels. Wherever the Chinese go, there are little restaurants and laundries. The difference is that besides the brothels the Japanese have also got steamships, banks and big businesses. The Chinese haven't got any industry apart from cuisine and clothes-washing. That's why the Japanese are forever looking smug while we never dare to straighten our shoulders! But the Europeans and Americans look down on the Japanese and Chinese equally. The only difference is that they call the Japanese "Japs" behind their backs and flatter them to their faces, while they say nasty things about the Chinese directly to them; it's downright uncivil.

'But let's not go on about that. If we can't sort ourselves out, it's no good blaming others. Ask me about something else, will you? It's enough to send me into a fury.'

'Well, you ought to be telling me something about the shop.'

'Right. Listen – your uncle was really on the ball, a very smart man indeed. He didn't just rely on selling antiques. Antiques aren't like bread: you can't expect regular day-to-day sales with them. He dealt in stocks and shares as well, and bought various goods for merchants in Canton. This shop barely managed to earn him two hundred pounds a year, after all the overheads were paid. The two thousand pounds or so that he left you all came from his other dealings. Now you've inherited his money, the best thing you could do would be to expand the business. If you really throw yourselves into it, you might have some hope of making a quid. But if you just stick with the shop as it is, I'm afraid you won't even earn enough for your own living. And once the two thousand pounds has been frittered away, you'll be in a real fix.

'What you've got to do, Ma, old chap, is persuade your father to decide right now to expand the business or to open up another little line of trade. My view is that it'd be best to go in for this same business in a bigger way, because there aren't any fixed prices with curios and antiques, and with a bit of luck you can earn a few hundred pounds on one item alone. Of course, it all depends on your skills and ability, but it's certainly not easy opening up any other line of business. Look at the small shops along this street: tobacconists, pubs and so on. They're all branches of a few big companies whose capital runs into millions. Trying to compete against them with only hundreds or even a couple of thousand pounds behind you would be a sheer waste of effort, wouldn't it?'

'My father's no businessman, and it's very difficult to discuss anything with him.' Ma Wei frowned, and his face had gone a bit paler, too.

'Seems like the old gentleman's got a mandarin complex, which makes things difficult. If the Chinese can't smash up their obsessions with mandarin values and jobs in government, they'll never get anywhere.' Li Tzu-jung paused for a moment, then continued. 'Luckily, there's us two as well. We'll just have to put pressure on him to get to it. Otherwise the shop'll start running at a loss, and as soon as that happens, your future will really be in danger. But look here – what are you planning on doing?'

'Me? Study.'

'Study what? Are you going to be another one of those who wrangle themselves a degree by translating a chapter of our old Taoist philosopher Chuang Tzu?' asked Li Tzu-jung with a smile.

'No, I'm thinking of studying commerce. What do you think?'

'Commerce, eh? Fine. First go and brush up your English, and then, when you're confident, go and study commerce. Not a bad idea.'

The two of them talked for ages, and the more Ma Wei got to know Li Tzu-jung, the more likeable he found him. As they spoke, Li Tzu-jung grew increasingly enthusiastic and lively, and they chatted until four o'clock before calling it a day. As Ma Wei was on the point of leaving, Li Tzu-jung told him he'd accompany him and his father to the police station tomorrow morning, to help them report their arrival.

'Lawyers and doctors are two indispensable treasures to the English, but you're better off using neither while you're here. I warn you: don't break the law, and don't get sick. The two most vital things when you're in England!' Li Tzu-jung carried on hastily, 'Look here, from tomorrow we'll speak English when we see each other. You've got to practise it. There are lots of Chinese overseas students who can't stand speaking foreign languages, but luckily we're "working-class" students with no need to imitate the gentry.'

The two of them stood outside the shop, talking for ages. As they were chatting, the manager of the shop next door came out, and Li Tzu-jung hastened to introduce him to Ma Wei.

Ma Wei raised his head and glanced at the dome of St Paul's. Without waiting to be asked, Li Tzu-jung launched into a history of the cathedral.

Having listened to the history of St Paul's, Ma Wei made to leave again. Li Tzu-jung came after him, as eager as some Robinson Crusoe who's met his Man Friday.

'Can I ask you something, Ma, old lad? Has your father given you that ring of yours?'

'No, he's still got it,' said Ma Wei quietly.

'Ask him to hand it over. Your uncle left it to you, and what's yours is yours.'

Ma Wei nodded his head, and slowly made off along the street. The clock of St Paul's Cathedral struck five o'clock.

PART THREE

I

SPRING DEPARTED with the flowers and summer, wrapped in a suit of green leaves, came dancing along upon the warm breezes. And what do you know – even London came in for its share of clear skies. Carloads of Americans in straw hats sped the streets, catching a fleeting glimpse of London on their tours of the continent. The leaves of the city's towering plane trees shimmered in the sun as they stirred to and fro, radiating a green sparkle. All around the edge of the blue sky over the buildings hung a white vapour of mist. It was all quite exhilarating, but somehow made you feel rather impatient.

Huge, piteous, pitiful bulldogs, seeming to expend all their energy from their tongues, panted along by the legs of their young mistresses. There was more traffic than ever on the streets, with tourists – forty or fifty to one coach, and wearing little paper hats of different colours – haring around, yelling and screeching, cramming London to bursting point. In stations, at bus stops, in the main streets and on the buses were hung gaudy posters advertising summer holidays. Besides dodging in and out of the traffic, people all seemed preoccupied with trying to manage a few days by the sea or in the countryside.

The girls looked especially pretty, with their white arms bared and wearing big straw hats with brims that swept down to their shoulders. And the hats themselves had all kinds of wonderful decorations – embroidered purses from old China, china dolls from Japan, ostrich feathers, huge daisies . . . If you sat upstairs

93

in the bus and looked down, it appeared as if countless large, bright mushrooms were walking along both sides of the street.

In the midst of such exciting bustle, Ma Wei's eyes would brim with two hot tears, and he'd say to himself, 'Look at them all: earning money; enjoying life. Happy, full of hopes. And just look at us, all suffering and hardship, scrimping and scraping. Save a couple of coppers, and the military bigwigs grab it from you. Huh . . .'

From May onwards, Miss Wedderburn spent a lot of time working out where to go for her summer holiday. Every evening she discussed it with her mother, but they never reached any decision. Her mother wanted her to go to Scotland to see some of her relatives, but the daughter thought the train fares would be too expensive, and was in favour of going to a nearby seaside resort for a few days. The mother changed her mind, and decided to go with her daughter to the seaside, but then the daughter felt it would be more interesting to go to Scotland than to the sea. The mother was on the point of writing a letter to her relatives in Scotland when it occurred to the daughter that there'd be much more excitement to be had at the seaside than in Scotland.

Young ladies take summer holidays not to enjoy a restful interlude, but to find a crowded place where they can skip around, having a ball, showing off their new dresses, exhibiting their slim, pale arms, and – it being the seaside – taking the chance to display their fair, bare thighs. So mother and daughter fought like cat and dog, in accordance with that English independence of spirit whereby each person must have his own idea and never yield to the other, which results, as the argument proceeds, in an ever-increasing distance of opinion between the two parties.

'Mary' – that was Miss Wedderburn's first name – said Mrs Wedderburn one day, 'we can't go together. If we both go away, who's going to cook for Mr Ma?'

'Tell them to go and have a summer holiday too,' said Miss Wedderburn, twinkling her dimples like a mischievous child.

'I've asked Mr Ma about it, and he's not taking any time off.' Mrs Wedderburn uttered the word 'not' with particular vehemence, and stuck the dainty tip of her nose into the air as if to shoo some fly that had settled on the ceiling. There was a fly there, too, as it happened.

'What?' Mary's eyes popped so wide that her eyelashes shot up. 'Not taking a holiday? I've never heard of such a thing!'

Yes, the English really have never heard of such a thing – that there should be people in this world who work for their living all year round, and never, ever stop working. She paused for a moment.

'That young Ma Wei,' she said with a giggle, 'told me he wanted to take a trip to the seaside with me. I told him I wasn't going with any Chinaman! Go with him – what a laugh!'

'Mary! You shouldn't be so rude to people. Actually, Mr Ma and his son really aren't so bad.' Although Mrs Wedderburn didn't like Chinese people, she had an argumentative spirit. If somebody said that red roses smelt the best, she'd unfailingly declare that white ones had the most marvellous perfume, or at least that pink ones were the best – despite having been perfectly aware right from the start that neither smelt as beautiful as red ones.

'Oh-ho, Mum!' said Mary, cocking her head on one side and twisting her rosy lips sarcastically. 'You've fallen for that old Mr Ma, thanks to his tin of tea and that dinky teapot. If I were you, I'd never have accepted his gifts. Look at the old wretch's face: looks as if someone's punched it swollen. Have you noticed how he just sits there for ages without saying a word? And that young Ma Wei's even more horrible. When he's got nothing else to do, he asks me if I'll go out with him. Asked me again yesterday, he did – if I'd go to the pictures with him. I —'

'And when he does take you to the pictures, it's always him who buys your ticket, isn't it?' Mrs Wedderburn rebuked Mary, with a stern look on her face.

'I've never asked him to pay for my ticket. If I give him the money, he won't take it. And while we're on that subject, Mum, you still owe me sixpence.'

'I'll pay you back tomorrow, I promise.' Mrs Wedderburn felt around in her purse, but as she'd thought, she didn't have enough. 'You know what I think? The Chinese are more generous than us.

You just watch when Mr Ma gives Ma Wei any money. He just stuffs his hand into his pocket, and hands him money without even counting it. And when Ma Wei does any shopping for his father, he never pesters him to get the money back. What's more,' Mrs Wedderburn shook her head, then put her bun back in place with a gentle prod of her finger, 'every week when Mr Ma pays the rent, he takes the receipt and crams it into his pocket with barely a glance, and hands me the money. Never ever argues about the amount.'

'How quaint! How novel!' said Mary, smiling.

'What do you mean?'

'"Ethics alter in accordance with economics."' Mary stuck out her chest and put a hand behind her back, with the air of a university professor. 'Our forebears used to live with all the family, young and old, together in one house, with everything shared – including money – just like the Chinese do. Nowadays we've got a different economic system, with each earning his own money and eating his own food. And our ideas of what's good have changed along with it. We prize independence, so we stake our claim to our own money. And the Chinese aren't any more generous than us, either! It's just that their economic system hasn't developed to —'

'Where on earth did you get all that from? Trying to show off with your learned airs!'

'Never you mind where I heard it from.' Miss Mary rolled her eyes, tipped her head to one side and giggled. 'Anyhow, it's true isn't it, Mum? Isn't it?' Seeing her mother nod, she continued. 'It's no good you sticking up for the Chinese, Mum. If they weren't so horrible, why would all the Chinese in films and plays and books be murderers or arsonists or rapists?'

Miss Mary's economical and ethical notions derived from her reading of the newspaper, along with her hatred of the Chinese. As none of this knowledge was really the product of her own research, you couldn't really blame her. If China wasn't such a shambles of a country, where would the foreign newspapers get their bad news from?

'None of the things you see in films are true.' In her heart, Mrs

Wedderburn didn't exactly feel any great love for the Chinese, but she couldn't resist rebutting her daughter's arguments. 'In my opinion, it's very mean to laugh and make jokes about people from weak countries.'

'Go on, Mum! If it's not true, then every film and every play and every book is wrong, and even if fifty per cent of them are wrong, that still leaves fifty per cent that have to be telling the truth, doesn't it?' Mary was determined to win her mother round to her way of thinking, and, poking her head forwards, demanded, 'Doesn't it, Mum? Doesn't it?'

Mrs Wedderburn gave a feeble cough and said nothing, buying time as she formulated further arguments with which to assail her daughter.

A sound came at the door, then another, like a bit of hemp rope thwacking against the wood.

'Napoleon!' Mrs Wedderburn said to Mary. 'Let him in.'

Mary opened the door and in bounded Napoleon, wagging his tail.

'Napoleon, my darling. Come here and help me make her see sense.' Mrs Wedderburn clapped her hands and called to Napoleon. 'She's got no business going and listening to all that rotten twaddle, and then coming back here to try to show us how smart she is. Has she, darling?'

As Napoleon came into the room, Miss Wedderburn knelt down, knees together on the carpet, and started playing. As she crawled backwards, the little dog flattened his forelegs and got ready to leap forwards. She screwed up her mouth and suddenly let out a 'Whooh!' The little dog jerked himself back with a flick of his body, then gave a bark. She watched him sideways out of the corner of her eye as he sidled up to her and gently took her plump wrist in his mouth.

They carried on playing like that until Mary's hair had got all untidy with the bumping and romping, and all the powder had come off her nose. Then Napoleon went round behind her and nipped the heel of her shoe.

'Mum! Look at your dog – he's bitten my new shoes!'

'Come here quickly, Napoleon. Don't bother playing with her.'

Mary stood up, out of breath, and after tidying her hair she brandished her fist at Napoleon. The little dog took refuge under Mrs Wedderburn's legs, peeping out at Mary with his beady eyes blinking wetly.

Once she'd got her breath back, Mary launched into the holiday discussion again with her mother. Mrs Wedderburn was still suggesting that they go on their summer vacations separately so that the Mas could be catered for, but Mary wasn't having a bar of it.

'Anyway, I can't cook, can I, Mum?'

'Then you ought to start learning!' Mrs Wedderburn seized the chance to take a dig at her daughter.

'I tell you what,' said Mary. 'We'll go together, and we'll write a letter to Aunt Dolly and get her to come here and cook for them. How's that? She lives in the countryside, so I bet she'd love to spend a few days in the city. We'll have to pay her train fare, though.'

'All right then. You write her the letter, and I'll pay her train fare,' agreed her mother.

Miss Wedderburn went to wash her hands, looked at herself in the mirror, put her head to one side and powdered her face. Examining herself from every possible angle, she kept on till the powder was spread evenly and flawlessly over her whole face. Then she fetched her stationery, pen and ink, pushed the small table right up to the drawing-room window, sat down, pulled the pleats of her skirt straight, and stuck the pen in the ink bottle.

A man outside selling apples gave a shout, so she put the pen down and pulled aside the curtain to have a look. Then she picked the pen up again, put her head on one side, drew a few tiny apples on the blotting paper, then lightly flicked the stem of the pen with her middle finger so that the ink came off the nib drop by drop, slowly blotting out the little apples she'd drawn. Next, she stuck the pen back in the ink bottle and inspected her plump hands. She pulled out a nail file and filed her nails, then placed the file on the blotting paper, but, thinking better of it, picked it up again, blew on it, and placed it beside the envelopes. Picking up the pen once more, she flicked a few further blots onto the blotting paper. Some of the blots weren't perfectly round, so she carefully perfected them with the nib of her pen. And when she'd finished rounding off the blots, she stood up.

'You write it, Mum. I'll go and give Napoleon a bath, shall I?'

'I've got to do some shopping!' Mrs Wedderburn came across the room, holding the little dog. 'How is it that when you're writing to your boyfriends, you can dash off five or six pages with no trouble? Very strange, I must say!'

'Nobody likes writing to their aunts!'

Mary handed her mother the pen, took Napoleon from her and ruffled his ears. 'Come with me and have a bath, you filthy little creature!'

II

WHAT EXPERIENCE Mr Ma had gained from his three or four months in London didn't amount to much. He'd managed to find three or four little Chinese restaurants, and went to one of them every day for his lunch. He was by now able to reach home from the shop without needing Ma Wei to guide him. His English had made fair progress, but he'd forgotten quite a bit of grammar in the process, since a lot of working-class English people don't bother about proper grammar when they speak.

There were no fixed rules to his days. Sometimes he would hurry to the shop at nine o'clock in the morning, and on his own and at leisure rearrange the antiques in the window, as he always thought that Li Tzu-jung had set them out in a tasteless, incorrect manner. Li Tzu-jung had tried lots of times to demonstrate how things should best be displayed and how colours should be matched, so as to attract the attention of passers-by. Mr Ma would give a slight shake of his head, and pretend he hadn't heard him.

The first time Mr Ma set out the items on display, he held each in both hands as if he was bearing a funeral slab, with his tongue stuck slightly out, holding his breath, not daring to breathe again until he'd set the object down in its place. After he'd done the window a few times, he grew emboldened, and would sometimes deliberately test his own dexterity. He'd pick things up, purposely averting his eyes, just like some airily blasé waiter serving food in a restaurant. Once, when Li Tzu-jung was also in the shop, Mr Ma got even more caught up in his display of nonchalance, and, not content with carrying things in his hands, held a small teapot in his mouth. Twitching his little moustache in a superior smile, he sneaked a sidelong glance at Tzu-jung, thinking, *Oh I despise businessmen, of course. But when it comes to business, I'm up there with the best of them!*

At this point, just when he was feeling so pleased with himself, his mouth suddenly felt dry and he had to cough. Gravity took its toll on the little teapot and it was smashed to smithereens. In his anxiety to save it he panicked, and the small vase and two plates he was holding became extraordinarily slippery. Li Tzu-jung ran over to relieve him of the two plates, but the neck of the vase was delicate and broke as it hit the floor.

When he'd finished with his window-dressing, Mr Ma went out and took a surreptitious look at the window of the antiques shop next door. Twirling his scrappy string of a moustache, he nodded approvingly in the direction of his own newly arranged window, and confirmed that the other shop had laid out its windows in a most tasteless manner. Yet he had to admit that his neighbour did better trade than him. Unable to divine the reason why, he could only condemn all the English as vulgar and lacking in taste.

The managers of the shop next door were a big, fat old fellow with no hair on his head, and an old woman, also big and fat but with hair on her head, a considerable quantity of it. A number of times they'd chatted to Mr Ma in an attempt to get on familiar terms with him, but he would sharply turn his head away, delivering a considerable snub, after which he would sit in his little chair and reflect upon the matter with a quiet smile. *Your business may be doing well, but that doesn't entitle you to my attention. What rudeness!*

Li Tzu-jung advised him time and again to add to his stock, to print a few pamphlets and catalogues of his wares, and to broaden his range to include things other than Chinese curios.

Mr Ma put him in his place with a few acid remarks. 'Increase our stock? What we have already takes forever to display, doesn't it? There's enough here to make your eyes dizzy as it is!'

Sometimes, as the mood took Mr Ma, he'd stay away from the shop the whole day, and plant flowers and so on for Mrs

Wedderburn. When the Mas had first arrived in London, the small patch of garden behind her house had nothing growing in it but a strip of grass and two half-dead dogrose bushes. She was very fond of flowers, but had no time to plant and tend them. Nor could she bear to part with the money to buy seedlings. Her daughter was forever buying cut flowers in town, but likewise professed little interest in growing flowers.

One day, without mentioning it to Mrs Wedderburn, Mr Ma bought a bunch of young plants in town: five or six rosebushes, fifteen or so wallflower seedlings, a heap of dahlia tubers which had just started sprouting, and a few rather unpromising chrysanthemums with very straggly stems and leaves, not looking very green.

He left the flowers in a corner of the garden by the wall, and first watered them with a couple of buckets of water. Then he went into the kitchen, got out the spade and trowel and made a little mound of earth in the middle of the grass, around the edge of which he planted the roses. In the middle he planted the wallflowers in a cross formation. The dahlias he planted at the foot of the walls, and he stuck in all the hopeless chrysanthemums along both sides of the little path leading to the back door.

When he'd planted all the flowers, he put away the spade and trowel, collecting a bucket of water on the way, and gave everything a good watering. Then he washed his hands and went to the drawing room to smoke a pipe. After that, he hurried off to the shop, tracked down some small sticks and some string and came rushing back, puffing and panting, to give all the flowers some support by securing them to the sticks with the string. No sooner had he finished tying them than it began to rain softly. He stood in a dreamy daze, watching the flowers gently nod in the rain, and not till the drops had drenched his hair and he was dripping with water did it occur to him to get indoors.

That afternoon, after Mrs Wedderburn had let the dog out for a play in the garden, she came rushing upstairs with wide eyes and mouth agape.

'Mr Ma! Did you plant the flowers in the garden?'

Mr Ma shifted his pipe to the side of his mouth and gave a small smile.

'Oh, Mr Ma! It's so good of you! And very naughty too. Without saying a word! How much did the flowers cost?'

'I didn't spend a lot. It's nice to have a few flowers to look at,' said Mr Ma, smiling.

'Are the Chinese fond of flowers then?' asked Mrs Wedderburn. It would never ever occur to the English that there might be other flower lovers in the world besides themselves.

'Yes, of course they are!' Mr Ma caught the implication of her words, but, disinclined to argue, simply emphasised his words and squeezed out a rather pallid half-smile. He paused vacantly for a moment, then said, 'After my wife died, I used to amuse myself planting flowers when I'd nothing else to do.'

At the thought of his wife, Mr Ma's eyes moistened somewhat. Mrs Wedderburn nodded, recalling her husband. When he was alive, that little garden had been full of blooms all year round.

Mr Ma stood up and invited her to sit down, and the two of them chatted for more than an hour. She asked what sort of clothes Mrs Ma had liked wearing, and what sort of hats. He asked her what her husband's favourite tobacco had been, and what government post he'd held. They chatted on with ever-decreasing understanding but ever-increasing warmth and amity. He told her that Mrs Ma used to wear a long sleeveless jacket of purple Chiang-ning silk. She'd never seen one of those. She told him that Mr Wedderburn had never been in the civil service. Mr Ma couldn't for the life of him imagine why anyone should by choice have failed to become a government official . . .

That evening when Miss Wedderburn came home, her mother, without giving her any time even to take off her hat, rushed her into the back garden.

'Come here, Mary, hurry. I've got something new to show you.'

'Oh, Mummy, what've you been doing, spending money on flowers like this?' said Mary, bending down and sniffing at a flower.

'Me? Mr Ma bought and planted them. You're always on about

how bad the Chinese are, but now look!'

Mary hastily straightened up and stopped smelling them. 'Nothing particularly amazing about planting a few flowers.'

'I'm just trying to show you that the Chinese appreciate flowers like civilised people do . . .'

'If you like flowers that doesn't mean you don't also like murdering people and setting places on fire! It's true, Mum! I saw three photos in today's paper, all taken in Shanghai. It looked awful, Mum. They chop off people's heads and hang them on telegraph poles. And that's not all – in the photo there was a crowd of people – men and women, all ages – watching it just as if they were watching a film.' As she said this, Mary's face went very pale, her lips trembled uncontrollably and she fled back into the house.

After planting the flowers in the back garden, Mr Ma acquired a new duty: whenever Mrs Wedderburn was too busy, he took Napoleon out into the street for a stroll and some recreation. The little garden had originally been Napoleon's playground, but the dog, seeing an insect, would bound high into the air to try to catch it. And as he jumped, the insect would fly away but the flowers would get knocked over. So he just had to be taken out for a stroll each day, and consequently Mr Ma acquired the noble task of doing so.

Miss Mary tried again and again to dissuade her mother from letting the elder Ma take the dog out. She'd heard that the Chinese ate dog meat. What if it just so happened that the elder Ma got peckish on the walk, and cut Napoleon to bits with his penknife? What on earth would she do then?

'I've asked Mr Ma, and he says the Chinese don't eat dogs,' said Mrs Wedderburn, her face stubbornly set.

'I've got it! Now I know what's got you, Mum!' said Mary, deliberately teasing her mother. 'He's fond of flowers. He's fond of dogs. All he needs now is to be fond of babies!' (The English assumption is that a man who likes flowers, dogs and little children makes a good husband.)

Mrs Wedderburn said nothing, just glared at her daughter, half frowning, half smiling.

Ma Wei tried to persuade his father not to take the dog out, as he'd seen the crowd of children who would follow Mr Ma, jeering and hooting, when he led the dog along the streets or strolled with it around some vacant site.

'Look at old yellow face! Look at his face – all yellow and puffed up . . .'

One time a little mousy-haired boy with no front teeth even ran up and tugged at Mr Ma's coat. Another one, a miserable little waif, picked Napoleon up and ran off with him, to make Mr Ma chase him. And once Mr Ma started pursuing him, all the other children lifted their heads and shouted, 'Look at his legs! Just like a Pekingese! Tommy!' – the urchin must have been called Tommy – 'Hurry! Don't let him catch you!'

'Tommy!' shouted a shrill-voiced little girl, with hair nearly as red as her cheeks. 'Hold onto the dog. Don't let it drop!'

When they teach history at the average school in England, they don't teach anything about China. The only people who know anything Chinese are those who've been to China as merchants or as missionaries. These two types of people are usually not well disposed towards the Chinese, and when they return to England and talk about China, they don't talk about its better aspects. And since China's not a strong nation, and has no navy or army worth the name, how can it possibly avoid being an object of scorn for Europeans, who judge a nation's civilisation solely on the quality of its military? What's more, China still hasn't produced any trailblazing scientists, literary figures or explorers. It doesn't even send a team to the Olympics. Remember all that, and it's not hard to see why Chinese aren't held in high regard.

Ma Wei tried to talk his father out of his daily walk with Napoleon, but his father wouldn't listen. Mr Ma collected a large number of cigarette cards, intending to try to bribe that crowd of little mischief-makers with them. In the event, it only made the children enjoy their mischief all the more.

'Call him "Chink"! Call him "Chink"! When you call him that, he gives you fag cards!'

'Tommy! Grab his dog!'

III

IN THE small red house in Lancaster Road, Mrs Ely issued her command: the two Mas, Mrs Wedderburn and daughter, and her own elder brother were to be invited round for a meal. The first to jump to attention in response was of course the Reverend Ely.

Madam Ely held absolute power within the household. Her son and husband didn't question her. Her daughter, now grown up, wasn't quite as obedient as she had once been. Children get more and more difficult to deal with as they grow up, whereas husbands become easier to control as they grow old. Why otherwise would so many Western women choose to marry old fellows?

Mrs Ely didn't issue commands with her voice alone – frankly, her whole being was a command. She had only to widen her eyes – big fawny-brown orbs, at least three times the size of her husband's, and with permanently puffy eyelids – and husband, daughter and son would all shut their mouths, while the atmosphere would become as stern and solemn as in a court of law.

She had a little black moustache – very soft, very black and very heavy. That, surely, was the reason why the Reverend Ely had never grown a moustache? He didn't dare compete with her. She was a head taller than him too, tall, big, and strong to boot. Her face was gaunt, and her skin looked as tough as cement and chopped-hemp plaster. On either side of her nose ran a deep, narrow furrow, right down to her mouth. When she wept – even Mrs Ely occasionally wept! – her tears had these handy channels down which to flow, but, drying almost as soon as they left her eyes, they never made it far. Her hair was a dirty white, and tied very loosely in a bun at the back of her head. If you looked at it absent-mindedly, you'd imagine you were looking at the torn-up kapok stuffing of a padded slipper.

The Reverend Ely had met her in Tientsin. In those days, the furrows on either side of her nose were already deep but her bun didn't quite look like kapok. He'd been very impatient to have a family, and she'd no objection to having a husband, so they agreed to marry each other. Her elder brother, Alexander, hadn't been very happy about the match. Being a merchant, he naturally had little regard for a petty, moralising pastor of poor financial prospects. But he'd said nothing.

Lucky to get married at all, he'd told himself, as he looked at the furrows on her face and that nondescript head of hair. *So who cares if it's a clergyman? Another few years, and those ditches on her face'll be bloody riverbeds, and she won't be able to snag herself even a clergyman.*

This thought had sent him off into fits of private laughter. He'd said nothing to his sister, though, and on the day of the wedding he even bought her a pair of Fukien lacquer vases.

What good taste and discernment my brother has, Mrs Ely would think whenever she looked at that pair of vases. They must surely be worth at least five or six pounds.

Oh, and besides the vases, Alexander had given his little sister a cheque for forty pounds as a wedding present.

The Elys' children – the perfect combination, one daughter and one son – were both born in China, but neither could speak Chinese. Mrs Ely's fundamental pedagogic principle dictated that inferior languages bred an inferior mind. If children learnt languages such as Chinese and Hindi from the moment they opened their mouths, you could be certain they wouldn't grow up with a good character. (But if, for instance, a Chinese child spoke English from infancy, it could never grow up to be as loathsome as the average Chinese person.) If you watered English tomatoes with Chinese water they'd never grow big and juicy, would they? On no account would Mrs Ely permit her children to play with

Chinese children, and she only allowed them to speak the absolute minimum of indispensable Chinese words, such as those for 'Bring tea!', 'Go!', 'One chicken!', with the exclamation mark denoting the imperative of every such command.

The Reverend Ely didn't exactly favour this approach. With his traditional English utilitarianism, he was very willing for his children to learn a bit of Chinese. When some day they returned to England, it might provide them with the means to earn some money. But he didn't dare openly challenge his wife. In any case, Mrs Ely was well versed in the value of utilitarianism. It's true she wouldn't let her children learn Chinese, but she'd no objections to their learning French. Not that she'd ever thought highly of French, either – what finer language was there in the world than English? But even English aristocrats and scholars had to learn French, so she wasn't going to be outdone in that respect.

Her son was called Paul, and her daughter Catherine. When Paul had reached the age of twelve, he'd gone back to England for his schooling, and, once in England, had forgotten any scraps of Chinese he'd learnt, except for a few swearwords. Catherine, however, had gone to an international school in China, and had learnt a fair amount of Chinese behind her mother's back. She was even able, with the help of a dictionary, to read easy Chinese books.

'Kay!' commanded Mrs Ely from the kitchen, 'Prepare a rice pudding. The Chinese are fond of rice.'

'But they're not fond of having it with milk and sugar, Mum,' said Miss Catherine.

'What do you know about China? Do you know more than I do?' said Mrs Ely, holding her head stiffly erect. She didn't believe there was anyone else in the world who knew as much about China as she did. No British ambassador to China, no English professor of Chinese would show her up. She'd often say to the Reverend Ely – to others she might have expressed it rather less bluntly – 'What does Mr Manning the ambassador understand about such things! Or Professor Price either? Perhaps they know a few bits and pieces about China, but it is only we who are truly able to understand the Chinese, the Chinese soul!'

Aware of her mother's disposition, Catherine said nothing, just lowered her head and went off to prepare the rice pudding.

Mrs Ely's elder brother arrived. 'What? The two Chinamen not here yet?' Alexander found a small space between his sister's haywire hair and her nose, and gave her a kiss.

'No. Go in and sit down, will you?' said Mrs Ely, and went back to the kitchen to keep preparing the food.

The object of Alexander's visit was a free meal, and certainly not a chat with the Reverend Ely. There was nothing you could talk about with a missionary.

The Reverend Ely passed his tobacco pouch to Alexander in silence.

'No, thanks. Got some.' Alexander pulled out a six-inch gold case, selected a Manila cigar and handed it to the Reverend Ely. Then he took one himself, stuck it in his mouth, smartly struck a match, sucked his cheeks in and inhaled a mouthful as he lit it. Then, with an almighty puff of his cheeks, he sent smoke shooting out into the distance. He contemplated the smoke with a smile, and in the same casual way tossed the matchstick into the ashtray.

Alexander was as tall as his sister, broad-shouldered, bull-necked, bald-headed and with a mouthful of false teeth. His cheeks were forever bright crimson, as if he'd just been on the wrong end of two violent slaps. He dressed very smartly and was invariably immaculate from head to toe.

Cigar in one hand, the other pressed against his forehead, he seemed to be thinking something over. 'I say,' he said after quite some time, 'what was the name of that Chinaman? That commercial traveller from the Handsome Profit Company in Tientsin. A dumb-looking little fellow. Know who I mean?'

'Chang Yüan.' The Reverend Ely was still holding the unlit cigar. He didn't feel he could put it down, for fear of disclosing his ineptitude in smoking cigars.

'That's him. Chang Yüan. I was fond of the little beggar. Tell you what, though,' Alexander inhaled another mouthful of smoke, and made a magnificent show of it as he puffed it out, 'don't think he was a fool! Oh, no, he was sharp. You see, my Chinese wasn't up to much, and he hadn't a word of English, but businesswise we got on like a house on fire. He'd come and say, in Chinese, "Two thousand dollars." I'd nod, and he'd pass me the invoice for the goods straight away. Then I'd say in Chinese, "Write name?" He'd nod his head, and I'd sign the invoice. See, all tied up, neat as you like!'

And having said this, Alexander clutched his belly and roared with laughter. Countless layers of ash from his cigar dropped onto the carpet as he went on and on, his scalp soon matching his cheeks for redness, before he finally stopped, in a high state of hilarity.

The Reverend Ely, unable to detect anything that merited laughter, pushed his spectacles up, and, grim-lipped, stared at the ash on the carpet.

The two Mas arrived with Mrs Wedderburn. She wore a taupe dress and a broad-brimmed straw hat, and the instant she set foot in the house, the cigar set her coughing. Mr Ma was clasping a black trilby, at a loss as to where to deposit it. Ma Wei took it and hung it on the hatstand, much to Mr Ma's relief.

'Hello, Mrs Wedderburn!' exclaimed Alexander in gruff, hearty tones, standing up with cigar at the ready. 'Haven't seen you for years. Mr Wedderburn all right? What's his line these days?'

At that point Mrs Ely came in with Catherine and hastily interrupted her brother. 'Alec! Mr Wedderburn is no longer with us. I'm so glad you've come, Mrs Wedderburn. Where's Miss Wedderburn?'

'Hello, Mr Ma!' Ignoring his sister, Alexander pounced on the elder Ma and shook his hand. 'Often heard my sister talk of you. From Shanghai, aren't you? How's trade in Shanghai? Been a lot of trouble there lately, eh? Has old Chang still got Peking firmly in hand? There's a splendid chap for you, now! I tell you, if he'd been in charge of Manchuria all these years, there'd never have been any trouble. I can tell you that when I was in Tientsin, we never had a spot of bother with —'

'Alec! Dinner's ready. Will you all please come into the dining room?' shouted Mrs Ely at the top of her voice, knowing that otherwise she'd never make herself heard over her brother.

'Eh? What? Dinner ready? Got any drink?' Alexander threw his cigar down and followed everyone out of the drawing room.

'Ginger beer,' replied Mrs Ely, stiff-necked. She was somewhat in awe of her brother, otherwise she wouldn't even have provided ginger beer.

Once all were seated, Alexander renewed his bellowing. 'We ought to at least have a bottle of champagne!'

The English actually give a great deal of attention to manners, and as a young man Alexander had possessed flawless manners and etiquette. But when he went to China, he felt that being polite to the Chinese wasn't worth the bother, and was forever bawling and glaring at the Chinese working under him, with the result that he was now past changing even if he'd wanted to. Because of his wild bellowing and general rudeness, many of his former friends had cut him off, which accounted for his having agreed to come to dinner at the Reverend Ely's house. Had he had plenty of friends, his brother-in-law, the Mas and the ginger beer could all go and jump in a lake.

'Where's Paul, Mrs Ely?' asked Mrs Wedderburn.

'He's not yet back from a trip to the countryside,' said Mrs Ely, then, aiming her nose in her husband's direction, added, 'Reverend Ely, say grace!'

The Reverend Ely had up to this point suffered Alexander in silence, but now he had the chance, he began an interminable prayer, perfectly aware that this irked Alexander, and deliberately letting him go hungry for as long as he could.

Alexander kept on opening his eyes to look at the ginger beer on the table, inwardly cursing the Reverend Ely. The moment the clergyman had uttered his 'Amen', Alec grabbed a bottle and began pouring it out for everyone.

'How do you like England?' he asked Mr Ma as he did so.

'Most beautiful!' Of late, Mr Ma had been learning with Mrs Wedderburn to answer every question with a 'Splendid!', 'Most beautiful!' or 'You're absolutely right!'

'What d'you mean, "beautiful"?' Alexander looked somewhat bemused, unable to comprehend the meaning of the word unless he knew how much "beauty" was worth per pound. He knew that the big coloured vases in the antiques shops were beautiful, and that the paintings in the art exhibitions were beautiful, because they all had price tags on them.

'Er . . .' Not knowing what to say, Mr Ma just rolled his eyes helplessly.

'Alec!' said Mrs Ely. 'Pass the salt to Mrs Wedderburn.'

Alexander grabbed the salt shaker and handed it to Mrs Wedderburn, knocking over the pepper pot in the process.

'Do you like fat or lean meat, Ma Wei?' asked Miss Ely.

Giving Ma Wei no time to reply, Mrs Ely jerked her head up stiffly and declared, 'The Chinese always prefer the fat!' Then, securing the meat with a fork in one hand, she carved with the knife in her other. Her lips were pursed grimly and one eyebrow was cocked, her expression implying that she was about to kill someone.

'Splendid!' Mr Ma suddenly put Mrs Wedderburn's term to use. Nobody knew why he'd said it.

When they'd eaten the beef, the rice pudding was brought out.

'Can you eat this?' Miss Ely asked Ma Wei.

'Yes, all right,' said Ma Wei, giving her a smile.

'All Chinese like rice. Is that not so, Mr Ma?' asked Mrs Ely, of Mr Ma but looking straight at Catherine.

'You're absolutely right!' said Mr Ma, nodding his head.

Alexander went off into hoots of laughter until his cheeks were purple. No one took the slightest notice of him, not even his sister, and he carried on laughing till his mouth ached, at which point he automatically ground to a halt.

Ma Wei took a spoonful of rice pudding and brought it to his lips, not daring for ages to put it into his mouth. The elder Mr Ma swallowed a mouthful of the pudding and stiffened at the neck, his eyes fixed and frozen for a long while, as if he were about to pass out.

'Would you like some water?' Miss Ely asked Ma Wei.

Ma Wei nodded.

'Would you like some water, too?' Mrs Wedderburn inquired warmly of Mr Ma.

Mr Ma's neck was still craned rigidly forwards, and the smile he gave Mrs Wedderburn was strained. Alexander went off into peals of laughter once more.

'Alec! Another helping of pudding?' asked Mrs Ely, shooting him a sidelong glare.

The Reverend Ely said nothing, but slowly poured two glasses of water for the two Mas. By combining a mouthful of rice pudding with a mouthful of cold water, they more or less managed to survive the dessert.

'I'll tell you a funny story!' said Alexander, addressing all and sundry, totally unconcerned as to whether anybody wanted to hear one. Mrs Wedderburn gave a light clap with her dainty hands in anticipation. Seeing her applaud, Mr Ma quickly uttered a series of 'Splendid!'s.

'It was the year I went to Peking.' Alexander stuck his thumb in his waistcoat pocket, stretched out his legs and positioned his spine squarely against the back of his chair. 'It's a poverty-stricken hole is Peking, I can tell you. Not a single big store, not a single factory, and the streets are filthy. Someone had told me Peking was an attractive place. Saw no signs of that. Filth and charm don't go hand in hand, what!'

'Kay!' said Mrs Ely hastily, noticing that Ma Wei's face was reddening somewhat. 'Take Ma Wei to have a look round your study, and when you come back, we'll be having coffee in the drawing room.' To Ma Wei she said, 'Paul has collected a good number of books, and his study is really quite the little library. You go and have a look with Catherine.'

'Listen to me!' Alexander looked a bit disgruntled. 'I was staying in the Peking Hotel. Now that's what you'd call a decent place. You can have a drink, play billiards, dance or gamble. If you wanted, you could do the lot. And do you know, there's only one good hotel like that in the whole of Peking. Well, when I'd finished my dinner, and had nothing else to do, I went downstairs for a round of billiards. There was an old chappy with black whiskers standing in the billiard room – a Chinaman. One of the old school of Chinamen. That's the sort I like, the old-school type, what! As I started playing, he curved up his moustache in a smile. Interesting old chappy, I thought to myself. When I'd finished the game, he was still standing there, so I went over and asked him, in Chinese, "He-chiu pu-he?" Would you like a drink?'

As Alexander pronounced the four words of Chinese, he did so with his face turned to the ceiling, his fist resting on his hip and his eyes closed, mumbling in a stifled wheezing voice, imitating a Chinese person.

While her brother was preoccupied with his Chinaman impersonations, Mrs Ely hastily said to her guests, 'Please come and sit in the drawing room.'

The Reverend Ely stood up with alacrity to open the door. Alexander made a beeline for Mr Ma, intent on continuing his funny story. Mrs Wedderburn, very eager to hear someone who'd actually been to China talk about the country, said to him, 'Tell us when we're in the drawing room, so that we all can hear.'

'Mrs Wedderburn! Your dress is quite gorgeous!' Mrs Ely was trying her level best to interrupt Alexander's tale.

'Most pretty!' added Mr Ma.

When they were all in the drawing room, Mrs Ely poured them coffee. The Reverend Ely smiled at Mrs Wedderburn. 'Shall we listen to the gramophone?' he asked her. 'Which record would you like to hear?'

'Lovely! But let's ask Mr Lanmore to finish his funny story first.'

His efforts falling flat, all the Reverend Ely could do was pick up his coffee and sit down. Alexander said 'Ahem!', and proceeded with his story, now in a thoroughly merry mood.

'Well, Mrs Wedderburn. You see, when I asked him if he would have a drink, he nodded his head and smiled again. I forged on to the bar, with him tagging behind me like an old dog —'

'Alec, pass Mrs Wedderburn a – Mrs Wedderburn, would you like an apple or a banana?'

Alexander passed the fruit bowl and carried on speaking, not for a moment breaking his stride. ' "What are you drinking?" I said. "What'll you drink?" he said. "I'll have a whisky," I said. "I'll join you," he said. So the pair of us got drinking. Fine chappy, that old fellow. Drank five with me. Never flinched.'

'Ha ha! Oh Mr Lanmore, do you mean to tell me that when you were in China you actually taught Chinese people to drink whisky?' asked Mrs Wedderburn, laughing.

The Reverend and Mrs Ely both opened their mouths to try to interrupt Alexander's anecdote, but as both of them started up simultaneously, nobody heard what either of them said, and Alexander grabbed his chance, and carried on.

'What was even more extraordinary, when we finished drinking the old chappy paid for the drinks. Settled the bill. Then he really opened up – asked me how he could buy a betting ticket for the Shanghai horseraces. You Chinamen are all for gambling, eh?' he asked Mr Ma.

Mr Ma nodded.

Mrs Wedderburn, chewing a piece of banana in her mouth, murmured, 'Teaching people to go horseracing and bet, and then you say they're —'

Before she'd finished whatever it was she was going to say, the Reverend Ely cut in quickly, 'Mrs Wedderburn, is the Reverend Chamberlain still —'

Mrs Ely opened her mouth, too: 'Mr Ma, which church do you go to for Sunday service?'

Alexander slurped noisily at his coffee. The more he thought about it, the funnier his story seemed, so that he ended up going off into great guffaws of laughter once more.

IV

IN PAUL'S study, Miss Ely sat on her brother's swivel chair, and Ma Wei stood in front of the shelves, looking at the books. There were probably twenty or thirty of them, of which a complete collection of Shakespeare's works accounted for half. On the walls hung three or four coloured prints of famous paintings, all bought by Paul in the market for sixpence each. On the small table next to the bookshelves lay an opium pipe, a new pair of shoes usually worn by Chinese women with tiny bound feet, a shabby snuff bottle, and a pair of old embroidered purses.

Paul's friends knew he'd been born in China, and Paul felt obliged to play this up a little. Whenever his friends came by, he'd weave a whole concocted tale round the curios: when the Chinese bound their feet and smoked opium, this was the little pot into which they stuffed the opium, and these were the purses that they put the little pots in . . . Fortunately, English people know nothing about China, so he could tell them whatever he liked and it didn't matter.

'So this is Paul's collection then?' said Ma Wei, turning round to Catherine with a smile.

Miss Ely nodded. She was probably about twenty-six or twenty-seven. Like her father, she wasn't tall, and she had big eyes. She had as much hair as her mother, and as she wasn't as tall, that head of hair seemed to weigh down the rest of her, depriving it of frivolity or lightness. But she wasn't at all unattractive, and, especially when she was seated, with her back very straight and her shimmering tawny hair hanging down behind her, she had quite a lot of that passive, still beauty of Oriental women. When she spoke, there was always the hint of a smile on her lips, but she didn't often laugh aloud. Her hands were particularly smooth and pretty, and she'd often raise them to sweep back her long hair.

'Are you all right here in England, Ma Wei?'

'Of course.'

'Really?' She gave a faint smile.

'I don't take much notice of English people's attitudes towards us. But my father's business, it's . . . It worries me every time I think of it, Elder Sister.'

When they had been in China together he'd called her this, and found he couldn't shake the habit.

'The Chinese tend to look down on businessmen, and my father's not the slightest bit interested in running a business. But now we rely on the shop for our livelihood, it's no good his being indifferent. He won't listen to what I say, and he won't listen to what Li Tzu-jung says either. Sometimes he doesn't go to the shop all day, and when he does go, he's likely to give a customer something for free if he hears them praising Chinese antiques. We've only been here a few months, and already we've spent more than two hundred pounds of the money my uncle left us. One day Father's shouting someone a meal, and the next he's inviting someone to have a drink on him. People only have to say the Chinese are nice, and he invites them out to dinner. And when they tell him the food's good, he has to go and invite them out again!

'Quite apart from all that, whenever anyone asks him a question, he tries too hard to answer them the way they want. English people by and large think the worst of China, and they're only too delighted to hear confirmation of their suspicions from the lips of a Chinese person. For instance, when people ask him how many wives he's got, he says, "Five or six"! And if I ask him about it, he gets all hot under the collar and says, "People are convinced the Chinese have a lot of wives. So why shouldn't I tell them what they want to hear?"

'And sure enough some old folks have got so fond of him he's become their proper darling – just because he always tells them what they want to hear.

'There was the day not long ago when General Gower was giving a lecture on the British troops sent into Shanghai, and he made a point of inviting my father to come along. Halfway through his talk, General Gower pointed at my father, and said, "Would it not be a good thing for the Chinese were British troops to remain permanently stationed in China? Let us put the question to a Chinaman. Mr Ma, what would you say?"

'And my father stands up and says exactly what's expected of him: "We welcome the British forces!"

'Another time, an old lady told him that Chinese clothes were lovely, so the next day he traipsed round the streets in a big silk jacket, and collected a crowd of little children shouting "Chink!" at him. If he'd worn the Chinese clothes because he wanted to, all well and good, but no – he was just wearing them to please that old lady. You know, Elder Sister, my father's generation's had the scares put into them by foreigners, and all they need is to hear those same foreigners bestowing faint praise and they feel tremendously honoured. He hasn't got an atom of national feeling, not an atom!'

Miss Ely sighed, smiling.

'Nationalism, Elder Sister,' continued Ma Wei. 'Nationalism's the only thing that can save China. Not like the Japanese, manufacturing big guns, aeroplanes and all those lethal weapons, but then again, in this present day and age, guns and aeroplanes are a sign of civilisation. The average English person sneers at us because our military's no good. If we're ever going to lift up our heads, we're just going to have to fight. I know it's not humane, but if we don't, we can forget about ever being able to hold our own in the world.'

'Ma Wei!' said Catherine, taking his hand. 'Ma Wei, just stick to your studies, and you needn't bother about anything else. I know how you suffer, and the irritations you have to put up with. But losing your temper can't do anything to help China, can it?

If your country's in a shambles, nobody's going to show you any sympathy. You could go on forever, telling the English, the French or the Japanese, "We're an ancient land, and it's not easy for an ancient land to modernise. You ought to show us some sympathy instead of taking advantage of our tribulations", but it'd be a sheer waste of effort, wouldn't it? If others see you as weak, they'll take advantage of you, and if you have a revolution, they'll mock you. Relations between countries are all about one-upmanship, and unless China becomes stronger without outside help, nobody's going to respect the Chinese, and nobody's going to be friendly to you.

'I'm telling you, Ma Wei: only study and learning can save a country. China isn't just short of big guns and aeroplanes – it also lacks all kinds of capable people. Unless you can make yourself into someone of ability, you've no right to talk about saving your nation! At least you've had the chance to come abroad. Take a look at other countries, and take a look at what's wrong with your own country – we've all got our faults, haven't we? – and then think things over calmly and coolly. You can't just fly off the handle.

'The problem here in England is that people *don't* study. Look at all these rotten books of Paul's, hardly any of them ever opened, and my mother has the nerve to tell you to come and look at them. All the same, England's certainly got a few people who really know their stuff, and it's those people who make it possible for England to stand her ground in this world. An Englishman discovered a medicine for cholera, and that's something that benefits people throughout the world. Another invented the telephone, so now the whole world can communicate. No matter what, there will always be those who lead the way, and there'll always be the ordinary people following in the wake of those few real innovators.

'It's the same trouble with the Chinese – they don't study. But where China falls short of England is that it doesn't even have one leading light. Don't get impatient, Ma Wei. Study and learn, that's the only thing to do, study and learn. What are you studying? Commerce. Right then – when you've got a real understanding of commerce, you'll be able to help China compete with other countries in trade.

'As for Mr Ma, you and Li Tzu-jung ought to force his hand. I know that it's hard for you; you want to be the obedient and loving son, as is expected in China, yet at the same time you can see the dangers ahead. But you can't have your cake and eat it too. As we English see it, slavish obedience is a danger too. I was born in China, and can claim to know a bit about the place. And being English, I can also say I understand England. And if you compare both countries, you can reach some very clear and relevant conclusions. Look, Ma Wei, if you have any problems, come and see me, will you? I may not be able to help, but at least I can suggest some ideas.

'You see, Ma Wei, I'm not exactly happy in my home life. I don't get on with my parents, let alone my brother. But I've got my own job, and when I've finished work and can quietly read in my room, I don't feel upset about anything. In my view, there are only two really satisfying things in life: using your knowledge and gaining more knowledge.'

At this point, Catherine gave a slight smile. 'Ma Wei,' she continued warmly, 'I'm still trying to learn Chinese. Why don't we have an exchange? You teach me Chinese, and I'll teach you English. But —' She scooped back her hair with her hands, and thought for a while. 'Where, though? I wouldn't like you to have to come here. To be honest, my mother doesn't like the Chinese. What if I came to your place? Would you —'

'We've got a small study,' Ma Wei quickly broke in, 'But surely, asking you to trek all the way there and back again would be —'

'That wouldn't matter – I often go to study in the British Museum, and that's not far from you. Wait a moment. Let me think. Tell you what: wait till I write you a letter, will you?'

While on the subject of English, she mentioned a number of useful books that Ma Wei ought to study, and also explained how to go about borrowing books from the library.

'Well, Ma Wei, we ought to go and see what's going on in the drawing room.'

'Thanks, Elder Sister. I feel a lot more cheerful after our talk together,' said Ma Wei in a quiet voice.

Catherine said nothing, just gave another faint smile.

V

MRS ELY'S and Mrs Wedderburn's foreheads were by now almost pressed against each other. Mrs Ely was pointing so vigorously at Mrs Wedderburn that she was nearly slicing off the teeny tip of Mrs Wedderburn's nose. Mrs Wedderburn had her nose in the air and her pretty mouth open, and her head was following the movements of Mrs Ely's finger, left, right, up, down, as if she were trying to take a bite out of it. The two of them were chattering away, but about what, none of the others had any idea.

Alexander was sitting on his chair, his legs sprawled out, the cigar in his hand burnt out. Both his eyes were shut, his cheeks were redder than ever and a steady snore was issuing from his mouth. Mr Ma and the Reverend Ely were engaged in quiet conversation, and the Reverend Ely's spectacles had nearly slipped off the end of his nose.

As Miss Ely and Ma Wei entered, Mrs Ely promptly served Ma Wei some coffee, while Miss Ely sat down next to Mrs Wedderburn and joined in the chat.

Alexander's snores grew louder and louder till he woke himself up with a start. 'Whassat?' he exclaimed loudly, blinking his eyes.

His question made everybody laugh. Even his sister laughed, so heartily that the bird's nest on her head shook and shuddered. Realising what had happened, Alexander went off into peals of laughter as well, a tone louder than everyone else.

'I say, Mr Ma, come and have a couple of glasses,' he said, putting his hand on Mr Ma's shoulder. 'You coming too, Reverend Ely?'

The Reverend Ely pushed back his spectacles and looked at Mrs Ely.

'Reverend Ely still has some business to attend to,' said Mrs Ely. 'You pop off with Mr Ma now. But you mustn't get Mr Ma drunk, do you hear?'

Alexander winked at Mr Ma and made no reply.

Mr Ma gave a little smile and stood up. 'You go home with Mrs Wedderburn,' he told Ma Wei. 'I'm going for a drink. Just one. No more. I've never been a drinker.'

Ma Wei said nothing, just shot a glance at Catherine.

Alexander kissed his niece and grabbed Mr Ma by the arm. 'Off we go then!'

'Bye-bye,' said Mrs Ely to her brother, without getting up. Her husband saw them to the door.

'Sure you won't come?' asked Alexander at the door.

'No, I won't,' said the Reverend Ely, and turned to Mr Ma. 'I'll see you some day soon. I've something I want to discuss with you.'

The pair of them left Lancaster Road, crossed the main highway and followed the iron railing of Hyde Park westwards. Being summer, it still wasn't very dark and there was a large number of people in the park. Not a single faded leaf was visible amid the tree foliage, and the flowerbeds were blooming with late tulips, like one unbroken strip of golden-red sunset. The tiny white flowers on the ground at the edge of the flowerbeds resembled flakes of newly fallen snow, giving a welcome cooling impression.

Visible in the distance through the grove of trees lay a stretch of water, over which flew a flock of seagulls, soaring and dipping. On the far side of the water, a military band was playing, and through the leaves you caught occasional glimpses of the red uniforms of the musicians. A cool breeze brought the sound of the music in waves to your ears. The sky was cloudless but a faint mist hung over the treetops to the west, in strips of red and white, as cheerful in colour as the hats of the girls in the park.

The hotel opposite the park stood with all its windows open and its awnings down. Under these pink- and green-striped canopies sat bare-armed girls, balancing teacups and enjoying the evening scenery of the park.

Looking between the park and the bright awnings, Mr Ma nodded his head in approval. The scene was very poetic, but Mr Ma, having never composed any poetry before, was unable to produce a single line in his mind.

Alexander marched on straight ahead, giving a sardonic smile now and then in the direction of the park revellers. But when he caught sight of the pub at the far end of Empress Gate, his face really lit up. He licked his lips, signalling with his head to Mr Ma. Mr Ma nodded.

Outside the pub there was a lame man playing the violin and asking for money. Alexander turned his head sharply away, pretending not to have seen him. An old white-whiskered man with a wry look was shouting, 'Evening paper! Evening paper!' Alexander bought a paper, and stuck it under his arm.

As they went into the pub, they found the bar crowded with people. One man was holding a glass of beer in his hand, talking and joking as he drank. A red-faced, toothless old lady was pushing through the crowd asking everybody, 'Have you seen my little child?' She'd been so engrossed in her drinking that she'd not noticed her child run off. Alexander stood to one side as she came rushing past, then drew Mr Ma further into the pub, to the saloon.

Chairs lined the walls of the saloon, and there was a carpet in the middle, on which stood a glass-topped table and a dark-purple piano. A couple of old men, each hugging a corner of the room, smoked with their eyes shut and a glass in their hand. A tall, fat woman, her eyes red with drink, was rocking her head as she played the piano. At her side stood a ruddy-faced bearded fellow, holding his glass high with his mouth wide open – wherein dwelt a small collection of black and imperilled teeth – and singing soldiers' songs in a loud voice. His voice was ample and his delivery most expressive, only the tune he sang hadn't the slightest relationship to that of the piano.

Seeing Mr Ma come in, the face of the woman playing the piano suddenly turned red then white. 'Cor! Lord love us! A Chink in here!' she said, hunching up her shoulders. She gave her head a shake, and played on with yet greater frenzy, her fat thighs plonking up and down on the little stool.

Without warning, the singer stopped and took a swig of beer, and the old men in the corners, without opening their eyes, jabbed their pipes in the direction of the piano and chorused, 'Come on, George. Sing.' George took another swig of beer, banged the glass down onto the table, and proceeded to sing once more. This tune had no greater relation to that of the piano than the last.

'What'll you drink, Mr Ma?' asked Alexander.

'Anything you like,' said Mr Ma, sitting on a chair by the wall, with very proper decorum.

Alexander ordered beer, and, as they drank, he recounted his stories of China. The old men in the corners opened their eyes, glanced at Mr Ma and shut them again.

Alexander's speaking voice was louder and fuller than George's singing voice, and, in a fit of exasperation, George stopped singing. The fat woman, likewise frustrated, stopped her playing, and they both listened to Alexander. Mr Ma, taking quick glances all round him, creased his lips into a smile and took a sip of his beer. George came up to join in the conversation, since he knew a bit about China – his brother-in-law had been a soldier in Hong Kong – but Alexander didn't pause for breath and George couldn't get a word in. Tightening his lips grimly and snarling menacingly through his sparse black teeth, he sat down.

'Have another?' Alexander asked, at the conclusion of one of his funny stories.

Mr Ma nodded.

'Have another?' Alexander asked, at the conclusion of yet another funny story.

Mr Ma nodded again.

As Mr Ma and Alexander drank and drank, the old men, legs like dough-twists, made their swaying way out of the pub. Then the fat woman stuck her hat on her head and staggered out, three teeters per step. George was still waiting for his chance to tell Alexander about China, but Alexander never left him any opening. Looking at his watch, George gave up and skulked silently outside, where he started singing away to himself again.

A young barmaid came in and said with a smile, 'Sorry, gentlemen. Time, please!'

'Thank you, miss.' Alexander still hadn't drunk his fill, but government regulations required pubs to close at ten o'clock, so there was nothing for it but to leave. 'Let's go, Mr Ma.'

The stars in the sky were so closely packed together they seemed on the verge of bumping into one another. The leaves of the trees lining the street were rustling in the cool breeze with a soft, pleasant sound. There wasn't much traffic, and when every now and then a car did approach, its two big headlights seemed to transform the deserted road into a shimmering glacier. And once the car had hurtled past, the black shadows on either side converged to hide the shiny surface. In the park, the trees were shrouded in darkness, stirring up the scent of flowers and plants and turning the whole place into one sweet, beautiful dreamland.

Holding onto the park railing to keep himself upright, Mr Ma looked into the park. The bushy black trees seemed to have grown legs, and were swaying and rolling wildly back and forth. Not only that, but the trees were surrounded by crazily flying sparks that were there whichever way his eyes turned. He leant against the railing and rubbed his eyes with his hand. The golden stars continued to zoom around in front of him, and all the gas lamps along the street strangely had two flames to each lamp. And some lampposts were bent, like stalks of sorghum blown by the wind. His head refused to obey him, and unless he leant against something, it would jerk forwards, as though trying to visit his feet. If he weren't careful he would indeed visit his feet at close quarters. As long as he had his hand on the railing, the forward movement of his head wasn't so violent, but meanwhile, his legs were staging a mutiny. From the knees upwards they were still hanging onto his body, but below they seemed disinclined to obey their superiors – a veritable workers' revolution!

The people in the street were odd too. Not a soul was walking alone – they were all in pairs. Funny. And someone or other had put a gramophone record inside Mr Ma's head, and it was whirling round, making a constant *buzz-buzz*, *zing-zing*, buzzing in his ears.

He was still very alert, and felt very cheery. Everything he looked at struck him as funny. Even if he looked at nothing, that seemed hilarious too. He looked at the lampposts, and they sent him off into peals of laughter. When he stopped laughing, he took one of his hands from the railing, waved it in a circle, pointing ahead, and announced from the side of his mouth, 'Home's that a'way! Take it slowly. No hurry. What's the hurry? Why hurry . . . ? Alexander . . . No, that's wrong . . . Yes, Alexander – where's he got to? Fine fellow.' With these words, he bent his head down low, and searched all over the place.

'Who was that speaking just now?' He looked around him for a good few moments, then, whirling his hand up, caught himself on the nose. 'Ah, now, here we are. That's where the talking was coming from! Isn't it, old fellow?'

VI

MA WEI and Mrs Wedderburn arrived home. Mrs Ely had talked so much that Mrs Wedderburn was feeling rather weary. There was no sound to be heard from inside the house as they entered, only Napoleon barking in the back garden. Without bothering to take off her hat, Mrs Wedderburn strode quickly out the back door. Napoleon was sitting under a rosebush, his forelegs straight out in front of him and his head raised, barking at the stars. Hearing his mistress's footsteps, he scurried up to her, whirling and twisting wildly round her legs, like some frenzied ball of fluff.

'Hello, my darling. Have you been left all on your own? What's happened to Mary?' asked Mrs Wedderburn.

Napoleon leapt up and yapped for all he was worth, seeking to convey the message, 'Pick me up quickly! Mary went out, and didn't care about me. In total I've caught three flies and scared off one black cat.'

Mrs Wedderburn carried her dog into the drawing room. Ma Wei was looking out through the curtains when she came in.

'Why hasn't my father got back yet?' he asked.

'And I wonder where Mary's gallivanting about too,' said Mrs Wedderburn, sitting down.

Napoleon still kept on jiggling round madly on his mistress's lap, rubbing his neck against her chest.

'Napoleon, do behave yourself a bit! I'm worn out. Go and play with Ma Wei.'

She handed Napoleon to Ma Wei, and Napoleon took the opportunity to whack her new hat with his tail in passing.

Ma Wei took the little dog, who was still wriggling like mad, not behaving himself in the slightest. Ma Wei tickled him under his chin, and after he'd done that a few times, Napoleon became much calmer, bumping his nose against Ma Wei's chest and stretching out his neck for Ma Wei to tickle him more. As he tickled away, Ma Wei felt something wedged under the dog's collar. He realised it was a tiny rolled-up ball of paper, tied on with two strands of red cotton. He slowly untied it while Napoleon waited, completely motionless except for the gentle wagging of the tip of his stubby tail.

Ma Wei untied the paper, and handed it to Mrs Wedderburn, who unfurled it. It was a note, which said,

> *Mum,*
> *I've burnt all the supper, and the eggs got stuck to the pan and I can't get them off. Washington called for me, and we're going to have some ice-cream together. See you tonight. Napoleon's in the backyard looking after old Ma's roses.*
>
> *Mary*

Mrs Wedderburn tore it up as she finished reading it, then gave a yawn, hiding her mouth behind the back of her hand.

'You go to bed, Mrs Wedderburn, and I'll wait up for them,' said Ma Wei.

'Yes, you wait up for them. Are you going to have some coffee?'

'No, thank you. Not just now.'

'Come on, Napoleon.' Mrs Wedderburn walked out carrying the little dog.

Mrs Wedderburn had taken a liking to Ma Wei, partly because he was so well behaved and polite and pleasant-spoken, and partly because Mary didn't like him. Mrs Wedderburn, as we know, was somewhat wilful, and very fond of deliberately being contrary.

Ma Wei opened the drawing room window slightly and sat on a chair next to the table, facing the street. Whenever he heard footsteps, he glanced outside. He did this quite a number of times, but it was never his father. He took a novel down from the bookcase and turned over a few pages, but, finding himself unable to read, put it back where he'd got it from. He thought of having a tinkle on the piano, but it was probably too late in the evening for that, so he simply sat by the window, frowning. *Young people of other countries are so cheery,* he thought. *No cares, no worries. Cigarettes to smoke, and money for the pictures, and football for relaxation, and what more do they want? But us?*

His thoughts then turned to the evening past. *That bloke Alexander! All that hair of Mrs Ely's. Miss Ely. Was she speaking from the heart? Must have been. Her smile was so genuine. Isn't she happy, either? Anyhow, she's better off than me!*

At this point in his ruminations, the image of Miss Ely appeared before him, her hair hanging on her shoulders and her lips stirring in a smile. It made him feel a bit more cheerful, and a new thought started to come to him, but he blushed before he managed to think it. Mary was so . . . but . . . she was beautiful. Who'd she gone out with? Letting someone else gaze at her face, and perhaps even enjoy her rosy lips? His eyebrows arched, and he clenched a fist and swung a couple of punches. A cool breeze wafted in through the window, and he stood up and took a deep breath of air.

A car approached, making Ma Wei's heart give a sudden jump. He poked his head out and took a look. Presently, a taxi was at the door.

'Here we are!' someone in the taxi said – Mary's voice!

The taxi door opened but instead of Mary, out leapt a policeman. Full of anxiety, Ma Wei rushed outside. Before he'd said a word, the policeman gave him a nod. He bounded to the taxi door, and, at that moment, Mary stepped out of the cab, holding her hat in her hand, her face pale and her eyes very round and wide. Despite this she didn't look too alarmed or panic-stricken. She pointed into the taxi. 'Your father,' she said.

'Dad – what's wrong?'

Before he'd time to speak, it sprang to mind that his father must have been knocked down by a car, and injured at the very least. Then something seemed to stick in his throat. He couldn't get any words out and his lips trembled uncontrollably.

'Let's lift him out,' said the big policeman, very solid and unperturbed.

At the policeman's words, Ma Wei ventured a look at his father. The elder Mr Ma's head was wedged into a corner of the cab and his legs sprawled sideways, so that he looked uncannily long. One hand was placed limply on his lap, and the other lay palm upwards on the cushion of the seat. There was a blue patch on his forehead and some flecks of blood on his face, and his mouth with its scrappy moustache seemed fixed in a smile.

'Father! Father!' Ma Wei shouted at him.

Mr Ma's hands were icy-cold, but there was some chilly sweat on the palms and congealed blood where one of his thumbs had been cut.

'Cart him out. He ain't dead. Nothing to worry about,' said the big policeman, grinning.

Ma Wei put his hand over his father's mouth. Sure enough, he was still breathing, and the scrap of moustache was twitching. Ma calmed down quite a bit. He glanced at the policeman, and went very red.

The policeman, Ma Wei and the taxi driver carried the sozzled Ma out. The elder Ma's head wobbled wildly, as if about to escape from his neck. A constant glug-glug sound issued from his throat. The three of them carried him upstairs and put him on the bed. Another gurgle came from his throat, and he spat out a blob of white foam.

By now, Mary's face had regained its ruddy hue. She brought up a jug of cold water from downstairs. Ma Wei took the jug from her but she hastily pushed back her hair and took the jug from him again.

'I'll give him some water,' she said. 'You pay the taxi driver and send him away.'

Ma Wei felt in his pockets. He'd only got a few pence, so he hurried over and fumbled around for his father's wallet, took out a pound, and handed it to the taxi driver. The man smiled broadly, clumped down the stairs and hurried off. Ma Wei stuffed the wallet under his father's mattress and as he did so he noticed something hard and small in the corner of the wallet. Most likely that diamond ring, but Ma Wei didn't feel like checking.

He promptly thanked the policeman, and offered him several cigars his father had just bought. With a smile, the policeman took one, put it in his pocket, then went over and felt Mr Ma's forehead.

'Nothing much,' he announced. 'Had a big night, eh?' After which he looked round the room, and then left leisurely, giving a 'Cheerio!' as he went.

Mary poured a little of the cold water down Mr Ma's throat, pushed her hair back again, and puffed out her cheeks in relief. Ma Wei undid the buttons of his father's collar.

'Miss Wedderburn,' he said, turning to her, 'you don't need to say anything about this to Mrs Wedderburn.'

'Oh, I wouldn't.' Her cheeks were very red, and as pretty as ever.

'How did you bump into my father?' asked Ma Wei, but before Mary could answer Mr Ma had brought up the water he'd just swallowed.

With a glance at Mr Ma, Mary walked over to take a peek at herself in the mirror. 'I went to Hyde Park with Washington,' she said. 'When the park was closed, we went walking along the path round the outside of the park, and I trod on something soft. Proper scared me, it did. I looked down, and it was him, your dad. Crawling around on the ground like some great crocodile. I kept an eye on him while Washington went to call a cab. The policeman wanted to take him to hospital, but Washington told him your dad was drunk and it'd be best if we just took him home. That was a lucky coincidence, wasn't it? I was scared stiff. I know my lips were all trembly.'

'I don't know how to thank you enough, Miss Wedderburn. When you see Washington next, give him my thanks,' said Ma Wei, leaning with one hand on the bed, looking at her. Inwardly, he hated Washington, but all the same he had to say what he did.

'Right. I'm off to bed now.' Mary shot Mr Ma another look, and as she reached the door, she turned her head. 'Give him a bit more water,' she said.

Mrs Wedderburn had heard the voices upstairs, and as soon as Mary got downstairs, she asked, 'What's the matter, Mary?'

'Nothing. We all got back late. Where's Napoleon?'

'Well, he's not in the garden, I don't mind telling you!'

'Give it a rest! See you in the morning, Mum.'

Ma Wei removed his father's coat and covered him with a blanket. Mr Ma's eyes opened slightly, and his lips made a small movement. His eyes immediately closed although his eyelids carried on fluttering, as if he couldn't bear the light. Ma Wei was sitting by the bed, and seeing his father stir, he was somewhat relieved.

That bloke Washington takes Mary out every day, thought Ma Wei, frowning. *But they rescued my father. She was really quite nice this evening, so maybe she's not so bad at heart. But what about my father? What a debacle! What if he'd got run over by a car? That Alexander! Right – tomorrow I'll go and see Miss Ely.*

As he was caught up in his roaming thoughts he noticed his father's hand moving under the blanket, as if he wanted to turn over. Then Mr Ma's lips parted, and he uttered two croaks.

'No more drink for me, Ma Wei!' he said in blurred tones. And his head slipped back onto the pillow, and he said no more.

VII

SOME TIME after three a.m., Mr Ma came round. He raised a hand and felt the blue spot on his forehead. It was now swollen, blue in the middle and red all round the edge, like a duck's-egg yolk going bad. He seemed to have a pile of dry tinder burning in his chest, blazing up and threatening to crack his throat, like a newly lit fire roaring up an old chimney. His hands were rather stiff, and one of his thumbs hurt. His head, resting on the pillow, felt suspended in mid-air, wobbling all over the place without any support. His mouth was as parched as his throat, his tongue stuck to the bottom like some bone-dry wooden bung. He opened his mouth, gulped some fresh air and felt much better. But a searing acidity rose in his mouth from deep inside him, making him wonder if he'd got a sour jube in there.

'Ma Wei! I'm thirsty! Ma Wei, where are you?'

Ma Wei was dozing on the chair, his head floating around as if he were dreaming, though it was no dream. As he heard his father call, his head dropped, then suddenly jerked up, and he opened his eyes. The light was still on. He rubbed his eyes.

'Are you a bit better now, Dad?'

Mr Ma shut his eyes again, and rubbed his chest with his hand. 'Thirsty!'

Ma Wei handed him a cup of water. Mr Ma shook his head, and, through parched lips, squeezed out the word, 'Tea!'

'There's nowhere to boil the water, Father.'

For a long time Mr Ma said nothing, resolved to endure his

sufferings. But his throat was burning terribly, and he couldn't hold out. 'Water'll do!'

Ma Wei held the cup for him, and Mr Ma bent his body slightly upwards. Eyes staring fixedly ahead, he drank all the water in one draught. Then he licked his lips, and let his head loll back against the pillow.

There was a short pause.

'Pass me the jug of water, Ma Wei.'

Mr Ma poured three fifths of the jug of water down his throat, until bubbles were popping from his mouth and drops of water were forcing their way out of his nose. His stomach emitted gurgling noises, and he placed his hands back in the middle of his chest. *Haah!* He sucked in a deep breath.

'Ma Wei, I won't die, will I?' Mr Ma grimly twisted his lips under the scrap of moustache. 'Pass me the mirror,' he said in strangled tones.

He looked in the mirror and nodded. It wasn't too bad except for his eyes, which were in poor shape: bleary, with fine streaks of blood across the eyeballs, and large yellowish smudges underneath them. The bad duck's-egg yolk on his forehead was of no account; a superficial wound. Yes, a superficial wound. But his eyes certainly did tell a tale.

'Ma Wei, I'm not going to die, am I?'

'Of course not!' Ma Wei was on the point of saying something else, but felt it wouldn't be quite appropriate.

Mr Ma put the mirror down, then picked it up again and stuck out his tongue for examination. It gave him no help in deciding whether or not he would die.

'Ma Wei, how did I — When did I get back?' Mr Ma could still vaguely recall Alexander, the pub and the park, but he couldn't recall how on earth he'd got from the park back home.

'Miss Wedderburn brought you back in a taxi.'

'Ah!' was all that Mr Ma said.

He felt rather inclined to reprove himself inwardly, but saw no need for him to make a public confession. Anyway, a father had no business apologising to his son. As the saying went, 'When old, one should be impulsive and wild. Youth's the time for steadiness.' It was quite in order for an old man to get drunk. Anyhow, he hadn't done any harm, had he? By this stage, he was feeling much easier in his mind. He put on a deliberate air of concern and generosity.

'You go to bed, Ma Wei,' he said. 'I . . . won't die.'

'I'm not tired yet,' said Ma Wei.

'Off with you!'

It delighted Mr Ma to see that his son refused to leave him and go to bed, but he felt duty-bound to address him in such a way. Excellent – 'a kindly father and a loving son', and no mistake.

Ma Wei pulled the blanket across his father again, wrapped another blanket round himself and sat down on the chair.

Mr Ma went off once more into a fitful doze, and when he woke, he ached terribly. Of course his thumb and forehead ached – that was to be expected – but the back of his knees, his elbows and his back all hurt too, with a twisting, wrenching pain. He felt himself all over, expecting to find some broken and splintered bones. There were none. No injuries anywhere; only the pain. He knew Ma Wei was in the room, so he was reluctant to groan. But it was no good – he just had to groan. And groaning with his parched throat felt singularly disagreeable. When he had a headache or fever, his groaning was usually as melodious as if he were reciting poetry. But not today, oh no. Each time he stretched his legs, he groaned before he'd had time to get in tune. But once he had groaned, he felt much better. That was all that mattered; never mind whether he was in tune today!

After one series of groans, he filled in the interval by contemplating death. People always groan when they're about to die. The one thing he mustn't do was die. Our Father who art in Heaven! Lord God above! Having never enjoyed good fortune in his life, it would be too unjust were he to die like this . . . He mustn't drink so much next time. It was no fun. But if you were with someone, you couldn't avoid keeping pace with them. It was a matter of social etiquette – as long as he didn't die, that's all. *Don't groan, groaning's a bad sign*. He drew his head back down into the pillow, and slowly drifted off to sleep again.

The dew-moist air was warmed by the rosy breath of the sun. London began to busy itself for the day. The milkmen and green-grocers hurried round, clattering their trolleys and barrows. Workmen came bobbing along, little pipes in their mouths, pack after pack on their way to work.

By now, a lot of the flowers in the backyard were covered with buds and blooms. As soon as Napoleon got up, he went into the garden and took a good sniff of the scented air. In passing, he caught two large, half-awake flies to eat.

The street noises startled Mr Ma from his slumber. He still felt a bitter burning inside, his mouth was dry and his tongue was stiff like the new sole on a shoe. His stomach was quite empty but his chest felt frightfully tight, he was constantly on the verge of retch-ing and his mouth was full of saliva he couldn't swallow. The lump on his forehead wasn't so prominent any more, but still ached.

'I'm not dying, I know. But I still feel unwell.'

The realisation that he was an invalid was a considerable con-solation to him, since everybody sympathises with an invalid. *Even Li Tzu-jung'll have to come and see me before long,* he thought. *If a lad eats apples when they're still ripening, he's asking for a thrash-ing. But if he eats so many of them he makes himself ill, he's in the clear. Nobody can beat a sick child, can they? He not only gets away with it but everybody buys him sweets as well.* And his being an elderly man, an elderly invalid would surely guarantee all the more sympathy and affection.

Yes, he was ill. So Mr Ma began to groan again, and most me-lodiously too. Ma Wei wiped his father's hands and face with a warm, wet flannel, and asked him what he wanted to eat. Mr Ma just shook his head. He wasn't going to die, it was true, but he was ill, and that meant he couldn't talk, could he? So he said nothing.

By this time, Mrs Wedderburn had heard the story of Mr Ma's adventures, which she found both funny and annoying. When she came upstairs and perceived his state, she at once was filled with motherly compassion, and asked him what he wanted to eat and drink. He just shook his head. She strongly recommended call-ing a doctor, but he shook his head at that, too, and very fiercely.

When she'd had her breakfast, Miss Wedderburn also put in an appearance upstairs. 'I say, Mr Ma, are you going out on the booze again today?'

Mr Ma suddenly let out an explosive chuckle, which gave Mrs Wedderburn quite a visible shock. But then he felt it had been rather out of place, so he groaned and said, 'Aah! I'm very much indebted to you, Miss Mary. When I'm better, I'll buy you a hat.'

'All right. Don't forget, now!' said Mary, and hurried out.

Mrs Wedderburn did bring up some breakfast in the end, but Mr Ma only drank one cup of tea, and as the tea reached his stomach, it stung quite badly.

Ma Wei went to call on Li Tzu-jung to ask him to go to the shop a bit earlier. Mrs Wedderburn busied herself with her housework downstairs, leaving Napoleon upstairs to keep Mr Ma company. Napoleon leapt onto the bed, sniffed the invalid thoroughly from head to toe, then stealthily drank up all the milk that Mr Ma had left.

Ma Wei came back an hour or so later, and, hearing his father still groaning, suggested calling a doctor. His father would have none of it.

'What's there to call a doctor for? Each groan I give cheers me up, and that does me good.'

Mrs Wedderburn brought up a few roses and a bunch of wall-flowers from the garden, and put them in a vase, which she placed by the window. Smelling the scent of the flowers gave Mr Ma much pleasure, and as he groaned he said to Napoleon, 'Just smell those! Just look at them! Is there anything more beautiful in this world than flowers? Who made the flowers so beautiful? I don't suppose you know. And me . . . I don't know, either. When flowers come into bloom, they smell so fragrant. Then all of a sudden they fade and disappear. People are like that. And you dogs are, too. No one knows what it's all about . . . Ah, dear me! Don't die. You don't think I'll die, do you?'

Napoleon wasn't saying. His eyes were riveted on the lumps of white sugar on the tray. He was licking his lips but didn't hazard to make a move.

That evening, Li Tzu-jung came round. He'd bought a bunch of bananas and a punnet of strawberries for Mr Ma. Afraid that Li would give him a telling-off, Mr Ma groaned away for all he was worth. Li Tzu-jung said nothing at all, just went and whispered with Ma Wei in the study for a while.

Alexander, too, had learnt from some quarter that Mr Ma was ill, and very proudly turned up with a bottle of brandy that he'd bought for him.

'Can't have that, Mr Ma – just a few glasses and you fall flat in the street, eh? Well, here's a bottle for you.' He placed the spirits on the table and lit up a cigar. A few puffs were enough to fill the room with smoke.

'I didn't drink much,' said Mr Ma, ceasing his groans and forcing a smile. 'I've never been much of a drinker, and throwing myself into it like that, I hadn't built up any tolerance. Just you watch next time. You'll see how much I can take!'

'Plenty of policemen on the streets, anyway,' said Alexander, and went off into roars of laughter.

At the sound of his guffawing, Napoleon sneaked up and took a good sniff of Alexander's large shoes. But he didn't dare to take a bite of his heel, even though such a fat pair of legs was well worth tasting.

VIII

LONDON'S WEATHER doesn't vary much, but it changes very quickly. As soon as the sky goes dull, a chill wind at once brings up tiny goosepimples on the bare, pale arms of the young ladies, while the old men and ladies adjust to the change by vying to be the first to catch a cold.

The Reverend Ely had never had much difficulty catching a cold. On the way home from a visit to Mr Ma, he sat for a while under a big tree in the park. As he did so, his nose became a little itchy, then he shivered and gave a sneeze. He hastened home and went straight to bed. Mrs Ely gave him a glass of hot lemon juice, and put a hot water bottle under his bedclothes. His sneezes grew louder and louder, and more and more violent. Had his nose not been so robust, he would several times have sent it flying.

He never fought with Mrs Ely. Only once or twice had he dared to have a row with her, when unwell and out of sorts. He was already rather peeved about how Mr Ma had got drunk, and the cold added fuel to the fires of his wrath. His train of thought became increasingly irate.

At last I managed to get a Chinese Christian shipped here, at long last, then Alexander goes and gets him blind drunk! We have enough trouble trying to convert people to Christianity, then he comes and ruins them for us! It's all his fault, that blasted Alexander! A-tchoo! If he hadn't got old Ma drunk, I'd never have got this cold . . . It's all his doing. A-tchoo! Alexander is her brother! I'll just have to have it out with her. He should never have taken him boozing, and she should never have invited Alexander to dinner. Just you see, a-a-tchoo! I'll put her in her place.

At this juncture in his thinking, he pulled the bedclothes aside to march down and confront Mrs Ely. But the instant he raised the blankets, a stream of chill air crept in, then *a-tchoo! Take it easy, now,* he thought. *Main thing's to survive. Bide your time till tomorrow . . .* But when he felt a bit better, would he still be as brave? Hard to tell. Experience told him that the only victories he'd scored in fights with Mrs Ely had all been on occasions when he'd been ill. She would say, 'Don't say anything more. You're right, all right? I'm not squabbling with an invalid!'

No matter if she was cutting him some slack, it was he, all said and done, who came away triumphant on those occasions. If he'd waited till he was better, though . . . you can bet she wouldn't have cut him any slack. He'd really have to have it out with her this time. He'd absolutely have to! With her? Or with her brother? Take them both on!

I baptised old Ma, and your brother takes him boozing. What've you got to say to that, might I ask? Catherine's sure to stick up for me. Paul's his mother's boy – but he's not home . . . To tell the truth, old Ma's not worth fighting over, but if I don't do it, how shall I look the Lord in the eye! And what if Ma Wei tackles me about it? Those Chinese youngsters are much smarter than the old yellow-faced de-mon horde, blast'em. And what if Mrs Wedderburn asks me awkward questions? Yes, I must give Mrs Ely a dressing-down. Anyway, never could bear the sight of Alexander.

With his feet, he pushed the hot water bottle further down, and the heat of it gave his feet a remarkably pleasant, tingly feeling. He closed his eyes and gradually fell asleep.

He awoke during the night, and it was drizzling outside. *More wretched rain.* A pure-scented cool breeze blew in through the window, quite chilling his nose. He wriggled down in bed and began to think about tackling Mrs Ely the next day. Instead, he quickly shut his eyes. *Don't think about it. The more you think about it, the more your will weakens. And then what chance have you got of standing your ground in this world? What a world!*

The neighbour's dog gave a few barks. *What are you shouting about? This world's not made for cringing curs* . . .

The next morning, Catherine brought his breakfast up. He hadn't intended to have any, but the eggs and bacon smelt remarkably nice. *Ah, better eat up. Who in the world can possibly make such a fine breakfast as we English? Not eat breakfast? What sort of an Englishman do you call yourself? Eat up! And don't leave a crumb.* After the meal, his mettle rose. Now he'd simply have to take on Mrs Ely, if only out of due deference to the breakfast.

Catherine came in again to ask if he'd had enough to eat, and he had a word with her.

'Where's your mother, Kay?'

'In the kitchen. Why?' asked Miss Ely with a smile as she picked up the tray. She hadn't combed her hair yet, and it was tangled in an unruly mass on her snow-white neck.

'Her brother got old Mr Ma drunk.' Without his spectacles, the Reverend Ely didn't know where to focus, and his eyes were moving frantically.

Miss Ely gave a smile, and said nothing.

'I put all I had into converting Ma to Christianity, and now in one go Alexander's swept it away.' He stopped speaking and stared hard at her.

She gave another smile. In reality she moved her lips only very slightly, but the smile was there, and a very pretty one it was, too.

'Give me a hand, will you, Kay?'

Miss Ely put the tray down again, sat herself on the edge of the bed and gently patted his hand. 'I'll help you, Daddy. I'm always on your side. But why do you have to have a go at Mummy? Next time you see Uncle Alexander, just have a word with him.'

'He'd take no notice of me. He always laughs at me.' The Reverend Ely wondered why he was speaking so forcefully and frankly today. 'Your mother will have to talk to him. And unless I kick up a fuss with her, she's not going to say anything to him.'

It seemed he was in a right mood today.

Noticing her father's nose thrust forwards and the veins on his temples pulsing, Miss Ely had no doubt: he was well and truly worked up.

'First get better, Daddy. Wait a couple of days,' she said slowly and calmly.

'I can't let it wait.' He knew that if he waited, he'd lose his chance of a victorious encounter. Then, afraid his daughter might see through him, he added hastily, 'I'm not afraid of her. I'm the head of the family. This is my household.'

'I'll mention it to Mummy. You can trust me, can't you, Daddy?'

The Reverend Ely said nothing, just moved his hand to wipe off the egg yolk from the sides of his mouth. With a smaller mouth, he'd have looked like a baby sparrow in the nest.

'Don't you want another cup of tea, Daddy?' Catherine picked up the tray once more.

'I've had enough. Go and tell your mother, do you hear?' Reverend Ely knew that he was speaking rather wildly, but he was an invalid – it was only to be expected. 'Go and tell your mother!'

'Very well, I'll go and tell her straight away.' Smiling, Catherine nodded and tiptoed out, bearing the tray.

After his daughter had left the room, the Reverend Ely fumed to himself. *Yes, you go and tell her. If that has no effect, then we'll see what I can do. What'll she say? Ah, I forgot to ask Catherine to pass me my pipe.* He leant forwards to look, but couldn't locate his pipe. *Yes, that Alexander . . . Gave me a cigar that day. Still haven't smoked it. That Alexander! His cigar! Why, the very thought of him makes my blood boil!*

After lunch Paul arrived home. He was twenty-three or twenty-four, even taller than his mother, and with a head full of thin brown hair, which was parted very neatly and combed very carefully. His hazel eyes glinted as they roamed about, but you couldn't be sure he was really looking at anything. He wore a sky-blue blazer above a pair of flannel trousers, with a soft-collared shirt and a red- and yellow-striped tie. Both hands were stuck in his pockets as if permanently fixed there. His mouth held a pipe, long since gone out.

As he entered, he removed one hand from his pocket, pulled the pipe from mouth, and casually kissed his mother and elder sister. Mrs Ely and Catherine had been discussing Mr Ma's drunken episode.

'Hello, Paul, what have you been up to these last few days?' At the sight of her son back home again, Mrs Ely flushed, a definite hint of pink spreading across her arid cheeks, and she very nearly smiled.

'Oh, just the same old.' Paul squeezed the words through his teeth as he sat down, put his pipe back in his mouth and jammed one hand back in his pocket.

His remark sent Mrs Ely off into peals of appreciative laughter. He was such a man! The less he said the more male he seemed. To tell the truth, though, Paul really hadn't been up to anything new. There wasn't much to be said about a few lads going to the countryside and pitching a tent for a few days' larking about.

'Will you have a word with Daddy in a bit, Mummy? His cold's affected his temper.' Catherine was anxious to convey her message and be done with the matter.

'What's going on?' Paul asked his sister, with the manner of a judge.

'Mr Ma got himself drunk!' Mrs Ely answered for Catherine. 'What's that got to do with us?'

The bridge of Paul's nose crinkled in response.

'I invited them to dinner, and Mr Ma went out with Alexander.' Mrs Ely glanced at Catherine.

Paul pulled out a match and flicked it with his fingernail, lighting it first go. 'Tell Dad not to bring 'em here again. He's got no business letting Chinamen run around our house. It's just not decent.'

'Now Paul, don't look at me like that. We're true Christians, and not . . . Your uncle took the elder Ma for a little drink, and —'

'Did both of them get drunk?'

'Alexander didn't, but Mr Ma collapsed in the street.'

'Knew it! Fine chap, Alexander. I'm very fond of the old fellow; he's got what it takes.' Paul withdrew his pipe, which had gone out again, and sniffed it. Then he turned to his sister, and said, 'Are you blaming Uncle for this, old girl? Trust you to back the Chinamen. Remember when we were kids how we used to flick clay pellets at their heads, and make'em yell like mad?'

'No, I do not remember,' said Catherine very coolly.

All of a sudden, the door burst open and in came the Reverend Ely, pale and frowning, wrapped in a dressing-gown like a rather mundane ghost.

'Get back to bed at once! Just when you were on the mend! I won't have you coming down here.' Mrs Ely barred his way.

'Hello, old chap!' said Paul. 'Another cold, eh? Off to bed with you straight away. Come on, I'll give you a piggyback.' Paul threw down his pipe, and, by hauling and hoisting his father, got him upstairs.

It made the Reverend Ely all the more furious that he'd been carted back to bed by his son, unable to vent his mighty wrath. He lay in bed and smoked the cigar from Alexander in one go, all the while cursing his brother-in-law.

IX

WHEN CITY life has developed to the level it has in England, time equals money. To waste a quarter of an hour is to lose half a crown, so to speak. Apart from the very wealthy, who can fritter time away as it suits them – dancing, theatre-going, dining out, throwing parties, idle chit-chatting, gossip-spreading, hunting, swimming or playing the invalid at their own sweet leisure – people's lives in general have to march in step with the clock. Yes, the cornerstone of this terribly busy, terribly chaotic, and terribly noisy society is an icy-cold, cruel, calculating little wretch – the pendulum of the clock. This economy of time has considerably reduced face-to-face communication, making the telephone and the letter the two treasured talismans of these civilised people. When Mrs White's husband dies, it's quite normal for Mrs Black to only write her a letter of commiseration, since Mrs Black's busy. And Mrs White, busy herself, then telephones her thanks to Mrs Black.

The matter gave Mr Ma much food for thought. The postman would make four or five deliveries a day, and he'd knock on virtually every door. Where did so many letters come from? Almost every evening, Mrs Wedderburn would take her little pen, and, with a frown upon her brow, write letters. Who was she writing them to? What had she got to write about? He felt a bit suspicious, and, in spite of himself, somewhat jealous. Holding her pen and frowning like that, she looked very pretty. But she certainly wasn't writing to him. Foreign women all have illicit affairs . . . Mr Ma wouldn't go as far as to say that he'd fallen in love with Mrs Wedderburn, but

145

when he saw her writing letters to others, he did feel something of an ache inside. Odd . . .

Since the Mas had come to live with her, Mrs Wedderburn had certainly used more postage stamps than before. With two Chinese men living in her house, she no longer felt comfortable inviting her friends and relatives round to tea. What – have them eat with the Mas? It wouldn't be fair, making them eat with Chinese people. She could make the Mas eat on their own, she supposed, but that'd mean too much bother for her. Of course the Mas wouldn't mind where they ate, but why should she be put to such trouble? Just let things be, she thought, and write her friends a letter hoping they were all right. That would save trouble, and still keep her on good terms with everybody.

Since the Mas' arrival, she'd in fact asked people round twice, but they hadn't taken up the invitation. Between the lines of their letters of reply she could read, 'Do you think we're going to sit down to a meal with two Chinese fellows?' Of course, they never put it so bluntly, but she wasn't such a fool that she couldn't tell what they were implying.

When she wrote letters, she often thought of these snubs, and she reflected that Mary had been absolutely right to say she shouldn't have let the rooms to the two Chinese. Mary herself hadn't actually been affected in the slightest by it. Chaps continued to call for her every day, and she went gadding about with them.

But what about me? Mrs Wedderburn asked herself. What a miserable time I have of it! If I don't invite folks to dinner, I can't go round to theirs for dinner, can I? I don't have any social life. I'm sacrificing my social life all for two Chinese fellows.

She found herself spilling a tear. Could she get rid of them? There wasn't much you could complain about, though, and, anyway, they paid more rent than she could get from anyone else. She'd just have to carry on writing letters with a frown on her face.

Before breakfast, Mary, short hair in a tangle, went to see if there were any letters. There were two: a bill from the gas company, and a letter from the country.

'Mum, a letter from Aunt Dolly. Just look at the skimpy little envelope!'

Mrs Wedderburn was making breakfast, so she told Mary to read it out to her. Mary slit the envelope with a paperknife.

> *Thank you for your letter, my dear sister. My old complaint is troubling me again and I'm afraid I won't be able to get to London. I'm ever so sorry. Is it true you've got two Chinamen living with you?*
>
> *Your ever loving,*
> *Dolly*

Mary threw the letter on the table, and gave a huffy puff. 'Well that's that, Mum. She's not coming. "You've got two Chinamen living with you." Pretty clear why she's not coming.'

'We'll go on holiday whether she comes or not!' As Mrs Wedderburn tipped the eggs into the pan, the oil splashed out and scalded her tiny pale wrist. 'Damn!'

When breakfast was ready, Mrs Wedderburn put Mr Ma's on a tray to take upstairs to him. The effects of Mr Ma's big night had already passed, and the bump on his forehead had healed. But he remained fastidiously alert to the possible after-effects of his drunkenness, which meant he now never rose before eleven in the morning, and he took breakfast in bed.

Just as Mrs Wedderburn was coming out of the kitchen, tray in hand, Napoleon returned from his constitutional in the backyard and leapt up at her suddenly. Her legs gave way and she fell down in the doorway, while the tray changed from sempre legato to fortissimo in B flat as it crashed to the floor. The fried egg smeared all over the carpet and the toast scored a direct hit on Napoleon's nose. The little dog took one look at his mistress, sniffed at the toast and then, realising something was amiss, put his tail between his legs, and, eyes rolling with fear, returned to the backyard.

'Are you all right, Mum?' asked Mary, helping her mother to her feet and holding her upright. 'Mum, what's up?'

Mrs Wedderburn's face blanched for a moment, then suddenly turned scarlet. Beads of cold perspiration covered her nose and her lips trembled, even more than her hands. She stood there dumbfounded, staring at the things on the floor, and uttering not a sound.

Mary paled too. She helped her mother to a chair and got her to sit down, while she herself then hastened to clear up the things from the floor. Thanks to the carpet none of the plates and cups were broken, the sole damage being a broken milk-jug handle. 'What's the matter, Mum?'

Mrs Wedderburn's cheeks grew redder still, and she seemed at that instant to recall all her life's sufferings. Her lips suddenly stopped quivering, and the grievances inside her came bursting from her lips in one rambling monologue.

'Oh, Mary, I've had enough of this life! I can't put up with it, living like this! Money, money, it's all about money. Your dad wore himself to death for money, and I went out to work and drudge for money. And now I'm playing servant to two Chinamen, all for the sake of money. It's making my friends and family look down on me. Money! Can't the clever people in this world come up with a better idea? Can't they find a way of getting rid of money? There's no fun in life unless you're rich!'

Having said her piece, Mrs Wedderburn was immensely relieved, and the floodgates opened, string after string of pearly tears. Tears welled up in Mary's eyes, too, and she didn't know what to say, so just wiped her mother's tears with her little handkerchief.

'Mum, if you don't want them to stay, you can tell them to leave.'

'But the money!'

'If you rented out to others, you'd get money too, Mum.'

'Always money!'

Unable to understand what her mother was driving at, Mary wiped her own eyes.

'You have your breakfast, Mary,' said Mrs Wedderburn. 'I'm going to look for Napoleon.'

'What made you collapse, though, Mum?'

'Napoleon jumped up at me and gave me a fright. I didn't see him coming.'

Mary called Ma Wei to breakfast. Warned by the expression on her face, he didn't say anything. First he took up his father's breakfast, which Mary had done her best to remake, then he ate his own in silence.

After breakfast, Mary went into the backyard to look for her mother. Mrs Wedderburn, with Napoleon in her arms, was standing by the bed of roses. The sun had lit up all the flowers in the garden and a gentle breeze was trembling the petals and leaves, making the air fresh and light. The dandelions by the wall had grown several 'old men', their fluffy dandelion-fairy seeds, which were slowly dancing off with the breeze into the sky. Napoleon, one eye on his mistress and the other on the white-whiskered seeds, was crestfallen and ashamed of himself, and didn't dare utter a peep.

'Are you all right now, Mum?'

'Yes, I'm all right. You better head off. It must be quite late by now.' Mrs Wedderburn's face wasn't as red as before, but the sun made her look worn and harassed. She'd been crying again, standing there in the garden with Napoleon in her arms, and the sunshine had dried her tears and left salty marks. Napoleon's eyes seemed rather moist too, and at the sight of Mary, he feebly wagged his tail.

'Have you said you're sorry to Mum, Napoleon? You're a naughty rascal to knock Mummy over, aren't you?' said Mary, speaking to the dog, but looking at her mother.

Mrs Wedderburn gave a wan smile. 'Off you go to work, Mary. It's late.'

'Cheerio, Mum. Cheerio, Napoleon. You go and have some breakfast, Mum. You must.'

Seeing his mistress smile, Napoleon risked a couple of barks, by way of saying cheerio to Mary.

X

AFTER MARY had left, Mrs Wedderburn carried Napoleon into the kitchen and made herself a pot of tea and a boiled egg. She drank a cup of tea then took a mouthful of egg, but, unable to swallow it, gave the rest to Napoleon. She thought of clearing up the dishes, but felt too listless even to stand. She looked out the window and saw the sun still shining brightly.

'Let's take a stroll in the park, shall we?'

At the mention of a trip to the park, Napoleon pricked up his ears and saliva ran from the sides of his mouth. Mrs Wedderburn changed her dress, brushed her shoes and put on her hat. It filled her with impatience to do all this, but her innate English sense of propriety compelled her to dress properly when she went out, no matter what. Anyway, she was a woman. And what was woman but the very epitome of beauty? How could she neglect her attire! None of the young girls nowadays, not even Mary, understood the meaning of beauty, with their short skirts that showed their legs, and their itsy-bitsy hats like eggshells. But times had changed, and there was nothing anyone could do about it. Just imagine if she were still young herself! She'd be wearing her dresses short and her hats tiny too. Anyway, men love whatever women wear, no matter how short or tiny.

Men . . . Yes, the only thing that could cheer her up would be having a chat with a man about her troubles. The elder Ma? Never! An old Chinaman. She wondered if he was up yet. Oh well, no matter if he was.

'Come on, Napoleon. Mummy'll comb your hair for you. How have you managed to get yourself so dirty?'

Napoleon, his tongue hanging out, let her comb his coat. He raised his left leg and scratched under his chin, as if he had fleas, though whether he actually did, even he wasn't sure.

On reaching the main road, they took a bus to Regent's Park. Mrs Wedderburn sat in the open top of the bus, and as the warm wind whistled past her ears, she breathed in deeply. Napoleon sat leaning on the railing of the bus, trying to snap off the large green leaves of the plane trees that lined the roads. But the bus was going too fast, and he never managed it.

The flowerbeds of Regent's Park were packed with blooms. Deep-red fuchsias, pale-blue hydrangeas, and numerous other shrubs whose names one can never remember all seemed to be laughing in the sun. On the grassy slopes grew daisies, tall-stalked with big round leaves – single ones and double ones, lead-white ones and gosling-yellow ones, all seeming to crinkle their petals in smiles and declare, 'We are the epitome of nature, the summer's soul.' The tall trees on either side of the beds were delicately stirring their verdant leaves, printing ever-changing patterns on the fine gravel of the paths. The girls sitting beneath the trees all had their arms bared, and upon those pale arms, too, the trees cast their shadowy patterns.

Mrs Wedderburn found a bench and sat down, putting Napoleon on the ground. As she breathed the scents of the flowers and plants, and watched the sunbeams coming down through the foliage, she felt much more relaxed. Her mind was a mixture of clarity and confusion, and all kinds of thoughts came to her. The wind whisked her skirt up a little, and a thread of sunlight shone across her legs, sending a warm feeling through her, as if she were being tickled. She hastily pulled her skirt in place, her face rather flushed.

Yes, twenty years ago now. Sitting here with him. In the distance, she could hear a lion roaring in the zoo. Ah, it was a long time since she'd been to the zoo. *When Mary was little, he used to carry her in his arms while I followed on behind, and we would take some tidbits with us and feed the monkeys together. Oh, we were happy in those days. Even the flowers smelt sweeter then, I know it. What a life . . . Such cruel changes. It's always changing for the worse. Who'd have thought I'd be waiting on a couple of Chinese? Not me!*

I should go home. What's the point of all this useless thinking? Life . . . Oh, well, everybody's got to get through it. Am I getting old? Of course not. Just look at those rich ladies over fifty, still in the very bloom of life. Such worries would never occur to Mary . . . Oh dear – if Mary gets married, that'll leave me on my own, and I'll be lonelier than ever. Lonely.

The little birds in the trees chimed in with chirrups of 'Lonely! Lonely!' *I'll go home; go and see Mr Ma.* Why did he keep on cropping up in her thoughts all the time? *Funny the way it is between men and women. But he's Chinese – people'd laugh at me. Then again, why bother what other people say?* A tiny sparrow flew past, skimming the brim of her hat. *Poor little bird, having to fly to and fro all day looking for food.*

Where's Napoleon? He's disappeared!

'Napoleon!' She stood up and looked all around, but the little dog was nowhere to be seen.

'Have you seen Napoleon?' she asked a small boy. He had a jar in his hand, and was picking up little red seedpods from where they'd fallen under a tree.

'Napoleon? The French man?' The small boy's mouth opened wide as he stared at her with his little brown eyes.

'No, my Peke,' she said, laughing. 'A dog.'

The small boy shook his head, squatted down again, and said, 'Here's a big one.'

Anxious and flustered, Mrs Wedderburn walked further in towards the middle of the park. She looked in all the clumps of flowers and behind all the trees, but her beloved pet was in none of these places. Panic-stricken, she became oblivious to everything else except finding Napoleon.

She went through a second gate within the park to a small stream, her eyes roving both banks, but still saw no trace of Napoleon. Two boatloads of boys and girls were rowing out on the water, and the sight of her hat set them all laughing. Ignoring them, she carried on along the bank of the stream, peering into the distance. The little dog was still nowhere to be seen. She was on the brink of tears, and, feeling rather weak at the knees, she flopped down on the grass. The crowd of boys and girls were still laughing. Yes, laughing! Nobody showed her any sympathy. *Just look at them – so scantily clad. Where could Napoleon be?*

Two swans, leading a flock of cygnets, came floating beneath a little bridge towards a weeping willow, fragmenting the reflection of the bridge in their rippling wake. On the far side of the bridge stood a policeman, like some implacable bronze statue. *I'll go and ask him,* thought Mrs Wedderburn. She was on the point of standing up when she heard a call behind her, 'Mrs Wedderburn!'

Ma Wei! And holding Napoleon!

'Oh, Ma Wei! You! Where did you find him?' She grabbed the dog, and gave it two kisses. 'What are you doing here? Have a sit down and rest for a while, and we'll go home together.' In her delight, she forgot everything, even that Ma Wei was Chinese.

'I was watching the children catch fish over there,' said Ma Wei, pointing northwards, 'and suddenly something bumped against my legs. And I looked down and saw him!'

'You naughty thing! Worrying your mummy like that! Just you say thank you to Ma Wei.'

Napoleon gave Ma Wei two barks.

With the dog in her arms, everything looked rosy as Mrs Wedderburn now contemplated the stream. 'Just look at those boys and girls; they do look healthy. And look at that group of cygnets. Oh, how sweet! Do you row, Ma Wei?'

Ma Wei shook his head.

'Rowing's a first-class sport. Do you swim?'

'I can a bit.' Ma Wei gave a smile. He sat beside her, and watched the oily-looking water of the stream drift along with the swans.

'You've lost weight recently, Ma Wei, you know.'

'You're right, I have. My father – you understand —'

'Oh yes, I understand,' said Mrs Wedderburn, nodding, actually expressing sympathy for Ma Wei even though he was Chinese.

'Yes, my father . . . Oh dear.' Ma Wei stopped himself and instead shook his head.

'Have you settled yet where you'll be going for your summer holiday?'

'No. I intended to —' Ma Wei stopped himself once more. Inwardly he was saying, *I've fallen for your daughter. Did you know?*

The small boy who'd been collecting red seeds came by, and seeing Mrs Wedderburn holding the dog, wiped the sweat from his brow with his hand. 'Is that your Napoleon, miss?' he asked.

Hearing the boy call her 'miss', Mrs Wedderburn smiled.

'Hey, miss, what you doing sitting with a Chinaman?'

'Him? He found my dog for me,' said Mrs Wedderburn, still with a smile.

'Huh!' Without another word, the boy ran into the trees, a cheeky look on his face and mischief on his mind. Then suddenly he noticed the policeman by the bridge, and, losing his courage, picked up the little jar and ran off.

'He's only a child, Ma Wei,' said Mrs Wedderburn. 'Don't take any notice of him.'

'I won't,' said Ma Wei.

I don't hate you Chinese, anyway. The words were on the tip of Mrs Wedderburn's tongue, but she didn't utter them. *As long as you behave yourselves. Others may make fun of the Chinese, but I'm not one of them.*

Once again, Mrs Wedderburn's contrary disposition came to the fore, and these thoughts ran through her head while her eyes followed the white swans along the stream.

'Mary's holiday starts next week,' she said, 'and we want to go away for a few days. Would it be all right for you to eat out?'

'Oh! Oh yes, that'd be all right. Is Mary going with you, then, Mrs Wedderburn?' Ma Wei tore a tuft of grass from the ground.

'Yes, she is. You see, I was going to find someone to cook for you —'

'But nobody wants to wait on Chinese people?' Ma Wei gave a laugh. Mrs Wedderburn nodded. She felt quite surprised that Ma Wei should have guessed the reason. As the English see it, all others – apart from the French, who are sometimes slightly smarter than the English – are fools. In the eyes of the English, only the English are correct in their assumptions, and they alone are capable of understanding their own thinking. If outsiders manage to correctly divine matters preoccupying an English mind, that's not merely strange, it's downright astonishing.

'Ma Wei, whose is the prettiest hat, do you think: mine or Mary's?' Having new insight into Ma Wei's astuteness, Mrs Wedderburn now wanted to test the Chinese concept of beauty, if of course the Chinese had any such notion.

'I think they're both nice.'

'That doesn't answer my question.'

'Well, yours is the prettiest.'

'And when you see Mary, will you tell her that hers is the prettiest?'

'Honestly, Mrs Wedderburn, your hat's very nice indeed. My father says so, too.'

'Oh!' Mrs Wedderburn took off her hat, and dusted it with her dainty handkerchief.

'I'd better be going.' Ma Wei took a look at his watch. 'Miss Ely's calling round today for a bit of studying. Are you leaving now too, Mrs Wedderburn?'

'I am. We'll go together,' said Mrs Wedderburn, and then she thought to herself, *Let anybody make fun of me if they want. I don't care. I'm going to walk with a Chinaman, whatever they think!*

XI

LATELY MA Wei had been spending a lot of time at Regent's Park. He would find a secluded spot, sit down and open a book . . . but he didn't always read it. Sometimes he'd just read a few lines, knitting his brow, biting his thumb, and flicking back through the pages again and again, reading until golden flowers danced in front of his eyes and he no longer knew what he'd been reading. Then he'd put the book down on the grass and give himself a couple of fierce punches on the back of the head.

What did you come here for, if it wasn't to study?

Hating himself didn't help, and punching himself was a sheer waste of energy. It all boiled down to the fact that the words in the book weren't going into his head.

The impasse in his studies wasn't the only trouble. He was off his food, and tea tasted insipid, and he could hardly raise the enthusiasm to say hello to people. What was up? Her! That was what. The only time he felt cheerful was when he saw her. Was this what they call love? Two red blotches appeared on Ma Wei's cheeks, hot to the touch.

Mustn't let my father notice. Mustn't let anyone, not even Li Tzu-jung. But those two damned spots on his face still burned when he felt them. Li Tzu-jung must have cottoned on by now.

Ma Wei met her every breakfast, and every dinnertime. But how many hours were there from breakfast till the evening meal? One, two, three, four . . . on and on, an endless number . . . Sometimes in the evening, he would go and stand outside the door to wait for her coming home. But that didn't help him, did it? She'd give him a nod, and sometimes a smile. But sometimes not.

What was the good of waiting at the door for her? Why not go and see her in her shop? That wasn't very advisable. Why not go for a stroll round town, on the off-chance of meeting her? He might just bump into her at lunchtime. And then he could join her for a meal, couldn't he? But knowing full well that she worked in the shop, there wasn't much point his traipsing round town for her. But what if . . .

I could just stand in the street where she works for a while, then walk around a bit. She might be on a bus, or browsing in a shop.

And that was just what he'd started doing. Once he thought he'd seen her on a bus and nipped on to it without thinking, but on closer inspection, it proved not to be her. Sometimes, pursuing some girl, he'd squeeze his way through a crowd and chase her with grim determination, trampling on old ladies' toes without even bothering to apologise. But when he'd caught up with her, he'd discover it was someone else. The girl might be as fair as Mary, and wearing the same type of hat and clothes. *Bloody hell! Wearing the same clothes as her! Keep on walking. Keep on look-ing . . .* And all the while that ache inside him. And those two red blotches on his cheeks, burning away.

And what happened when it rained? That didn't stop him. He still went out, in case she might knock off early because of the rain. *You idiot, Ma Wei. Who ever stopped work early on account of the rain! Can't sit here, anyway. Out I go.* He didn't even take an umbrella. He hated using one, since it blocked off people's faces. He got soaked to the skin, and water poured from his hat, but still he didn't see her.

Yesterday he'd been certain. Her! It was her! Walking on the other side of the street. His heart had beat quicker, and his legs seemed to be spinning round inside his trousers. *After her! But what'll you say? Invite her for a meal? Nearly three o'clock now – she's bound to have had lunch. Invite her out to tea. No, it's too early. And what if she's got something urgent on? Hold her up, and she'll be grumpy. What if she just ignores me? And the other people in the street look at me? What if it makes her so angry she'll never even look at me again?*

He'd almost caught up with her when his courage failed him. He came to a halt and just watched her hurry away. Anywhere else but in that main street, he would have wept. How could he be such a coward! So dithering! With a hollow feeling inside, he wondered how to proceed: hate himself? Punish himself? Pity himself? But it didn't matter what he did. It was her that mattered. She held his heart.

Try to think negatively; put her to the back of my mind; try not looking at her. Plenty of girls in this world, so why should I be set on loving her? Someone like her, who wears such ugly red lipstick each Saturday. And she's English: what's the point? Why go and fall for a foreigner? Some day I'll have to go back to China, and what about her then? Could she go with me? Not likely! Right then: cast her into oblivion, far beyond the imagination.

But back she came. Not her, but her image, dimples twinkling, lips quivering, with one of her white teeth biting the edge of her lower lip, and curly brown hair like a sunlit pool of springtime ripples. Her soft pale neck, always so pretty. Nothing he said or thought was as sweet to him as saying 'Mary' and thinking Mary.

If I could hold her in my arms just the once. Life wouldn't matter then. I'd give my life just for that. I went to the cinema with her once, and stroked her hand in the dark. So beautifully smooth, it was. She didn't even seem to notice. Perhaps foreign women don't think anything of it when they let someone touch their hand. She rescued my father, so she must think something of me. Otherwise why'd she let me stroke her hand? Why was she so shaken by rescuing my father? There may be hope yet.

That punk Washington! I bet he doesn't stop at stroking her hand . . . I hate him! If she were a Chinese woman, I'd tell her straight, 'I love you!' Would I, though? Would I have the courage, even with a Chinese woman? Ma Wei! You're a useless bloke, a total chicken! Don't think about it any more. Just get down to your studying in earnest. If I don't make a go of it, what sort of future will I have to look forward to? Oh, damn the future! I'd do anything, absolutely anything to get her off my mind . . .

Before his eyes, water flowed, birds flew and flowers moved in the wind. The water, the birds, the flowers. Maybe they were all more beautiful than her, but people are people, things of the flesh. Love wasn't something to be understood with the spirit, but something to be enjoyed or suffered with the body. It was no good trying to suppress it, either.

Mrs Wedderburn carried Napoleon and with Ma Wei following behind, they made their way home together.

As they reached their door, they saw Miss Ely standing at the foot of the steps. She wore a blue straw hat with a pale-pink flower fastened to its brim, a blue blouse and a rice-yellow silk skirt. Her head was tipped very slightly to one side, and she was serenely and tranquilly contemplating her shadow, cast across the white stone of the steps.

She's pretty too, Ma Wei observed.

'Ah, Miss Ely! How are you? Do come in.' Mrs Wedderburn shook hands with Catherine.

'Sorry, Miss Ely. Have you been waiting a long time?' Ma Wei shook hands with her.

'No, I've only just arrived.' She gave a smile.

'You go on up, Miss Ely. Don't let me waste your studying time.' Napoleon in her arms, Mrs Wedderburn opened the drawing room door and went in.

'See you shortly then, Mrs Wedderburn.' Miss Ely placed her hat on the hatstand, gathered her hair back and went upstairs.

Mr Ma was on his way out to lunch, and he met her on the stairs. 'Ah, Miss Ely. How are you? How is the Reverend Ely? How is Mrs Ely? And how is your brother?' When making polite enquiries Mr Ma tended to go a little overboard.

'They're all very well. And are you much better now, Mr Ma? It was very bad of my uncle. You —'

'Not at all! Not at all!' Mr Ma gave a few throaty gurgles, by way of laughter. 'It was my fault. He meant well. Old boys painting the town red together! Ha ha!'

'Enjoy yourself, Mr Ma. I'm going to do some studying with Ma Wei.' Miss Ely stood aside to let Mr Ma go past.

'Well then, I'll leave you in peace. Won't keep you company. Ha ha!'

Slowly descending, he had a word with Ma Wei. 'I'll be going to the shop when I've had my lunch.' He spoke very quietly for fear of being overheard by Catherine. 'Going to the shop' was hardly something to be trumpeted from the rooftops. If he'd been 'going to my government office' – well, now, that really would be worth shouting about.

Sitting down on a chair, Catherine drew out a magazine. 'You teach me for half an hour, Ma Wei, and I'll teach you for half an hour. I'll translate a passage from this magazine into Chinese, and you correct me, sentence by sentence. How about you – what do you plan to read?'

Ma Wei opened the window and watched a strand of sunlight fall on her hair, forming a circle of golden light that set her off, making her look a bit like the Virgin Mary in pictures. He pulled a chair across, sitting further into the room, to avoid blocking the ray of sunlight on her head. *Her hair's very pretty, even nicer than Mary's. Don't know why, though, but Mary's still better-looking than her. Mary's prettiness gets at your heart, whereas Catherine's just a pretty elder sister.*

Then, as he registered her question, he rapidly pulled himself together and asked, 'What do you think I ought to read, Elder Sister?'

'Why not read a novel? If you don't have one already, go and buy a copy of Wells' *The History of Mr Polly*. You read it aloud and I'll listen, and as long as I can understand, you can keep on reading. If we do it that way, you'll learn to read every word exactly right. You look up the words you don't know beforehand, and if any of them aren't clear I'll tell you which of the dictionary meanings fits best. We'll do it like that, shall we? If you've got any other good ideas, so much the better.'

'We'll do as you suggest, Elder Sister. I haven't got any book to read from today, so I'll teach you now, and you teach me next time.'

'What, and let me get half an hour up on you?' Catherine looked at him with a smile.

Ma Wei smiled back.

'Mum! Mum! Have you bought a new hat?' As she came into the house, Mary had caught sight of Catherine's blue straw hat.

'Where?' asked Mrs Wedderburn.

'There!' Mary pointed at the hatstand, her blue eyes filled with admiration.

'That's not mine. It's Miss Ely's.'

'Oh, Mum! I'm going to buy one like that, too. What's she here for? Huh, I don't like that pink flower much.' Picking on a small flaw made her envy less potent.

'What's brought you home so early?' asked Mrs Wedderburn.

'Oh, Mum, I kept on worrying about you after you'd had that fall this morning. I'll have to rush back but I just wanted to make sure you were all right. You are, aren't you now? Mum, I want a hat like that. We don't sell straw hats in our shop. Wonder where she bought it?'

Mary was still standing in the doorway, her eyes riveted to the blue hat. The blue of the hat and the blue of her eyes seemed to have merged into one blue line.

'Have you had anything to eat, Mary?'

'I just had a slice of almond cake and a cup of coffee, because I was in such a hurry to come and see how you were.' Mary moved a step in the direction of the hatstand.

'I'm all right now, thanks, Mary. Don't worry about me. You be off.'

'Mum, what's Catherine here for?'

'She's learning Chinese with Ma Wei.'

'I'll get him to teach me some day.' Mary shot a glare at the blue hat.

Just as Mary was about to leave, down came Miss Ely and Ma Wei. Saying hello to mother and daughter, Miss Ely took her hat and put it on, all very naturally, with no trace of pride or any affectation in her manner.

'You're looking very well, Mary,' she said, smiling.

'Your hat is gorgeous, Miss Ely.' The left side of Mary's mouth lifted in a decidedly sour smile.

'Do you think so?'

Don't pretend you don't know it is! thought Mary, and glanced at Ma Wei.

'Bye, Mrs Wedderburn. See you, Mary.' Catherine shook hands with them, and nodded to Ma Wei.

'See you this evening, Mum.' Mary followed her out.

From the steps, Ma Wei watched their retreating forms. Apart from their both being girls, they had nothing else in common. Catherine's head was erect, with the brim of her hat trembling slightly. Mary's head poked forwards a little, and her skirt was wrapping itself round her thighs.

He put his hands in his pockets, and, with a frown on his forehead, went upstairs. It was lunchtime by now, but he wasn't hungry. Actually, it wasn't that he wasn't hungry – he couldn't say what it was . . .

'Mum, Gamages in Oxford Street have got that sort of straw hat. Let's both buy one, shall we?' said Mary to her mother in the kitchen, holding Napoleon in her arms.

'We're not rolling in money, Mary! Pass me the sugar bowl.' Mrs Wedderburn's little nose was baked bright red from the stove, and she was a bit snappy. 'We're going on our summer holidays, aren't we? If you're planning to spend all your money buying hats, we can forget about going away. That sort of hat must cost at least two pounds!'

She tipped a spoonful of sugar onto the vegetables and her eyes widened. 'There now! Just look! You come here disturbing me, and I've gone and put sugar —'

'If you go anywhere on holiday, you've simply got to have a new hat!' Mary spoke with earnest conviction, and in her vehemence squeezed Napoleon's legs so hard they must have hurt.

The little dog didn't dare utter a squeak. *If you don't get your way about buying your hat,* he said to himself, *it'll be all over for me, I can see. Dogs are better off than humans – no hat problems.*

'We'll discuss it when we've eaten, Mary. Don't hold the dog so roughly.'

Mr Ma didn't arrive home until dinner had already been served. For his lunch he'd had three immortals soup with noodles in a Chinese restaurant. After that he'd gone to the shop, where, in a solemn and businesslike manner, he'd smoked a few pipes of tobacco. It had been his original intention to rearrange the wares, but he reminded himself that he'd only just recovered, and mustn't overtire himself. Yet it didn't seem quite right not to be doing something or other.

Why not take out the accounts, and have a look at them? Forty pounds profit two months ago. Fifteen pounds loss last month. He *put the accounts away. Who could be bothered with such stuff! Sometimes you make a profit, sometimes you don't. That's trade. You can't always be turning a profit.*

After dinner, Mary was about to launch into the hat discussion with her mother when Mr Ma gave a slight nod in her direction.

'For you, Miss Wedderburn.' He handed her a small envelope.

'Oh, Mr Ma, it's a cheque for two pounds. What's that for?'

'I promised you a hat, didn't I?'

'Hooray, Mum! A hat!'

XII

SINCE HE'D recovered from his illness, Mr Ma had been very keen to please others. Breakfast over, he'd go into the backyard and water the flowers, remove caterpillars and cut the lawn, humming wordless hymns, with the air of some Taoist gentleman of Chinese antiquity rejoicing in thoughts of paradise and immortality. He felt so carefree and cheerful that if a bee landed on his forehead, he made not the slightest move to shoo it away. *As long as you don't sting me, I'll do you no harm. There now, see how placid and relaxed I am!*

He'd given Mary no less than two pounds to buy a hat. Fine, one vow fulfilled. Now should he buy one for her mother or not? *We made a loss of fifteen pounds last month, and that's no joke. Better be more thrifty, hadn't we? But you can't dismiss human obligations just like that. I gave Mrs Wedderburn considerable trouble when I was unwell, and I ought to buy her something to express my thanks. We'll see next month. Yes, next month. Hardly likely to make a loss of fifteen pounds again next month.*

Ma Wei's been getting thinner lately. Wonder what's the matter with him? Still a young lad, but he ought to eat a bit more. Plenty to eat and a lot of sound sleep, that'd fill him out. Yes, he'll have to eat more.

Ah, I ought to pop in at the shop. All that fellow Li Tzu-jung can do is grumble. A load of rubbish — grumbling morning till night. I'll go in early this morning, and give him no chance to grumble. Hey, it's ten o'clock already. I'll have to be off there in a hurry. Wait a moment, I'll take two pots of flowers to the shop. Splendid idea!

If he says I'm late, I'll have a ready excuse: I've been transplanting the flowers. Those hopeless-looking chrysanthemums have grown after all. Look quite nice now, too. That's it. I'll take a couple of pots of chrysanthemums. A few pots of chrysanthemums in the shop'll look very elegant. And perhaps they'll show up Li Tzu-jung's tasteless display all the more vividly!

If he had a long way to go, Mr Ma would always take a taxi. If his destination was nearby, he'd walk at a leisurely pace. Under no circumstances would he take a bus or tram. It'd be no laughing matter if he had an accident and died in London. Of late he'd even taken to travelling less by taxi, since the traffic was so chaotic and you could never be sure, even with a taxi. When he used to catch cabs in Peking, the police would halt the pedestrians and horses to speed the taxi on its way. So exalted, so grandly mandarin-like! But here in London, a big policeman had only to stick out a hand and all the traffic, even the prime minister's car, had to come to a stop. These foreign devils! No sense of the proper social distinctions! No notion of rank!

Hugging his two pots of transplanted chrysanthemums, his mouth with its stringy moustache twitched up in a little smile, he pushed his way through the crowds. *Bloody hell, where on earth have all these people come from? You can't get through them, and they're all walking so fast. That's a bad sign. They'll never get anywhere, the English. Not remotely sedate!*

By the time he reached the shop, his ears were buzzing, as they had begun to do all day, every day. *God have mercy, and grant me a return to my own homeland. I can't endure this chaos.* When he'd recovered his composure, he arranged the two pots of chrysanthemums at the front of the shop window, and, twirling his moustache, he contemplated them for a while. *Aha! That one's got a little yellow leaf – best nip it off. Can't allow the smallest bit of faded leaf. Must keep the lot perfectly green. You have to be particular about things.*

'Mr Ma!' Li Tzu-jung came out of the back room, with his sleeves rolled up as usual and his hands covered in muck. (*The young fellow always refuses to wear a jacket. So common!*) 'Last month we didn't make a penny, and we haven't sold much this month, either. I can't just stand by and watch it happening; we'll have to put our heads together on this. If you've got a plan for improving things, I'll be only too glad to help you, of course, but if you haven't, I'd best try and find another job, to save you my wages. There's not a lot of work to be done here, so you and Ma Wei could easily manage between the two of you. Whether in fact I'd be able to find another job, I'm not sure, but if you'd be good enough to give me two weeks' notice, I might manage to find something. Let's put our cards on the table and be frank with each other. Standing on ceremony'll do us no good.'

Li Tzu-jung spoke bluntly, but his manner was gentle and friendly. Even Mr Ma could see that. His words came straight from the heart – but all the same, they were distinctly ill-bred. Mr Ma removed his large spectacles, delicately wiped them with his handkerchief, and said nothing for a long time.

'Well, there's no immediate hurry, Mr Ma. You think it over, and let me know something definite soon, all right?' Li Tzu-jung knew it wasn't the slightest bit of good putting pressure on the elder Ma. Better to give him some time to think it over. Whether he actually would think it over, even given the time, was quite another matter, but suggesting that at least saved them from being locked there in awkwardness.

Mr Ma nodded, and continued to wipe his spectacles. 'I say, shop assistant Li,' he said with a half smile, putting his spectacles back on, 'If you feel your wages to be too low, we can discuss the problem.'

'Good grief! My dear Mr Ma, do I think my wages are too low? Really, there's just no way of getting you to understand me, is there!' Li Tzu-jung scratched his head, and stuttered a little as he spoke. 'You must see how things stand, Mr Ma. I've told you many times that we've got to think about the shop, but you've never taken any notice. And now we're running at a loss. I . . . I . . . really, I don't know how I can make it clearer. Do you know, our neighbour made a good few hundred pounds last month, just from selling Mongol and Manchu books. I —'

'But who on earth would buy Mongol and Manchu books?

What would be the point of buying such things?' Mr Ma now felt that, besides being ill-bred, Li Tzu-jung was slightly insane into the bargain. How ludicrous, selling Mongol books in an antiques shop! Who would buy them? 'If you feel the wages to be too low, we can come to some arrangement. We'll find a way. But on no account must we lose face with one another over it.'

Face!

It's funny how the Chinese concern for face often goes hand in hand with shamelessness. When in Peking, Mr Ma used to grovel to borrow a single dollar from someone. Why? He had to buy a drink at some relative's wedding, for the sake of face. When Field Marshal Chang gets reinforcements from Japan to help him out of a tight spot, he has to fight Field Marshal Kuo, for the sake of face. Department Head Wang knows perfectly well that Under-Secretary Li is a bad egg, but doesn't fire him, for the sake of face. All things Chinese bow down at the foot of face. As long as face can be maintained, who cares about the reality?

The Chinese way of doing things reminds one of the children's game of blind man's buff. You go round in circles trying to touch someone, and if you manage to, you've succeeded in preserving your face, so everything's fine and dandy. Who cares whether the person you've caught is Little Three, Little Four or Little Three's elder brother, Dopey Two?

Mr Ma was justly in a tight spot. The facts were simple: the business was running at a loss, and he had to think of some means of rectifying this state of affairs. But, being truly Chinese, he wouldn't allow himself to see things in this light. Only foreign devils would think in such terms. Li Tzu-jung thought like that, too, the yellow-faced foreign devil!

'So the business is running at a loss,' he said. 'Well, I never wanted to come and run such a dead-end business in the first place.'

Realising that Li Tzu-jung wasn't going to argue, he sat down on a chair, and, twirling his scrap of moustache, gave his thoughts free rein.

If I hadn't come to England, I might have become a government official in China by now. If I spend a lot, it's my money, and it's nobody else's concern. The vehemence of this thought jerked his hand so violently that he almost pulled a couple of hairs from his moustache.

No, I'm not acquainted with the ins and outs of commerce. The last thing a gentleman-scholar concerns himself with is trading! Trying to put the squeeze on me, Li? Bare-faced coercion, eh? Young fellow, Li Whatsit, if you were to study more you might reach a truer appreciation of your venerable Uncle Ma. Such commonness and vulgarity! He shot a glare towards the interior of the shop. *Selling Manchu and Mongol writings, eh? Ridiculous! What would the foreign devils be doing – reading the* Twelve Heads *in Manchu? Or preparing themselves to see Manchu soldiers on armoured horses? We live in the era of the Republic of China!*

So you want to resign, to quit my employ? In complete disregard of face? What more could you ask for here? Haven't I treated you well? Yet out of the blue you suddenly threaten me with your resignation. What impudence! What stupidity!

As his thoughts proceeded in circles, his anger grew ever more righteous and he distanced himself ever further from reality. And the further he strayed, the more he felt himself to be a truly good Chinese. That yellow-faced foreign devil Li Tzu-jung!

'I say, shop assistant Li.' Mr Ma stood up, his eyes glinting rather fiercely and his voice rougher than usual, giving Li Tzu-jung quite a start. 'I've offered to increase your wages, yet still you refuse to work for me. Very well then, I've given the matter some thought, and if you wish to leave, leave! Leave now, at once.'

He followed this speech with several titters in imitation of the famous strategist Chu-ke Liang as depicted in Chinese traditional theatre. As the titters trailed off, he wondered whether he had spoken too hastily. But the words were out now, so what was the point of remorse? Best carry it to its proper conclusion. 'Leave now. At once!'

Li Tzu-jung was in the middle of polishing a copper kettle. As he heard Mr Ma's words, he slowly put the kettle down on the table, and looked at Mr Ma for ages without saying a word.

Mr Ma grew somewhat ill at ease. The young upstart was giving him such a hard stare.

Li Tzu-jung laughed. 'Mr Ma, neither of us understands the

other, so it's best if we don't waste any more words. I can't leave at once. I'm asking you to give me two weeks' notice out of respect for our friendship. But there's also a legal requirement: I had an arrangement with your elder brother that no matter which of us decided to terminate my contract, he was to write the other a letter to that effect two weeks in advance. So with that in mind, Mr Ma, I'll do another fortnight's work here, starting today. Thank you.'

With these words, Li Tzu-jung picked up the kettle again.

Mr Ma reddened, glared at Li Tzu-jung's back, opened the door and marched out onto the street. He muttered curses to himself and his thoughts ran riot. *You shameless young peasant! Someone gives you the push, and you insist on two extra weeks! Right, I'll let you stay here two more weeks. But I'm not going to see you again. I've lost all face, and it will be quite impossible for us to work together. Quite impossible. That's it; I'll go back. I'll go back, and give him two weeks' wages, and tell him to leave immediately. Let's see you still refusing to leave when I give you that money for nothing!*

Let's make it clear: I never fired you. It was you who was unwilling to continue the job. You think you'll carry on for another two weeks and then hang around after that, but I see through your little plan. I'm no fool!

That's what I'll do. Give him a fortnight's wages, and tell him to leave. From what I've seen of him, though, even if I give him the money, he'll still refuse to go. If he says he's going to work two more weeks, then that's what he'll do. There's no way of dealing with such a person. He doesn't have the slightest concern for face! There's nothing I can do. Some day I'll take Ma Wei back to China – there's nothing good to be learnt abroad. Just look at Li Tzu-jung, brazen and shameless. You tell him to go, and what does he do but talk about the law and drag friendship into it, the glib rogue!

There's nothing for it . . . No face . . . I'll go and have a bowl of three immortals soup. Who cares about Li Tzu-jung and his type. He's not worth losing one's temper over. If I really did get angry, I'd show him what I'm made of!

XIII

'LI, OLD chap! Have you been arguing with my father?' asked Ma Wei with a very disagreeable expression on his face as he entered the shop.

'Me? How could I possibly have argued with him? Come on, now, Ma, old mate,' said Li Tzu-jung with a smile.

'Look here, Li!' Ma Wei's face was set sternly, brow knitted and lips quivering slightly. 'You shouldn't stir up trouble with my father. You know what he's like. You can always come to me first. All right, I know you've been quite a lot of help to us, but don't you try putting my father in his place! All said and done, he's over twenty years older than us, a generation our senior, and ought to be treated with some respect.' He suddenly stopped, and glanced at Li Tzu-jung.

Li Tzu-jung gaped at him for a moment, scratched his head and burst out into chuckles. 'What's got into you, Ma, old lad?'

'Nothing's got into me! But don't try to boss my father around again!'

'Oh-ho!' Li Tzu-jung was on the verge of losing his temper, but pasted a smile on his face again. 'Have you eaten yet, Ma?'

'Yes, I have.'

'Well, mind the shop a moment, will you? I'm going out to get a bite, then I'll be straight back.'

Ma Wei nodded stonily. Li Tzu-jung stuck his cap on and marched out, still smiling.

About ten minutes after Li Tzu-jung had left, a benign-looking old man entered the shop.

'Ah, young man! And might you be Mr Ma's son?' asked the old man, smiling and cocking his head to one side quizzically.

'Yes, sir,' replied Ma Wei, forcing a smile.

'Ah! Right first guess! You and your father have the same eyes.' As he said this, the old man glanced towards the interior of the shop. 'And where is Mr Li?'

'He's gone out for his lunch, and will be straight back . . . But if you'd like to look at anything, sir, I can help you.' Ma Wei was thinking, *I've got a head for business too. Li Tzu-jung's not absolutely indispensable!*

'No need to bother about me. I'll just have a look round on my own.' The old man gave a smile, and, with one hand stuck behind his back and the other in his jacket pocket, proceeded to tilt his head this way and that in minute examination of the objects on the shelves. After each inspection, he gave a slight nod.

Ma Wei didn't feel he could engage the man's attention with sales talk, yet he didn't feel right just waiting there either, doing absolutely nothing. He stared at the old man's back with a frown on his brow. Sometimes the old man would turn his head, and Ma Wei would hastily force a smile, but the old man never took any notice of him.

The old man wasn't particularly tall but was amply proportioned, with very broad shoulders that drooped slightly because of his age. His hair was as white as snow, and all combed backwards. A white beard covered his face from cheek to cheek handsomely. His nose wasn't very prominent but his eyes were exceptionally deep-set, with little eyeballs lying in wait, ready to rush to the aid of any smile that might appear below. His head seemed permanently cocked to one side.

He was remarkably well dressed, with a dark-grey woollen suit, a grey silk tie fastened by a fine gold tiepin, and a stiff single collar, so high that whenever he tilted his head, the tips of the collar would hide themselves in his white beard. He wore no hat, and his shoes were exceedingly big, at least two sizes bigger than his feet, so that when he walked he shuffled some-what, thus enabling the crease down the centre of each of his trouser legs to remain as straight as a rod, without the slightest wrinkling.

'I say, young man, this pot wouldn't be the genuine thing, would it?' The old man picked up a little earthenware pot from one of the shelves, and, holding it in one hand, gently felt round the lip of it with the other, his eyes shut, like a lady stroking her hair with the utmost care and pleasure.

'It . . .' Ma Wei hastened over in two strides, took a look at the pot, then uttered another long and useless 'It . . .'

'Ah, you can't tell me. Never mind, we'll wait for Mr Li.' The old man cupped the pot in his hands, and his lips in motion beneath his white beard, restored the little vessel to its original place.

'Where's your father? I haven't seen him for quite a few days.' He didn't wait for Ma Wei's reply, but carried on talking, his eyes looking at the pot from a distance. 'Your father is a very likable chap indeed. The only thing is, he has very little idea of how to do business. Yes, he has quite poor business sense. You're studying here, I suppose? What are you studying? Ah, Mr Li, how are you?'

'Ah, John – Lord Simon! How are you? I haven't seen you these last few days.' Li Tzu-jung's face was wreathed in smiles, and he shook hands with Lord Simon most warmly.

Lord Simon's eyes twinkled and he gave a smile in return.

'What would you like to look at today, Lord Simon? Have you finished analysing that I-hsing pot you took last time?'

'Yes, yes, I've analysed it. If you have any cheap-quality Cantonese porcelain, any kind whatsoever, I would be glad of it. Cantonese porcelain is the only sort I haven't done any experiments with as yet. I'll take whatever you have, so long as it's poor quality.'

Then he pointed to the little pot. 'Is that the genuine article?'

'With you asking me, I wouldn't dare to say what's genuine and what's not!' Li Tzu-jung was smiling so much that his face looked like a steamed flower bun. As he spoke, he fetched the little pot and handed it to the old man. 'The glaze is too thin, and the brown on the bottom's not thick enough, either. So it's certainly not Tz'u-chou, but it's early Ming at the latest. You know more than me,

Lord Simon. You do as you see fit, pay what you think it's worth. Mr Ma, bring a chair over for Lord Simon.'

'No need. I'm on my feet all day in the laboratory, so I'm used to standing up. Yes, used to standing, very used to it!' He smiled at Ma Wei. 'No, thank you, no need to bring a chair.'

Then he held up the small pot and scrutinised it once again. 'Yes, you are quite right. The brown on the bottom is not thick enough. Quite right. Very well, have it delivered to me in any case. How much do I owe you?'

'Name your price, Lord Simon.' Li Tzu-jung rubbed his hands and shrugged his shoulders gently, the very picture of a seasoned salesman.

Watching Li Tzu-jung, Ma Wei unconsciously nodded in approval. The old man looked at the price tag on the shelf. Then he winked and said, 'Let me have it at half-price, Mr Li, will you?'

'All right, Lord Simon. Shall I deliver it myself again?'

'Yes, please do. I shall definitely be home from six o'clock onwards. Come and have dinner with me, will you?'

'Thanks. I'll be round before half past six, I promise. Do you want the Cantonese porcelain delivered, too?'

'Yes – how much of it do you have? I don't want good stuff. To use for analysis, you know —'

'Of course, of course. We've only got two sets of teapots and teacups here at the moment. Not very good – genuine Cantonese goods. We'll deliver the two tea sets to your laboratory, and I'll bring this little pot to your study. Will that suit you, Lord Simon?'

The fellow's got it down pat! thought Ma Wei.

'Yes, quite right. Perfectly right, Mr Li.'

Li Tzu-jung took the little pot from him and placed it on the table. 'And I'll bring it to your study on the q.t., so Lady Simon doesn't catch wind of it, eh, Lord Simon?'

The old man burst out laughing, the first time he'd actually laughed out loud. 'Yes, indeed! You're familiar with all my domestic affairs by now!' He pulled out a silk handkerchief and wiped his eyes. 'You know, scientists ought not to get married. Brings them too much trouble, far too much trouble. Lady Simon is an excellent woman, but she comes and disturbs my work all the time. And my being both a scientist and a collector makes it even worse. Lady Simon likes diamonds and pearls, and all I do is buy broken pots and tiles! Ah, but women will be women . . .

'Yes, bring it to my study, and we'll have dinner there together. I may want to ask you about a few characters, too. The day before yesterday, I bought a bronze casket with Chinese characters on the lid, lots of little ones all squared off. I can't manage to make them out, so you translate them for me, will you? A shilling for every character, eh?'

'They aren't seal script?' Li Tzu-jung was still smiling, as if he could power the antiques shop, if not the whole world, with smiles.

'No, no, they aren't. I know you're afraid of seal script. Anyway, I'll see you this evening, and I'll pay you for the wares and for the translation together. Until then.' As he said this, Lord Simon walked over and patted Ma Wei on the shoulder. 'You still haven't told me what you are studying!'

'Commerce, sir – your Lordship!'

'Ah, good, good. The Chinese have the talent and stamina that business requires. Only thing is they don't understand modern methods. Try to learn'em. Good; get down to your studies, and don't go chasing after the girls, eh?' The old man winked one of his little eyes deliberately, and was about to laugh but stopped himself, merely grinning beneath his whiskers.

'Yes,' said Ma Wei, with a red face.

'Where's your hat, Lord Simon?' Li Tzu-jung opened the door, and, bowing at the waist, ushered the old man out.

'Ah, yes. It's in the car. I'll see you this evening, Mr Li.'

After the old man had gone, Li Tzu-jung lost no time in packing the little pot and the two tea sets in cotton wool and wrapping them up. As he wrapped, he said to Ma Wei, 'The old man's a good customer. He specialises in collecting bronzes and pottery. His study's got three times as many things in it as we've got here. He used to be a professor of chemistry at the University of London, but he's retired now. He's still doing some special research into the chemical composition of pottery clays, though. Very interesting old fellow. Buys the precious stuff for his collection, and the poor-quality stuff for his chemical analyses. Over seventy, he is, but a real livewire. Ma, old lad, could you make out two invoices and stick them with these two parcels?'

When Li Tzu-jung had finished his wrapping, Ma Wei brought the two invoices he'd made out. Li Tzu-jung looked at him.

'Ma, old lad,' he said, 'what was up with you this morning? I know it wasn't me that got you in a lather. You've got something else on your mind – you were just venting your spleen. Am I right? Love, most likely. I've seen it before. Blushing cheeks; frowning brow; a shortage of words, and a surplus of temper. Off your food and drink. All that's left for you to do now is . . . cut your throat or hang yourself!' Li Tzu-jung began to gurgle with laughter.

'"The eyes of the lovesick lover shine bright, while the eyes of the lonely and lovelorn are overcast. Being lovesick for one who loves you, has a certain sweetness of flavour. But yearning alone and unloved is naught but bitter pain." Which cap fits you, old Ma?

'Lovelorn and yearning alone?'

The teasing cheered Ma Wei no end. When you're pining away with no one to confide in, there's not much left but to cut your throat.

'Miss Wedderburn?' Li Tzu-jung guessed.

'Mm.'

'Ma, my friend, it's no good me trying to give you advice. I know it's no use. If I were to fall in love with a girl some day and she didn't take me seriously, I'd immediately cut my throat with my penknife.' Li Tzu-jung wiped his index finger across his throat. 'But I can tell you one thing. Every time you think of her, ask yourself, "Does she regard me, a Chinese man, as a human being?" And of course, the next step after that brings you to the highly pertinent conclusion: "If she doesn't regard me as a human being, where can love come into it?" That's my own unique method for the cooling of romantic fevers. Let's call it lovesick ice-cream.

'No English boy or girl can love a Chinese person, because nowadays the Chinese are the laughing-stock of the world. If somebody writing an article wants to raise a laugh, you can bet your life he'll say something nasty about the Chinese, because it's only about the Chinese that you can say nasty things safely, with impunity. University students haven't got any time for the Chinese, because the Chinese are the only people who can't help them in their pursuit of knowledge. What branch of learning do the Chinese particularly excel in? None whatsoever! And ordinary people despise the Chinese because the Chinese – well, they've got so many faults you could never list the lot.

'Now, we could make them admire us in one go by defeating England, Germany or France. But a better method would be for our country to become a haven of peace, packed with able men. What shall we take? Why not start with politics? Let's make China the most incorrupt and enlightened of all countries. What else? Chemistry. Let's make Chinese chemistry the best. Unless we can do that sort of thing, we've got no hope of others respecting us. And while we're pitied by the people of the world, we're not in a position to entertain any wild thoughts about their womenfolk!

'I've only met Miss Wedderburn once, so I can't judge whether she's pretty or not, or what her character's like. All I can tell you is this: she can't possibly love you. She's an average young English person, and the average English person looks down on the Chinese. Why should she prove an exception to the rule and love a young lad called Ma Wei?'

'You can't be so certain she doesn't love me,' said Ma Wei, head bent low.

'How so?' asked Li Tzu-jung, smiling.

'She came to the pictures with me, and she rescued my father.'

'What difference does it make whether she goes to the cinema with you or I go to the cinema with you? I ask you! Foreign boys and girls don't have such strict social barriers between them. You know that, no need for me to tell you. As for her helping your father when he was in trouble, no matter who it was she saw crawling around on the ground, she'd have been bound to take him back home.

'When the Chinese see someone in a state, they clear off – the further the better, because our education teaches us to worry only about ourselves. When foreigners see someone in trouble, they do all they can to get them out of it. They don't care whether it's a white-faced person, a black-faced person or a green-faced one. Normally, they look down on their black-faced and green-faced brethren, but at the first sign of their needing a hand, they forget all about the colour of their faces. She didn't rescue him because he was your father, but because that's her notion of what's moral.

'We think that if we see a person lying on the ground, it's perfectly acceptable for us to ignore them. The foreigners don't see things like that. Their morals are social ones, communal ones. That's one way we Chinese ought to imitate the foreign devils! The other day I read that an old woman collapsed in the street in Shanghai, and people just stood around watching the spectacle for a bit of thrill. In the end it was a foreign soldier who helped her up. No wonder they scorn us!

'Where was I? Let's get back to the subject. You needn't feel so chuffed with yourself, imagining she loves you just because she shakes hands with you. As if she'd have any time to fall in love with you! The best thing you can do is have a scoop of my ice-cream, and stop thinking crazy thoughts.'

Ma Wei cupped his forehead in both hands, and said nothing.

'Hey, Ma, old chap, I've given in my resignation to your father.'

'I know. You can't leave. You can't just stand aside and watch our shop going to rack and ruin like this.'

'I can't leave? If I go, it'll save you a good twelve pounds a month.'

'And who'll run the business for us?' said Ma Wei, raising his head and looking at Li Tzu-jung. 'When that old fellow Simon asked me about the bowl, I didn't have a word to say in response. I don't know a thing about antiques.'

'There's nothing to it. Study a few books, old Ma, and you'll get to know a lot about them. Do you think I ever used to know anything about antiques? Got it all from studying. No matter what subject foreigners study, they always manage to write some systematic and rational works on it. There are loads of books on Chinese porcelain and bronzes – go through a few and you'll be all right. Just study enough to answer a few main questions, and that'll do. Don't worry, Ma, old lad, we'll still be good friends once I've left, and I'll be only too glad to help you in any way.'

After a long silence, Ma Wei asked, 'Where will you look for another job?'

'Can't say. Depends what opportunities crop up. Luckily, I've just won a prize – it's fifty pounds, plenty for me to live on for a good few months. You see,' Li Tzu-jung gave another smile, '*Asia* magazine was asking for articles on modern Chinese labour conditions, and I slogged away day and night for a month and managed to write one. Turned out mine was chosen. Fifty pounds! I tell you, old Ma, the Lord above doesn't let a blind chicken starve to death, and that's the truth. So I've got fifty pounds, which is plenty for me to get by on for a while. No job'll come to you unless you go looking for it, but if I go job-hunting every day, something's bound to turn up, isn't it? Folks who are willing to have a bash at things never starve to death. The capable never go hungry. Lose the frown, Ma, old lad. Buck up, and get your act together!'

Li Tzu-jung went over, put his hand on Ma Wei's shoulder and gave him a few shakes.

Ma Wei, with a wry, mournful expression on his face, gave a smile.

XIV

AFTER HIS argument with Li Tzu-jung, Mr Ma rushed off to a Chinese restaurant, and there ate two dishes of three immortals soup with noodles. Normally, when not in a bad mood, he'd only have one helping. But as the first bowl reached his stomach, his wrath virtually vanished. It's a good sign if you feel like eating two lots of noodles even when you're in a temper; the thought almost turned his rage into joy. Finishing the noodles, he ordered a pot of tea, and sipped it slowly until all the other diners had left, before at last settling his bill and strolling out.

Once outside the restaurant, he was at a loss where to go. He couldn't go back to the shop, anyhow. If the manager fell out with the shop assistant, the manager at least was able to absent himself from the shop, in the same way that a department head can refuse to go into his government offices when he's annoyed. It's precisely the same.

But where should he go? Should he stroll around town? The traffic was too chaotic, and his mind was still somewhat clouded with indignation. It'd be no joke, getting knocked flat by a car. Should he go to the theatre? But who wants to go to the foreign devils' theatres! They haven't got any gongs or drums, and they don't paint make-up patterns on their faces either. It's nothing but a handful of men and women babbling a load of endless nonsense; nothing of interest. Should he go and call on the Reverend Ely? Yes, now there was an idea. The reverend had said that day that he wanted to discuss something with him, hadn't he? It didn't matter what it was. If Mr Ma took the trouble to go all that way to see him, it wasn't likely the reverend would turn him away.

He hailed a taxi to take him to Lancaster Road. As he sat in the car, his thoughts involuntarily turned to Peking. If he were in Peking, how fine it would be, his sitting in a taxi for all the neighbours to see. How exalted! But here, with cars all over the place, there wasn't anything remarkable about the mode of travel. In fact the taxi fare could even be called a sheer waste of money.

'Hello, Mr Ma.' The Reverend Ely opened the front door and showed Mr Ma inside. 'Feeling much better now, are you? Seen anything of Alexander since? Take a tip from me, Mr Ma, and be on your guard when you go out with him.'

'How are you, Reverend Ely? How is Mrs Ely? How is Miss Ely? How is Master Ely?'

Mr Ma got out all his solicitous enquiries in one breath before deeming it proper to sit down.

'They're not at home, so we can have a nice little chat without them.' The Reverend Ely pushed his diminutive spectacles upwards, and his nose crinkled in several places. After sneezing day after day during his cold, it seemed his nose had got used to the exercise, and since his recovery, such wrinkles had made regular appearances.

'Look here, now. There are two things I want to discuss with you. Firstly, I'd like to introduce you into the Reverend Bawley's church, as a member of his congregation, to give you somewhere to attend your Sunday services. His church isn't far from your place. Know Euston Road? Well, carry on in an easterly direction, straight along Euston Road, and it's opposite St Pancras railway station, to the side. Would you like me to introduce you there, then?'

'Absolutely splendid!'

Nowadays, whenever addressing foreigners, Mr Ma tended to use expressions of an absolute nature.

'Very well, that's what we'll do then.' The Reverend Ely's mouth curved in an unconvincing smile. 'Now the second thing's this: I plan that we two should do something with our spare time in the evenings. You see, I intend to write a book, which we can provisionally call *A History of Chinese Taoism*. But my Chinese isn't entirely up to scratch, and I'll need some assistance. If you'd agree to help me, I should be infinitely grateful to you.'

'Yes, yes, that would be fine!' said Mr Ma with alacrity.

'Now, I'm not asking you to help me for nothing. I must do something for you, too.'

The Reverend Ely pulled out his pipe, and slowly filled it with tobacco. 'I've been doing a great deal of thinking on your behalf for some time now, and I feel that while you're abroad, you ought to take the opportunity of writing something. The best thing would be a comparison of Eastern and Western cultures. That's a fashionable topic nowadays, and it doesn't matter particularly whether what you write's correct or not. As long as you say something with conviction, anything at all, you'll be able to sell it. You write it in Chinese, and I'll translate it into English. That way we can both be of help to each other, and once the books come out, I guarantee they'll earn us some money. What do you think of that?'

'I'll help you all right,' said Mr Ma, slowly, 'but as for me writing a book? That wouldn't be easy. Would a man nearing his fifties be up to such a strenuous undertaking?'

'My good friend!' The Reverend Ely's voice suddenly grew much louder. 'So you're nearly fifty? I'm over sixty! Bernard Shaw's over seventy, and still writing books nonstop. I ask you: how many old men in England do you see idling their time away? If everybody went into retirement at fifty, who on earth would run the world's affairs?'

'I didn't say it was out of the question.' Mr Ma beat a rapid retreat, but solely to appease the Reverend Ely. Actually, he was saying to himself, *You foreign devils have no proper respect for the aged. That's what makes you foreign devils!*

The English are reluctant to talk about their domestic affairs with outsiders, and the Reverend Ely had originally had no intention of telling the elder Ma his reason for wanting to write a book. But in view of Ma's apparent hesitation, he felt obliged to say a few words on the matter.

'I ought to tell you, my friend, that I simply have to do something or other. You see, Mrs Ely's secretary of the China section of the London Missionary Society, Paul's working in a bank and Catherine's an executive secretary in the YWCA. They're all earning money, so I'm the odd man out: idle, no job. It's true I have a pension of one hundred and twenty pounds per annum, but, all the same, I've no wish to remain a man of leisure . . .' He pushed his spectacles up again. Now he rather regretted having confided in the elder Ma.

Mr Ma was astounded. *So the children are earning money, yet their old man still insists on subjecting himself to needless toil and trouble! These foreign devils . . . Their psychology's beyond me.*

'My only hope's to obtain a post as professor of Chinese in some university. But I'll have to write a book first, to make myself something of a reputation. You see, the Chinese department of the University of London's lacking a professor at the moment, as they can't find anybody who can write and speak Chinese. Now I'm fully proficient as far as speaking's concerned, so all that remains is for me to prove my erudition by writing something. I may be over sixty, but I'm still good for at least another five or six years work, aren't I?'

'Yes, you're absolutely right. I'd be glad to help you!'

Mr Ma contrived to push aside the matter of his own writing of a book. 'Just think, if you become a professor of Chinese, it will be simply splendid! You'll be able to put in a good word or two for China.' Mr Ma was of the belief that the professional role of a professor of Chinese was to stick up for the Chinese.

The Reverend Ely gave a smile.

Neither of them spoke for some time.

'Look here, then, Mr Ma.' The Reverend Ely was the first to break the silence. 'That's the way we'll do things. Mutual assistance. If you won't let me help you, I won't ask you to help me. You know the English way – fifty-fifty, with neither party losing on the deal. I can't ask you to do it for nothing.'

'You say I ought to write about Eastern and Western culture, but, really, where should I start?'

'You don't necessarily have to write on that topic. Anything'll do, even a novel. You see, there are very few Chinese people who write in English, and your book, regardless of its quality, will sell all the better for it.'

'But I can't write anything slapdash, and risk losing face for the Chinese.'

'Oh . . .' The Reverend Ely's mouth hung open for a long while. He'd never for a moment expected such a statement from the elder Ma. Mr Ma himself couldn't have explained how such words had come to him.

English people who've never been to China picture the Chinese as sinister, underhand beings with disagreeable yellow faces. And English people who have been to China view the Chinese as dirty, smelly, bewildered fools. The Reverend Ely had never held Mr Ma in any high regard, and his reason for suggesting that Ma write a book was purely so that he might have Ma help him. He knew that Ma was a fool, and fools, naturally, can't write books. But unless they came to some mutually beneficial arrangement, it would be impossible for him to reconcile the matter with his conscience, as the English people's notion of 'fair play' is a powerful one.

Like other English people, the Reverend Ely was fond of the older people of China, because these older types never utter the word 'nation'. He loathed the young people of China, because these youngsters, although just as foolish as the old ones, forever have the words 'nation' and 'China' on their lips. Of course this national pride is quite futile, but that doesn't stop them from banging on about it endlessly. And for Mr Ma to come out with that sort of thing, well . . .

'Mr Ma,' said the Reverend Ely at last, after a long dumbfounded silence. 'You think it over first, and then tell me what you think. Fortunately, we don't have to reach any definite decision today. Anyway, how are things with Ma Wei? What's he studying?'

'He's brushing up his English, and he's probably going to study commerce,' replied Mr Ma. 'I told him to study politics, so that when he returns to China he can become a civil servant or something with rather more prospects. But the boy's stubborn, and insists on commerce. There's nothing I can do about it.

He's just a lad, and, having no mother, he's missing that stable parental background.

'He's become very thin lately . . . I don't know what's the matter. The boy's secretive, and I don't really like to question him too closely. Let him have his own way. Anyway, I give him the money for whatever he wants. It's my fault for being a father. You're helpless, quite helpless!'

Mr Ma spoke with great passion, his eyes fixed on the ceiling so as to prevent his tears from falling. Inwardly he was very much hoping that saying such things might encourage the Reverend Ely to act as marriage broker for him, arranging a suitable one with Widow Wedderburn, for instance. Of course, it wasn't entirely respectable to marry a widow, but with a foreign woman such a marriage mightn't entail the usual ill omens and calamitous fortune for the husband . . . He gave a sigh.

What's more, if the Reverend Ely took it upon himself to act as marriage broker for him, the clergyman would then have helped him, and the comparison of Eastern and Western cultures could fall by the wayside. *If you arrange a marriage for me, I'll help you read Chinese books. Surely that would suit you to a T, you foreigners and your 'fair play'!*

He stole a glance at the Reverend Ely. The Reverend Ely had his pipe in his mouth, and was quite silent.

'Mr Ma,' said the Reverend Ely eventually, standing up after they'd been sitting there in silence for ages, 'I'll see you on Sunday at the Reverend Bawley's place. You really ought to get Ma Wei to come along, too. The young must always have faith. Always! Paul goes to church three times a week without fail, you know.'

'Yes.' Perceiving that the Reverend Ely was politely dismissing him, Mr Ma stood up, inwardly most disgruntled. 'I'll see you on Sunday.'

The Reverend Ely saw him to the door.

Bloody hell! Call yourself a friend! Mr Ma swore under his breath as he stood out in the street. *Don't even wait for a sign from your guest that he wants to leave – just stand up and say, 'See you on*

Sunday', eh? Just you wait and see. It'll be a real miracle if you get this Ma inside a church!

BRRUMM, BRRUMM, FFSSSS!

A car hurtled past, brushing Mr Ma's nose.

XV

MRS WEDDERBURN and daughter went off on their summer holiday, both wearing new hats. On the band of Mary's hat was embroidered a Chinese character, which Mr Ma had written and her mother had stitched on. For half an hour or so after putting on her hat, Mary's mouth hung open, and for another half an hour she remained glued to the mirror. There were lots of hats similar to hers, but having a Chinese character embroidered on it made it something novel and unique. At the seaside the hat would be sure to make all the girls and ladies weep or even swoon with envy.

Mrs Wedderburn was delighted with it. Her daughter's hat was bound to cause a revolution; a hat revolution, so to speak! Her daughter's photograph would appear in the papers for certain, and a lot of people would sit up in jealousy and admiration.

'Mr Ma!' Just as Mary was about to depart, she came looking for Mr Ma. 'Look!'

With one hand she tweaked her skirt up so that its pleats flared out like a fan. She tipped her head to the side and stretched out her other hand, palm up, then lightly flicked that hand backwards from the wrist, at the same time gently shrugging her shoulders and gathering her lips in a little smile. 'Look!'

'Splendid! Most beautiful, Miss Wedderburn!' Mr Ma gave her a thumbs-up.

At Mr Ma's words, Mary abruptly drew both hands in, clasped them in front of her chest, threw up her head, gave a little giggle and vanished like a puff of smoke.

Actually, Mr Ma had only said half of what he might have. Yes, the character he'd written meant 'beautiful', but when Mrs Wedderburn had embroidered it, she'd done it upside down, and the 'beautiful' now looked like the three characters 'big', 'king' and 'eight' – the 'big' standing on its head – which together mean 'big bastard'. He burst out laughing. Never since coming to England had he had such a good chuckle.

Ah, so funny! Foreign women! Putting 'big bastard' on their heads, and with the character for 'big' doing a handstand . . . Dear me, how funny! What a laugh! As he shook his head in laughter, his tears of mirth flew into the air.

After laughing for ages, Mr Ma slowly went downstairs, planning to see mother and daughter off to the station. They were waiting for the taxi at the door. The first thing that caught his eyes was the 'big bastard'. He clenched his teeth and strained at the neck, and his face went very red. It was all right, though: he managed not to laugh.

'Ta-ta, Mr Ma!' chorused mother and daughter. And Mrs Wedderburn had a few extra words to say: 'Behave yourself. Don't do anything naughty! And whatever you do, don't forget to lock the back door before you go out!'

The taxi arrived and Napoleon led the way, bounding into it. 'Bye-bye,' mumbled Mr Ma. 'Have a good holiday!'

As soon as the taxi had gone, he shut the door and burst out laughing once more.

When he was quite worn out with laughing, Mr Ma went into the backyard to water the flowers. It hadn't rained for over a week, and the leaves of the flowers, especially those of the wallflowers, were looking worse for wear. He deftly picked off those that were brown, and while he was at it, debudded the chrysanthemums.

The sky was a clear blue one, with not a breath of wind, and in the distance there was the continual noise of cars. As he contemplated a rose and listened to the far sound of traffic, an inexpressible melancholy grew within him. He forced himself to think of Mary's hat, but somehow it could no longer raise a laugh. He lifted his head to look at the blue sky – bright, far away, infinitely far, and with a hint of pallid forlornness about it.

Will we ever get back to China? he asked himself. *Or am I going to see out my days like this, here in London? No, never! When Ma Wei's graduated, we'll go back to China. And we'll take my brother's coffin back with us.*

At the thought of his brother, he felt like going to have a look at his grave, but was hesitant about making the trip there by himself. Instead, as he gazed at the blue sky, his mind flew through the air to his brother's grave. That grey stone slab, that washed-out wreath and even the fat little old woman all appeared before his eyes.

Ah, what's the joy in living? Mr Ma gently shook his head, and murmured aloud, 'A stone slab? Why, even that's doomed to destruction before many years are out. Nothing survives forever in this world, and some foreign devils even say that the sun'll die one day . . . But where was I? No, being alive's not really so bad at all . . . Depends how you live, of course. If you're a high-up government official enjoying a fat salary, with a crowd of wives and concubines and chubby sons and daughters, there's not much missing. Life would be worth living then . . .'

Mr Ma's thoughts always progressed from the negative to the positive, and then from the positive to the middling; or taking life as it comes, the good with the bad, getting by the best you can and taking each day as it comes. He very nearly hummed some lines of Peking opera, to its lively Hsi-p'i musical accompaniment.

This attitude of taking life as it comes, the good with the bad, is one reason why China's only half alive. But of course no such thought would ever have occurred to the elder Ma.

Complete pessimism can at least produce a few great thinkers. And complete optimism can stir a nation into life, and add some joy and spice to living. One fears, though, that our four hundred million compatriots are, like the elder Ma, both too ambivalent and too listless to fire up and take action. This attitude of just living and making do is the most useless of outlooks, and a disgrace to the human race!

A protracted period of thought brought no enlightenment to

Mr Ma, so in a fit of pique he abandoned his thinking and went back to his study, gave the tables and chairs a wipe-over and smoked his pipe. He'd intended at first to sit down and read a book, but never having made a habit of reading, the moment he picked up a book he felt ridiculous. That put paid to that idea.

I'll just pop downstairs and have a look to see if all the doors are locked, he said to himself. *What was I thinking! Now they're away, it just won't do for me to be so neglectful.*

Mrs Wedderburn hadn't locked all the rooms, as she worried that it would impede a safe exit should a fire break out. Mr Ma took a look in at the drawing room, then looked round the kitchen and Mrs Wedderburn's bedroom. He'd never been into her room before, and felt rather timid, walking on tiptoe, with his hands hovering in front of him, as if he were afraid of being caught, although he knew perfectly well that there was no one else in the house.

Once in the room, he smelt the faint scent of perfume and powder, and a vague ache came over his heart. He stood in front of the mirror, just standing there in a daze for ages. Then he felt he ought to go, but couldn't bring himself to move. He was reluctant to think about Widow Wedderburn, but when he tried to recall his late wife his thoughts were blurred and wouldn't clear.

Without knowing how or why, he made his way out of the room, his mind in a haze of confusion, like in some siesta dream, thinking of something yet lost in a glazed numbness. His footsteps made no sound as he reached Mary's bedroom. The door was open, and through it he could see her little iron bedstead. And someone was kneeling by the bedstead, his head on the bed, the back of his head moving up and down as if he were silently crying. Ma Wei!

For a moment, Mr Ma stood frozen to the spot. His mind seemed to go blank, then, unable to restrain himself, he said in a quiet voice, 'Ma Wei!'

Ma Wei leapt to his feet. His face reddened, the colour starting at his earlobes and spreading right up to his forehead.

Father and son stood there, neither of them saying a word. Ma Wei, head lowered, wiped away his tears, and Mr Ma, hands trembling, rubbed at his scrap of moustache.

In many ways Mr Ma still regarded Ma Wei as a little boy of eleven or twelve. Whenever his son came to mind, he'd think, *Motherless little lad!* Noticing that Ma Wei had lost weight, he'd assumed it was because the boy didn't like English food. And seeing him with a frown on his brow, he'd just supposed he was out of sorts. Never once had it occurred to him that Ma Wei was now a youth of over twenty, let alone that his 'little boy' might —

Mr Ma couldn't think of any appropriate expression to convey that particular relationship between men and women. After a great deal of thought, he decided that it was best to stick to the familiar terms. *I'd never imagined he'd have woman trouble so young!*

He couldn't bring himself to reprove Ma Wei, his motherless, only son. No, he couldn't harden his heart to scold him. But neither could he, as a father who'd seen his son weeping on a young lady's bed, neglect to make some comment on the matter.

It wasn't proper. It was common; a fruitless course. But then what was stopping Mr Ma from giving his son a telling-off? He himself was partly to blame. Why had he persisted in viewing his son as a naive little innocent all this time? Hadn't he realised that times have changed, and that children are wicked in the womb? Why hadn't he seen it coming and taken due precautions?

Still, it wasn't as bad as it might have been. Nothing scandalous had occurred between Ma Wei and Mary as yet. If they'd . . . She being a foreigner . . . What on earth could he have done? True, he himself was sometimes enamoured of Widow Wedderburn's dainty pink nose, but that was merely a momentary madness. There was no question of marrying her! Marry a foreign woman? How could he face anyone again if he did that! But Ma Wei was just a boy. He couldn't think as far ahead as that . . .

With a glance at the younger Ma, the elder Ma slowly made his way upstairs. Ma Wei came out of the room too, and stood at the doorway, looking at the iron bedstead. Suddenly, he went back into the room again, and gently smoothed out the sheet, which was damp with his tears. Then he came out, head bowed low, closed the door and walked upstairs.

'Father.' Ma Wei went into the study, and called again in a subdued voice, 'Father.'

Mr Ma, himself on the brink of tears, uttered some response.

Ma Wei stood behind his father's chair. 'You don't need to worry about me, Dad,' he said slowly. 'I haven't had any relations with her. These last few days . . . I've been insane, quite mad! I'm over it now. I went to her room to . . . as part of my resolve to be done with it all. I'm not going to take any more notice of her. She looks down on us. None of the foreigners think anything of us, so you couldn't expect her to.

'From now on, we've got to knuckle down and really get serious about the shop. All that's happened before . . . that's over and done with. I was crazy. If Li Tzu-jung's set on going, we can't stop him, and if that's the case, from now on it'll all be up to us. He's agreed to help us, though, and I admire and trust him, and think he's definitely right in what he says. I was rude to him the other day, without really meaning to be, but I . . . I was crazy. And he didn't take the slightest bit of notice. He really is a good sort. I've let you down, Dad. If you had a son like Li Tzu-jung, you'd have nothing to bother about.'

'Ten thousand blessings that I haven't got a son like Li Tzu-jung!' Mr Ma shook his head, and gave a smile.

'Now, Dad, will you promise me that we'll really get down to it in earnest, both of us? We'll have to economise a bit, and be late to bed and early to rise, and really give it our all. And we'll have to ask Li Tzu-jung's advice – and take it. I'll go and see him and ask him whether he's found a new job. If he has, there's nothing we can do about it. We'll just have to let him leave. But if he hasn't, we've got to keep him on. That's what we'll do, eh, Dad?'

'Very well. Very well,' said Mr Ma, nodding, but not looking at Ma Wei. 'As long as you know what you're doing. As long as you don't entertain any wild notions about . . . you can do anything you wish. You're my only son, and your mother passed away before her time. You're all my hopes, and whatever you say goes. You discuss things with shop assistant Li, and if he says pull the house down, we'll do it straight away! Off you go and fetch him, and we'll have a Chinese meal together. I'll wait for you at the Top Graduate. Off you go, now, and here's a pound for you.'

The elder Mr Ma stuffed a note into Ma Wei's pocket.

These last few days Ma Wei's mind had been a wok full of boiling, frothing porridge. Love, affection and obedience towards his father, friendship, career, and studies all in conflict. Emotion, self-respect, self-loathing and self-pity at loggerheads. His father was wrong, but he was still his father, all the same. Li Tzu-jung was too blunt and forthright, but a fine chap through and through.

If Ma Wei helped his father run the shop, would he still have any time for studying? If he put his nose to the grindstone and got stuck into his studies, who'd run the business? And to cap it all, there was HER! She was forever in front of his eyes, on his mind, in his dreams, turning up and disappearing quite unpredictably. He tried constantly to forget her, but how could he? Love's the hardest thing to get rid of, as it sprouts in the heart's deepest recesses. *She doesn't love me, but that doesn't even come into it!* Her smile, her manner of speaking, her ways and her looks were all sweet dew nourishing those buds in his heart and making them grow.

When she's there, you're head over heels, completely infatuated with her. While she's in this world, you can't help thinking of her. Not think of her? Forget her? Only a man with a heart of steel could manage that. Ma Wei's heart was neither of steel nor of stone, and at the very quiver of her pale arms, his heart would tremble too.

All the same, I've just got to forget her. I can't think of loving her any longer; she ignores me. But I can't hate her: she was born lovable! Stuck between a rock and a hard place, what's left to do? A young man's got to have some fire in him, some self-respect. Why go trailing after her, begging for her love? Have a bit more regard for yourself than that! Why not help Dad with the shop? Why not take a leaf out of Li Tzu-jung's book? Right, enough's enough! I've cried on your bedclothes, and I've prayed to the gods to cherish you, but I'm not going to look at you, not going to think about you any more. I hope some day you'll find a good husband, and live happily ever after . . .

And that was when my father came in! I felt a bit resentful, but he didn't say anything. I've got to help him, though; I had to put it to him plainly. It took some of the load off my mind. I'll go and see Li Tzu-jung, and put things to him in the same sort of way.

And without further ado Ma Wei went to the shop.

'Li, old fellow,' called Ma Wei as soon as he entered the door, 'Li, old lad, it's all over!'

'What's all over?' asked Li Tzu-jung as he sat at the counter.

'The past. It's all history now. From now on, I'm taking my fate into my own two hands.'

'Come on, then, let's shake to it! You're a fine lad, Ma Wei! Come on, let's shake!' Li Tzu-jung took Ma Wei's hand and shook it vigorously.

'And what about you, Li, old chap? Are you leaving, or will you be giving us your help?'

'I've already promised Lord Simon I'd go and be his assistant,' said Li Tzu-jung. 'He's writing books now. One's about the results of his chemical tests on Chinese porcelain, and another's a catalogue of the antiques in his collection. My job's to help him write the catalogue of antiques, as he can't read the Chinese characters very well. I'll go in the mornings, and leave at one o'clock, which suits me fine.'

'And how are we going to manage with the shop?' asked Ma Wei.

'Let me make a suggestion. First, get in a large consignment of goods, and hold a big sale just before Christmas. Mark everything thirty per cent off, and when the customers come, hand them a printed colour catalogue free. I'll arrange for the printing, and all you'll have to do is give me a bit of money for my bus fares. Publish adverts for three months running in both *Asia* magazine and the bulletin of the School of Oriental Studies.

'As for getting hold of the goods, tell your father as a first step to invite Wang Ming-ch'uan out for a Chinese meal. After which I'll go and have a word with old Wang, and ask him to get the goods for you. He's an old pal of your uncle's. Runs an antiques shop of his own, and also imports stuff. Give him five hundred pounds to get the goods, and when they arrive, get the sale underway.

'If you make a success of it, your business'll be back on its feet.

Even if you come out of it badly – but I'm sure that's not likely. You'll have to be here every afternoon, and study in the mornings and evenings. It's no good if you leave it all to Mr Ma. After the goods have arrived, I'll come and help you sort them out and fix their prices, but you'll have to shout me a lunch. How about it?'

'Li, old lad, we'll do whatever you say. We'll pin all our hopes on this move, come what may. Oh, my father's waiting at the Top Graduate for us if you'd like a meal. Are you coming?'

'No, thanks. Same old reason: eat one meal like that, and I'll want another. Too expensive a habit, I couldn't afford it. Look here, Ma, old lad, you ought to go for a week's holiday in the countryside, have a spot of leisure and relaxation. Luckily I'm still here for a few days, so there's nothing to stop you going.'

'Where to?' asked Ma Wei.

'There's loads of places! Go to the station and ask for a travel brochure, pick yourself a place and go and stay there a week. It'll do your health good. Right, old Ma, off you go and have your meal, and give Mr Ma my thanks. And eat a bit more now!' Li Tzu-jung started laughing.

As Ma Wei went off, alone, Li Tzu-jung was still laughing.

PART FOUR

I

FROM THE onset of autumn right through to winter, there are all kinds of things going on in London. Once the theatres have shown all their best plays, the shops start their autumn sales, and straight after that come the preparations for Christmas. Wealthy men and women go to London to see the plays, to throw parties and to buy their Christmas presents. Hard-up men and women likewise go to London, to do things that cost no money, such as watching the Lord Mayor's Show and watching the King open the Houses of Parliament. And even if they've got no more than a shilling in their pocket, they'll put it on a horse, or make a bet on some football team. A large part of the evening paper is devoted to horseracing and football results, and these people buy a copy – at nine o'clock in the morning – to check whether they've won or not. When they see they've lost, they purse their lips and read a bit of the anti-foreign news to make themselves feel better.

As well as all that there are ice-skating rinks, circuses, dog shows, chrysanthemum shows, cat shows, leg shows, car races, grand contests and special competitions, one after the other, providing people with plenty to see all the time, plenty to talk about and plenty to entertain them. The English could never have a revolution. With so much to do and talk about, who's got the time for inciting revolution?

Mrs Ely, too, was very busy, collecting charity for the poor so that people with nothing to eat might have a good dinner on Christmas Day. The untidy kapok on top of her head was more dishevelled than ever, and increasingly threatened to fly completely out of control. The Reverend Ely was terribly busy as well. Day after day, a little dictionary clutched in his hand, he'd be reading Chinese books, all the time encountering more and more Chinese characters that he didn't know.

It's difficult to describe the way in which Paul was busy. He was fully capable of standing for three hours in the rain waiting for a glimpse of the Prince of Wales, and when he got back home, he'd stand in front of the mirror with a slight smirk on his face, because someone had said his nose was the image of the Prince's. When the Prince of Wales gave a broadcast on the radio, asking for contributions to charity for unemployed workers, Paul at once donated two pounds. If the Prince hadn't told him that the workers were suffering great hardships, such a gesture would never in his life have entered his head. In fact he sometimes even ridiculed his mother for dashing round so wildly on behalf of the poor. As for himself, come wind come rain, he would go and watch football or hockey, or see an anti-Chinese film.

Miss Catherine continued as serene as ever, but she too was busy, doing things for the YWCA. Despite this her hair wasn't in the slightest unkempt, and hung, still as long, lightly covering her snow-white neck.

Mrs Wedderburn and daughter were likewise busy. The mother was stoking fires upstairs and downstairs from morn till night, leaving a perpetual smut of black on the tip of her nose. There weren't many days left to Christmas, and she had to snatch whatever opportunities she could to go Christmas shopping in town. And she bought a lot now, because you can save money by buying your presents a little early. Also, the Christmas cake had to be made more than a month before Christmas.

Mary was busy with her eyes, so busy her eyes almost couldn't cope. Every shop in town was decorated with cheer and colour, and everywhere you looked was so pretty. Each week she'd put by a few shillings, and, after some fifteen or sixteen hours' research on the matter, she'd buy a nice little something, bring it home and secretly stow it away in her suitcase as a present to give at Christmas time.

She also wanted to buy a new hat for herself, and that was no easy matter. Savings booklet in hand, she'd do sums night and day, but, try as she might, she could never manage to find herself any extra. In secret, she bet a shilling on a horse, hoping to win some money that way. As it turned out, her horse got halfway round the course then tumbled head over heels, and she lost the shilling. The less money you've got, the more you lose. They ought to get rid of money, or else they'll never solve the problem. In her anger, she almost turned socialist.

Even the weather in London grew busier. It was either windy or raining, and if it was neither of those, there was a fog. Sometimes, to keep people on their toes, it'd be both rainy and foggy. London fog's fascinating. Just take its colours, for instance – it may be several all at once. In some parts it's light grey, and you can still see things within a range of forty or fifty feet. In other parts, it's such a dark grey that there's no difference between night and day. In some places it's greyish yellow, as if the whole of London city is burning damp wood. In yet other places, it's a reddish brown, and when the fog is this colour you can forget about being able to see anything any more. All you can spot if you're standing indoors, looking out the windowpane, is the reddish brown colour.

If you walk in the fog, it's dark grey just ahead of you, and it's not until you raise your head and make an actual effort to pick out a lamp shining somewhere, that you can see the faintest yellow tinge to it. That sort of fog doesn't come in wisps, but in one whole mass, and blocks out the world. As you walk, the fog follows you. You can't see anything, and nobody can see you. You don't even know where you are. Only the fiercest-burning gas lamps penetrate the gloom, and all you can distinguish are the wisps of steam from your own breath before your lips. The rest is hazy and unidentifiable.

The cars crawl along slowly, one foot at a time, declaring their presence only by the sounds of their horns. If not for those horns, you might feel really afraid, wondering whether the whole world had been suffocated by the fog. You're conscious that there are things to the right and left of you, and in front and behind, but you simply can't pluck up the courage to move in any of these directions. That object in front of you may be a horse, a car or perhaps a tree, but unless you put your hands on it, you won't know which one it is.

Mr Ma was London's leading man of leisure. When it was rainy, he didn't go out. When it was windy, he didn't go out. And when it was foggy, he stayed at home. He'd stick his pipe in his mouth, stoke up the fire till it was burning brightly, and through the windowpane minutely savour the beauty of the rain, fog and wind.

Wherever they may be, the Chinese can always discern the beauty in things. Beauty, in any case, is a living phenomenon, a combination of emotion and scenery, something that radiates from the aesthetic force of the individual's mind. The homeward boat 'mid the mists and rain! Treading o'er the snow in quest of plum blossoms! And amid the mists and rain and snow there's always a skinny bloke with a smile on his face. This gaffer's the Chinese god of beauty. Not a god who dwells in heaven, but one who dwells in the mind of the individual. Hence the gentle smile that would unconsciously appear on Mr Ma's face as the cars made their way through the fine silk strands of rain; as the young ladies' umbrellas were blown askew by the wind; it was all beautiful. As a ray of lamplight wafted in the fog, it was like fireflies on an autumn night; beautiful.

Pipe in mouth, Mr Ma stared out the window, then looked a while at the flames in the fireplace, and forgot all sorrow and care. All that was missing was wine. 'Must get half a catty of vintage Shao-hsing, eh?' he muttered to himself. But you can't buy Shao-hsing wine in London. *Oh dear!* he thought. *Really ought to be getting back to China.*

The elder Ma could never forget about returning to China, to that place where everybody is capable of treading o'er the snow in quest of plum blossoms and the homeward boats 'mid mist and rain. If the Chinese could keep both 'beauty' and 'China' forever in mind, and allow both to fully prosper, then China might yet know a golden age some day in the future. If science and beauty could be blended together, and if loyal sentiments towards the motherland could be fostered by incorrupt and enlightened politics, things would be very hopeful for China.

It was a pity that the elder Ma, a representative of China, possessed no more than some muddled intuitive appreciation of beauty, without the vital common sense and knowledge. It was a pity that the elder Ma merely desired to return to his country, and had no understanding of the meaning of country. A pity that the elder Ma had the urge to become a government official, and yet no knowledge of the duties and responsibilities that being a government official entailed. A pity that the elder Ma loved his son without having any notion of how to educate him. A pity that . . .

As Christmas approached, yes, even Mr Ma grew a little busier. He was delighted to hear that the English gave one another presents at Christmas. What a good opportunity for making friends! Naturally, the four Elys, Mrs Wedderburn and daughter, and Alexander would all have to be given presents. He couldn't forget even Li Tzu-jung either. *Common, that young fellow, no taste . . . I'll give him a vulgar present. That's it – a pair of shoes. Ill-bred people like to receive useful things. Who else was there, now? The manager of the Top Graduate. Washington . . . That's right, have to give him something. He carried me into the taxi that day I got drunk . . . The young chap's bought a new motorbike recently. Bound to come off it and kill himself sooner or later. Hey, now, better stop that – putting curses on people! But motorbikes are extremely dangerous. I hope he doesn't come off and get killed, but if he does, there's nothing I can do about it, anyway.* The elder Ma twitched up his lips and scrappy moustache into a smile.

How many's that now? Mr Ma bent up his fingers as he counted. 'Four plus three makes seven, plus Li Tzu-jung, the manager of the Top Graduate and Washington, makes ten. Who else is there? Wang Ming-ch'uan. If a chap gets my wares for me, I can scarcely avoid giving him a little something or other. Eleven. Let's leave it at eleven for the moment. If any more come to me, we'll see. Shall I buy Mrs Wedderburn a new hat?'

Here, Mr Ma stopped mumbling to himself, closed his eyes, and embarked upon a deliberation as to what kind of hat would further enhance Mrs Wedderburn's charms. He thought for ages, but all that came to mind was the tip of her little nose, her dear brown eyes and her rather long face. For the life of him, he couldn't work out what kind of hat would make her face look not quite so long. No, he just didn't know. Leave it at that then, and see when the time comes. *Ah, and there's Napoleon, too!*

Mr Ma utterly worshipped Napoleon – Napoleon being Her dog. *That's tricky, though. A present for a dog? Never given a dog a present before, to tell the truth. Aha – I've got it! I've got it!* In his triumph, he knocked the tobacco from his newly filled pipe out into the fire.

Get a bit of coloured paper, and wrap up seven shillings and sixpence in a parcel. Tie some ribbon round it and hand it to Mrs Wedderburn. Heard her say the other day that she'd have to buy a new annual licence for Napoleon after the new year, and it'd cost her seven and six. Well, I'll be paying for it for her! Ho-ho! There's a marvellous idea for you, eh? Bloody hell, though – seven and six every year, all for one little dog. The things the foreign devils get up to. Anyway, it'll be me paying for it, so you can bet it'll make her . . . make her . . . Yes, that's it!

He was highly pleased, and indeed for him to have actually managed to think up such an ingenious idea by himself was no small feat.

It was nearly lunchtime, but the fog outside was still very thick. He thought about asking Mrs Wedderburn to make a meal, but he strongly objected to eating cold meat. Then he thought of going to have a look at the shop, but was afraid he might get run over by a car. Anyway, he'd simply not dared show his face in the shop this last month. Ever since Li Tzu-jung had suggested organising a massive Christmas sale, Ma Wei and Li Tzu-jung – who was snatching some time each day to come and help – had been so busy they'd been run off their feet, but they wouldn't let the elder Ma lift a finger to help them.

One day, Mr Ma had wanted to take a small vase home to put flowers in. Without so much as a word, Li Tzu-jung had forcibly snatched the vase from his hands. And what's more, Ma Wei's face had gone all stern, and he'd given him, his father, a telling-off.

Another time, when both Ma Wei and Li Tzu-jung were out of the shop somewhere, Mr Ma had taken down all the gaudy notices and posters from the window, feeling they were in poor taste. And that had earnt him another dressing-down from Ma Wei.

It was no good. If even your own son didn't side with you, what could you do? What on earth had made him come to this foreign-devil country? *There's nowhere here you can lay a charge of 'obstreperousness and unfiliality' against your child! I'll just have to put up with it. Of course, Ma Wei does it because he's trying to get ahead and make some money. But trying to get ahead doesn't mean you can entirely ignore the requirements of face. I'm your father, I'll have you realise!*

He's a good boy, Ma Wei. Wants to make a go of things. Mr Ma nodded his head and sighed in approbation. *But all the same, stick to making a go of things, and don't forget I'm your dad.*

The dense fog outside the window turned from grey to dark grey, to brown and to red. The houses were now invisible. Lights were on everywhere, but seemed to be half out, which lent an uneasy, unsettled feel to the scene. A coalman in the street called out in a hoarse, choked voice, his voice seeming to come from immediately outside the window, but he himself and his coal cart were in some other world.

That's settled it. Mr Ma sat down by the fire again. *I'll only get told off if I go to the shop. So I think I'll stay here, and patiently while away the time.*

Yes, Mr Ma was London's leading man of leisure.

II

NO MATTER whether you're an important person or an insignificant one, you can accomplish something if you strive onwards with the utmost resolution. Although the magnitude of these accomplishments varies, they're alike in the force of spiritual determination behind them, and in their success, for which they deserve our respect.

But merely waving flags and shouting battle cries without really doing anything is disgraceful. Only people lacking in ideals, only people devoid of constructive ideas or those who delight in vainglory, wave flags and shout battle cries. Such things are not only doomed to fruitlessness, not only undeserving of respect, but they can't even raise a laugh in others.

When did any of those foreigners in China, the foreign devils with their big guns, their aeroplanes and their science, their knowledge and their financial resources, ever laugh at all those students waving paper flags, shouting about justice, vying to become president of their students' union and neglecting to study? Laugh? It wasn't worth a single laugh. The less they study, the better. As long as they fail to study, the foreign devils' knowledge will remain superior to theirs. And their paper flags, come what may, will never overcome the foreign devils' artillery. If those students had a go at the foreign devils' big guns with some little guns, the devils might perhaps manage a laugh. But if they merely clutched a little stick with a bit of red paper pasted on it, and tried to repel the cannons with that scrap of paper, they could hardly expect the foreign devils to crack a smile. No, that's not the way people who truly care for their country set about things.

Love. What a terrible thing love is. At its altar, life and wealth may both be sacrificed, sacrificed for the sake of a woman. Even love, however, may be overcome by firm resolution. Life's a complex, many-sided thing, and besides love it involves ambition, duty, vocation . . . Those who are fortunate may proceed from the fulfilment of their love to the attainment of their duty, and the accomplishment of their vocation. The unfortunate can only acknowledge their bad luck, and turn their attentions to their ambition, duty and vocation.

If someone abandons all his sacred ambition, duty and vocation, gratuitously discards his golden life simply because he can't kiss someone's cherry-sweet lips – such a person is a fit hero for a novel, but a social criminal. Real society and novels are two quite different things. To drop the paper flags to study and work, and to quiet one's sad wails of disappointed love and take a look at one's ambition, duty and vocation; those would be two salutary doses of medicine for the youth of China, of shattered China, decrepit but charming China.

When in China, Ma Wei had held up a paper flag and shouted battle cries along with the rest of them. But now he'd come to realise that the strength and prosperity of England was in large measure due to the fact that the English don't shout battle cries, but put their heads down and get on with it. The English are passionately committed to freedom, but oddly enough their university students have no right of free speech with regards to their school authorities. The English are passionately committed to liberty, but oddly enough there's order everywhere. When several million workers went on strike, it could be done without the firing of a rifle, and without the death of a single person. Order and discipline are the secrets of a strong country, as Ma Wei now realised.

In his heart, he couldn't forget Mary, but he also realised that if he went to pieces over her, he and his father would starve to death, without question. And he would be unable to render the slightest service to his motherland.

Ma Wei was no fool. He was one of the new youth, and the new youth's highest aspiration was to achieve something for their nation and society. Such a duty was more important than anything else. To lose your life for old China would be a million times more noble than dying for a beautiful woman. Sacrificing yourself for love would be to add one more flower to the garland of poetry, but sacrificing yourself for the nation would be to add a most splendid page to the history of China. Ma Wei realised that now.

His approach was simple: to resist his spiritual depression by means of physical labour. First thing in the morning, he'd get up and go for a run around the park, and sometimes he'd also do half an hour or so of rowing. The first time he rowed, he almost knocked himself flat on the bottom of the boat with all the exertion. Wind or rain, he'd go out running, and after three weeks of it, his cheeks had acquired a ruddy glow. On coming back from his run, he'd take a cold-water bath (Mrs Wedderburn had now granted them permission to use her bath) and rub himself bright red all over, till he looked like a fresh lobster in a fishmonger's. After the bath, he'd go down to breakfast. Mary would look at him, and he would look at Mary. When Mary spoke, he would reply with a smile. He knew that she was beautiful, so he decided to regard her as some beautiful little ragdoll.

You look down on me, but I scorn you even more, he told himself. *You're beautiful, but I'm seeking glory and the fulfilment of my duty. Beauty can scarcely balance glory and duty on heaven's scales. Ha!*

Noting the ruddiness of Ma Wei's cheeks, how his wrists grew daily thicker and more muscular, and the remarkable sparkle of his eyes, Mary now made deliberate excuses to engage him in conversation. Foreign girls do like tough young lads. Ma Wei deliberately ate quickly, and as soon as he'd finished his breakfast, he would go upstairs, three steps at a time, to do some studying. When he met Mary in the street, he'd just lift his hand and hurry on past like a gust of wind.

Ha! Good fun, this. Seem to have worked that lot out of my system! thought Ma Wei.

If you can see the funny side of things, life's much more enjoyable.

After a few hours study, Ma Wei would go out and run all the way to the shop. He put all Li Tzu-jung's suggestions into effect, one after the other. The goods that Wang Ming-ch'uan had obtained for them reached London just before Christmas, and he and Li Tzu-jung set to work with a vengeance, decorating the shopfront, pricing things, printing the catalogue . . . Each day without fail, he'd put in seven hours' work.

The wares weren't all antiques, but included Chinese embroideries, trinkets and old embroidered garments. When elderly ladies in search of something Chinese for their relatives and friends came to hear of the Mas' shop, they found many things to choose from. One day they'd buy a small purse, and the next a circular fan. Sometimes as they picked up such gifts, they'd also buy something expensive in passing.

As soon as Li and Ma Wei got all the goods sorted out, Li Tzu-jung called Lord Simon in to take his pick of the best. Head cocked to one side, Lord Simon wandered round the room for a good half of the day. In addition to the porcelain that he wanted for himself, he bought an old embroidered Chinese skirt costing twenty-five pounds as a Christmas present for Lady Simon. On that occasion alone, he bought a hundred and fifty pounds' worth of goods.

'It's worked, Ma, old lad!' said Li Tzu-jung, raking his hair.

'Yes, it's worked, old Li!' Ma Wei was already smiling so much that those were the only words he could manage.

The two of them then got into a long discussion of how to attract the attention of passers-by to their shop. Li Tzu-jung proposed putting flashing lights at the end of the street, a red light alternating with a green one, shining out the message BUY CHINESE ANTIQUES, followed by GIVE THEM SOMETHING CHINESE AS A PRESENT.

Young people move quickly, and three days after this discussion, the lights were installed in position.

As the Mas' shop trade got busier, the manager of the antiques shop next door grew rather worried. He'd always known that the elder Ma was a useless layabout, and was just biding his time, fully expecting Ma to declare that he was giving up the business, so that he himself might take over the Mas' shop. Seeing the two young men now making such a wonderful go of things, he decided that he'd have to take action. If he waited until the Mas' shop was really going great guns, the matter wouldn't be so easy to pull off. Hatless, his bald head shining and his hands clasped round his ample belly, he secretly invited Li Tzu-jung out for a meal and had a little word with him, tête-à-tête.

'Go and buy yourself a bottle of hair-restorer,' Li Tzu-jung told him smiling, 'and when you've grown some hair, we'll talk again!' The old manager stroked his bald pate, burst out laughing – the English do have their good points – and said nothing more on the subject.

Mr Ma dropped by a number of times, pretending that it was to help them, but in reality it was only to get a couple of delicate little trinkets for Mrs Wedderburn. On one occasion he paced around the shop, posture upright, steps measured, looking at this, looking at that, feeling this and shifting that.

He snatched a furtive glance at Ma Wei. Ma Wei's eyes were riveted on him. He gave a couple of feeble coughs, stuffed his hands in his trouser pockets, and moved off on his rounds once more with his erect posture and measured tread. A customer came in, and the elder Ma gave him a deep bow. He intended at the conclusion of his bow to advance and begin his sales pitch, and thereby demonstrate his talents. But by the time he'd straightened up, Ma Wei had already led the customer past him. Well, then!

'He's got the drive. The boy's certainly got what it takes. But don't you forget that I'm your dad,' Mr Ma muttered to himself.

When Christmas was only a few days off, business grew even busier. Of the things they sold, eighty or ninety per cent had to be packed up and delivered to the customers. Sometimes, Ma Wei and Li Tzu-jung would be wrapping up parcels till ten o'clock at night. Some they took to the post office, but other more fragile things they had to deliver themselves. Li Tzu-jung volunteered to undertake this difficult mission, and went to the bicycle shop to hire a wonky bike, upon which he hared round for all he was worth, delivering parcels around town. When Mr Ma saw Li Tzu-jung on the battered old bike, squeezing his way through the traffic, he shut his eyes and prayed to God on his behalf.

'Tell that Li Tzu-jung,' said Mr Ma to Ma Wei, 'not to hurtle round at such a speed! It's no game going round like that, pushing his way in and out of gaps in the traffic. Tcha! He shouldn't try to do a Washington. He'll be thrown off and killed sooner or later.'

Ma Wei communicated his father's well-meant advice to Li Tzu-jung, who burst out laughing.

'Thank Mr Ma for his kind advice. But it doesn't matter – I'm insured. So if I get run over and killed, the insurance company'll give my mother five hundred pounds. You know, Ma, old lad, it's a marvellous feeling edging between two big vehicles. And if I wasn't carrying the goods, I'd be able to move even faster. Last night I was having a proper race with a crowd of boys and girls on bikes, when suddenly I noticed that I was hurtling towards the back of a car. What do you think I did? Don't know how I managed it, but I brought the bike up sharp, so that its wheel rammed against the car while I jumped off. The whole crowd of youngsters raised their heads and gave me three cheers, they did!'

Ma Wei told his father about this, and the elder Mr Ma said nothing, just nodded his head and gave a couple of sighs.

Seeing Ma Wei so busy gave Mr Ma pause for thought. One day, after finishing his evening meal, the elder Ma went back to the shop.

'Ma Wei,' he said as he entered, 'I absolutely must do something. I may be no good at the business side of things, but you can't tell me I'm not capable of wrapping up parcels, can you now? I insist on giving you a hand!' With these words, he placed his tobacco pouch and pipe on the table, and picked up a few sheets of paper. 'Give me some of the easier things to pack,' he said.

Ma Wei gave his father some things. Mr Ma stuck his pipe in his mouth, screwed his nose up a bit, surveyed the size of the paper, then examined the articles. He wrapped away for ages, but for all his efforts, he couldn't manage to wrap them up neatly. He stole a glance at Li Tzu-jung. Li Tzu-jung had already wrapped quite a number of things into tidy parcels. Actually, all he was doing was putting one hand on the object, to hold it in place, then, it seemed, chopping at the paper with his other hand.

Hmm, don't know how on earth the paper obeys him like that. In one movement it was all wrapped neatly and evenly round the articles. Mr Ma, too, chopped with his hand, and hastily tied up his parcel with string. Remarkably, the string tied itself into one great tangled knot, and the ends of the paper curled up out of the parcel, as wildly as Mrs Ely's hair.

'"The mason spake: is it even or nay? All we need now is one handful of clay." There we are!' Having somehow or other managed to wrap an object, Mr Ma weighed it in both hands. Then he took a look at the other two. Both were smiling.

'Don't you laugh! When you get old, you'll understand. You're young and strong, nimble-fingered and agile. Whereas me . . . well, I'm getting on in years.'

He proceeded to walk round in a circle, clutching the parcel in both hands, not knowing where to put it. Li Tzu-jung dashed over, took it from him, and told Ma Wei to stick on the address label and write the name on it. Ma Wei took it and placed it to one side.

'Now, where's my tobacco pouch?' asked Mr Ma.

'Haven't seen it. Under the paper perhaps?' they said, by complete coincidence in perfect unison.

Mr Ma lifted up the paper, sheet by sheet, but his tobacco pouch wasn't there. 'Don't bother about me. I can look for it. I'm always losing my tobacco pouch.'

He hunted all over the room, but couldn't find it.

'Odd! The busier you are, the more mishaps occur. Why, bl—!' The parcel that he'd just wrapped caught his eye. Without a word, he opened up the parcel and took out his tobacco pouch.

'Ma Wei, I'm going home. Don't stay up too late, either of you.'

The instant he'd left, Li Tzu-jung leapt high into the air and laughed himself hoarse. Ma Wei laughed too, so much that he knocked the ink bottle over.

'Shall I tell you something, old Li? Those things I handed my father didn't need to be wrapped anyway. Nobody'd bought them! I knew full well the old man wouldn't be able to wrap them properly.'

'Buy our stuff . . . ha ha! . . . and you get a free gift . . . ha! A tobacco pouch! Ha ha!'

The two young men laughed for a good quarter of an hour. Or maybe more.

III

ON CHRISTMAS Eve, London was astir with great excitement. Male and female, young and old, all went into town. It was as though the things in the shops were being handed out free, in big bunches and little parcels, carted away on backs and clutched under arms, for you couldn't see anybody in town walking along empty-handed, except for the policemen. Buses and trams came past all the time, but, even so, old ladies couldn't push their way onto them, and in the process of trying to, would send things from their baskets tumbling all over the street.

None of the postmen were using their bags now – they all had another man to push a trolley for them, as they went door to door delivering parcels. Some of the citizens of London had already dispatched their presents and taken a trip to the countryside to spend Christmas there. At the same time, country people came into London for a few days' celebration and entertainment. So the main roads to the countryside were crammed with traffic.

The weather was very dull, and a cold east wind was blowing. But nobody noticed the dullness of the weather or the coldness of the wind. All the shops in town had put up their coloured lights, which lit up the goods with sparkle and vivid colour, radiating good cheer. Father Christmases hung everywhere, wearing big red hoods and carrying magic sacks filled with presents. So preoccupied were people with looking at the shops that they were oblivious to the gloominess of the sky. And once you'd pushed your way through the crowds, you'd be covered in sweat, so nobody even noticed how cold the wind was.

People forgot about everything: politics, society, court cases, sorrows, opinions . . . all fell by the wayside. People suddenly turned into little children, eager to give their friends something novel, and at the same time hoping they'd receive some nice trinket themselves. Everyone's faces seemed open and generous, completely free of worries and cares, and their only concern was to eat and drink well. Those with surplus wealth even gave a little of it to the poor. That evening it was indeed as if the redeemer of humankind was about to be born on earth, as if the world was about to know a great peace, with all people living in harmony with one another.

The shops didn't close till midnight, and the buses and trams were still running in town right until dawn, all crammed with passengers. The side streets were as bright as the main streets, every shop adorned with a Christmas tree and at least a few coloured balls. Poor children were singing Christmas carols, going from door to door asking for money, while the children of the better-off were still awake at midnight, waiting for Father Christmas to come and bring them some nice presents. There's a gap between rich and poor, but on this day both the haves and the have-nots might receive a gift to render their hearts as joyous as a newborn Jesus. The sounds of bells and carols from the churches rang out in the air all around, and even those not religiously minded were filled with a sense of solemnity and beauteous concord.

Mr Ma had already sent off his presents ten days earlier, because, once he'd bought them, it would have nagged on his mind to have them around. Only those for Mrs Wedderburn and her daughter remained in his study. Mrs Wedderburn had told him that they weren't to be brought out until Christmas Day. After he'd sent off the rest of the presents, he waited eagerly for people to send him presents in return. As soon as the postman knocked, Mr Ma would have a race with Napoleon to see who could be first to the door.

In the two days before Christmas, presents kept coming. From the Reverend Ely he got a bible, from Mrs Ely a book of hymns, from Miss Ely a handkerchief and from Master Ely no more than a Christmas card, although Mr Ma had given Paul a box of cigars. It's English custom to exchange presents, but Paul, utterly despising the Chinese, had made a special point of not giving Mr Ma a present. Mr Ma's first thought was to send the bible, hymnbook and Christmas card back again. But he thought better of it. *For Miss Ely's sake, I won't do that.*

These last few days, he hadn't been to the shop at all, there being nothing much for him to do there. When customers came, all he could do was open the door for them, bow, and see them out. Although a good many old women remarked, 'What a well-mannered old man! So nice!', Mr Ma felt differently about the matter.

Do you imagine all a manager's here for is opening the door for people? he grumbled to himself. *I know you're doing fine, but don't forget I'm your father. Fancy making your own dad open the door and bow to people!* Feeling put out, he'd ceased going to the shop.

Strolling idly round town, he looked at the men and women, young and old, all so bustling and busy, and he felt a bit dismal inside. *Ah, it'd be so nice if I were in China. Just the sort of bustle and excitement we have at New Year. No matter how much others are enjoying themselves, I can't get into the spirit of things, celebrating a festival abroad. I only hope I can make a fortune. Then I'll go back to China and celebrate the festivals there.*

Watching others rush around made him feel more and more inclined to go home. And the more his thoughts turned to home, the more people kept treading on his toes.

Let's get back. Go home and see Mrs Wedderburn. Give her a helping hand. Leisurely he sauntered back.

Mrs Wedderburn was in such a hustle she was run off her little feet, the veins of her temples were throbbing and the delicate tip of her nose was bright red. She beat the carpets, polished the tables, and wherever there was anything brass, she gave it a rub – from oven door to doorknocker. Above the pictures in every room she hung a twig of holly, and she bought a bunch of chrysanthemums, which she set reverently before her husband's photograph. And from the light in the drawing room she hung two sprigs of mistletoe.

Having no small children, she couldn't very well have a Christmas tree, but she insisted all the same on having some decorations in every room. In some places it was a string of coloured balls, in others a couple of paper lanterns. The whole house took on a festive air. In the oven she was steaming a Christmas pudding and baking mince pies, and every now and then she took a peep at them. So, what with one thing and another, she was flying round in a flurry, up the stairs and down the stairs, like a little swallow. In the evening, after rushing around the whole day long, she had to write Christmas cards and wrap the Christmas presents, and she was in such a flap and fluster that she didn't even have time to dab any powder on her nose.

As Miss Wedderburn's shop was extra busy with the seasonal trade, young Mary went out early and came home late, and couldn't give her mother any help at all. Napoleon kept running madly up and down the stairs, barking at the coloured balls, and then giving another few barks at the little lanterns. And when his mistress was elsewhere engaged, he'd seize the opportunity to go into the kitchen and steal one or two of the shelled walnuts to eat.

'Mrs Wedderburn!' called Mr Ma as soon as he came in, 'Mrs Wedderburn! I'll come and give you a hand, shall I?'

'Thank you, Mr Ma!' said Mrs Wedderburn, wiping her tiny red nose. 'Take Napoleon out to have a play first, will you? He's doing nothing but giving me trouble here.'

'All right, Mrs Wedderburn. Napoleon! Here!'

Mr Ma took the dog out for a stroll. Luckily no children played any pranks on him, as they were all celebrating Christmas and had no spare time for mischief-making. He brought the dog back, and, just as he reached the door, Alexander appeared in the street. He was carrying lots of things in his arms, parcel upon parcel piled right up to his big red nose.

'Ma! Ma!' he shouted, while still a good way off. 'Take the parcel on top. It's your present!'

Mr Ma went and took the parcel down, and Napoleon came up too, to have a sniff at Alexander's large feet.

'Thanks for your present, Ma, old chap!' bellowed Alexander.

'How about dropping over to my place for Christmas, eh? We'll have a good old booze-up together!'

'Thank you very much,' said Mr Ma, smiling, 'but will it be all right if I come after Christmas? I've already promised Mrs Wedderburn that I'd keep her company here for the festive merry-making.'

'Aah!' Alexander took two paces forwards, and said in a low, confidential tone, winking each eye in turn. 'So you've taken a fancy to the little widow, Ma, old chap. Well done! Well done! Right, we'll leave it at that, then. I'll be expecting you at my home the day after Boxing Day. Make sure you come. Cheerio! Ah – hang on a moment! Pull out the fourth parcel from the bottom, and give it to Mrs Wedderburn with my wishes for a Merry Christmas. Cheerio, Ma!'

Mr Ma took the two parcels, and Alexander, clutching the remaining ones, charged off like a path-clearing demon effigy at a funeral.

'Mrs Wedderburn!' called Mr Ma again as he came in.

'Hello!' shouted Mrs Wedderburn from upstairs, at the top of her high voice.

'I'm back. And I've a present for you.'

Clitter, clatter, Mrs Wedderburn sped downstairs like a flash of greased lightning. 'Oh,' she said as she took the parcel, 'it's from Alexander. And I've nothing to give him. What shall I do?'

'Don't worry. I have a box of cigars in the house. You wrap them up as a present for him. That'll solve your problem.' Mr Ma's smiling eyes riveted themselves on her dear little red nose.

'Oh, yes, that would be lovely! How much did they cost you? I'll pay you whatever it was.'

'Don't mention the money,' said Mr Ma, still gazing at the red tip of her tiny nose. 'Don't mention money! It's Christmas. What's a box of cigars between friends? We are friends, eh?'

Smiling, Mrs Wedderburn nodded.

The elder Ma let the dog off its lead, and went upstairs to fetch the box of cigars.

On Christmas Eve, Ma Wei and Li Tzu-jung were still working at four o'clock in the afternoon, at which point they made a halt.

'Li, old fellow, lock the doors. We must go and enjoy ourselves now!' said Ma Wei, smiling.

'Right, shut the door!' replied Li Tzu-jung, smiling.

'Shall I switch off the sign at the door?'

'Yes, but leave on the one at the end of the street.'

'I've got to give you a present, old Li. What would you like?' asked Ma Wei.

'Mr Ma's already given me a pair of shoes. Don't give me anything more.'

'That's from my father. I've absolutely got to give you something. You've gone to so much trouble for us.'

'Look here, Ma, old lad,' said Li Tzu-jung with a smile, 'one thing we mustn't do is start getting all stuffy with one another. I've been helping you, but you've been seeing to my lunch every day.'

'I don't care. I insist on giving you a present. What do you want?'

Li Tzu-jung scratched his head for ages, without saying anything.

'Speak up, old Li!' said Ma Wei, trying to pin him down.

'If you've really got to give me a present, then buy me a watch.' Li Tzu-jung pulled a shabby old watch from his pocket, put it to his ear and gave it a shake. 'Just look at this watch. When it feels like it, it loses a couple of hours or more per day, quite apart from the fact it's only got an hour hand, no minute hand. If you're so inclined, fork out a few shillings and get me a new one, will you?'

'A few shillings, Li, old mate!' said Ma Wei, his big eyes opening even wider. 'If we buy one, it's got to be a good one. Now then, no call for you to make any fuss. Let's go and buy one together. Come on!'

Ma Wei began to drag him to the door. Li Tzu-jung was never at a loss for words, but today he seemed timid and bashful, and his face was bright red.

'Hold on. Wait till I've taken that old bike back first.'

'We'll do it together. You ride, and I'll stand on the back.'

The two of them mounted the bike and took off, wobbling and

swaying, to the bicycle shop, where they returned the bike and settled the bill for its hire.

As they came out of the bike shop, Ma Wei grabbed hold of Li Tzu-jung, fearing he might make a bolt for it, and the two of them headed off, walking a bit, then stopping a bit, arguing as they walked, and coming to a standstill to keep arguing. Ma Wei maintained it was right to give presents at Christmas, and Li Tzu-jung said one shouldn't spend much on presents. Ma Wei countered that if you bought something, you had to make sure it was good, while Li Tzu-jung declared that he'd been carrying his shabby old watch around for three years and saw no need to buy a good one now. Ma Wei was steadily losing patience, and his eyes grew fiercer and fiercer. Li Tzu-jung was steadily losing patience, and his face was getting redder and redder. From St Paul's Cathedral, the two of them crossed Cheapside and continued on till they came to Charing Cross, from where they traversed Piccadilly and arrived at Regent Street. Noticing a watch shop, Ma Wei wanted to go in, but Li Tzu-jung hurried on past, dragging Ma Wei with him.

'Look here, old Li, you can't do that sort of thing!' Ma Wei was getting really worked up.

'You've got to promise me that any watch you buy won't cost more than ten shillings. Or else I'm not letting you go in!' Li Tzu-jung was getting really worked up too.

'All right, that's settled then.' Ma Wei had no choice but to agree. In the Grand Watch Emporium they bought a watch for ten shillings. Ma Wei felt so embarrassed that his face was scarlet, but Li Tzu-jung, quite unperturbed, put the watch in his pocket, and marched out with a back as stiff and straight as that of some Grand Marshal of the Army. 'Thanks, old Ma . . . Thanks.'

Outside the shop, he took hold of Ma Wei's hand and wouldn't let go, but kept on repeating, 'Thanks. But I haven't bought you anything. Haven't got you a thing.'

Ma Wei almost wept with frustration but he said nothing, and just shook hands very vigorously with Li Tzu-jung.

'Ma, old mate, have you taken all the money from the shop to the bank yet?'

'Yes, I have. Where are you going for your festive fun tomorrow, old Li?'

'Me?' Li Tzu-jung shook his head.

'Come round to my place tomorrow then, eh?'

'The buses and trams are only running for half the day. It'll be awkward getting about.'

'Tell you what: you come round on Boxing Day, and we'll go to the theatre together. You've been busy all Christmas. Surely you can slack off and enjoy yourself for one day?'

'Righto then! See you the day after tomorrow. Thanks, old Ma.' Li Tzu-jung shook hands with Ma Wei again, then rushed off into the crowd as if he were running to catch a train.

Ma Wei watched him till he was out of sight, before at last, his head well down, he slowly made tracks for home.

IV

THE SKY was still overcast, and a few snowflakes drifted through the air. There were hardly any people or cars in the streets, as everyone was celebrating Christmas Day in their homes.

Mrs Wedderburn had invited Aunt Dolly to come for Christmas, but she'd not replied. Not until the Christmas morning post was delivered did she receive an answer – a brief note, along with a parcel of presents. The gist of her letter was that one's life wasn't safe in the company of Chinamen, and that Christmas being the season of joy and good cheer, it didn't seem right to go looking for terrors and perils.

After reading the letter, Mrs Wedderburn pursed her lips very visibly. But you could hardly blame Aunt Dolly; the average English person speaks of 'the Chinese' and 'murder' in the same breath.

Pale brow furrowed, Mrs Wedderburn opened the parcel. A pair of knitted gloves for her, and a pair of flesh-coloured silk stockings for Mary. She called her daughter in, and the two of them pronounced judgement on Aunt Dolly's presents.

Miss Mary was as fresh as a flower, with the perfect shade of lipstick on her red lips, deep-black kohl and mascara on her eyebrows and eyelashes, and rouge on her dimpled cheeks, which looked like nothing more than two bashful cherry-apple blossoms. The sight of her daughter looking so pretty cheered Mrs Wedderburn up again, and she curved her lips into a smile as she gently placed a kiss on Mary's forehead. They gathered up Aunt Dolly's gifts and set about preparing the grand Christmas lunch.

The cooking was left to Mrs Wedderburn, while Mary put her pale hands into service shelling nuts, fetching plates and so on, keeping her distance from the stove. As she shelled, she munched, her two red dimples moving in and out, never idle.

After breakfast, Mr Ma took a seat in the drawing room to smoke his pipe, curious to see what the grand Christmas lunch would be like. After a quarter of an hour he got chased out by Mrs Wedderburn.

'Off to your study with you!' she said, laughing. 'Lunch will be ready in here soon enough, but don't come down until I ring the bell. Do you hear?'

Mr Ma knew how English women loved to flaunt their skills, and how they like to surprise, evoking one's astonished applause. Pipe in mouth, he went upstairs, chuckling.

'And don't forget to bring your presents down to lunch!' said young Miss Wedderburn, as he went. 'Oh, and what about Ma Wei?'

'Ma Wei! Ma Wei!' shouted Mrs Wedderburn from downstairs.

'Here! What is it?' asked Ma Wei from upstairs.

'Don't go into the drawing room until lunchtime, all right?'

'All right. I'll take Napoleon for a stroll round the block, shall I?' asked Ma Wei, running down the stairs.

'Oh, lovely. Off you go, then. Lunch's at one on the dot. Don't be late!' Mrs Wedderburn handed Ma Wei the dog, and gave it a tender kiss on the ear.

As Ma Wei took Napoleon out, mother and daughter busied themselves downstairs, and Mr Ma, pipe in mouth, sat alone in the study.

Well, it's Christmas . . . Ought to take a look in at the church, thought Mr Ma, *so that I'll have something to say for myself when I see the Reverend Ely tomorrow . . . Huh, the Reverend Ely. Fancy giving me a bible for Christmas! He could just have given me some little knick-knack or other – at least that'd have some spirit of the season about it. A bible! Do you think I can eat bible or drink bible? Silly fool!*

So Mr Ma decided against going to church. He took out his presents for Mrs Wedderburn and Mary, opened up the parcels to have a look, then rewrapped them the same as before. When he'd finished doing that, he felt that the string was a bit thick and didn't look nice. Pipe in mouth, he went to check in his room, but couldn't find any thinner string. Returning to the study, he gave the matter extensive thought.

Got it!

He hurried into Ma Wei's room to look for some red ink, which he used to dye the string red, then he put the string by the fire to dry.

Red's such an eye-catching colour. And all women love red. When the string was dry, he retied the parcels with it, and put them on the table. Then he put the bottle of ink back. As he did so, he took a close look at Ma Wei's room. The table was covered with books, but Mr Ma had no idea when Ma Wei'd bought them. On the wall hung Li Tzu-jung's photo, a small one, four inches square, with his hair all dishevelled and untidy, and a most vulgar smile on his face. Mr Ma gave a snort in the direction of the photo. Under the bed were piled cases and boots, and even a pair of ice skates.

That boy. He's game for anything . . . even learning ice-skating now! Dangerous on ice, though. When he gets back, I must tell him not to go ice-skating any more. Why, he might fall through a hole in the ice. No joking matter, that.

Mr Ma returned to the study, put some more coal on the fire and sat down again to smoke his pipe.

Somehow feel I've forgotten something or other. What was it? he thought, tapping his forehead with his pipe. *I know! I've forgotten to put any fresh flowers on my brother's grave! Too late now. Today's Christmas, and everybody's on holiday, so there's no telling whether you'd be able to buy any fresh flowers in town. Growing old's a curse. You keep on thinking about something, and then in the end it slips your mind after all . . . Ah, I look forward to the day we make our fortune. Then I can take my brother's coffin back to China. I can't wait for the day when we can return home . . .*

Now, if she and I . . . no, never! Wouldn't be fair on others. Wouldn't be fair on Ma Wei if I married, and gave him a foreign mother. Anyway, if I married her, I could say goodbye to ever returning to China. And that's unthinkable! Not go back to China . . . Foreign women certainly are pretty, though. Not that you could say she was the ultimate in prettiness, but she's neat and lively, oh yes. Yes, foreign women are an improvement on Chinese women. Even if they don't have a nice-looking face, they at least have a good figure. Real waists, real thighs; pale, bare bosoms, and arms like slender lotus-roots ... Hey now, it's Christmas! Mustn't think such naughty thoughts.

Think something good. Wonder what we'll be eating in a bit? Turkey, most likely. That's nothing very special. But as long as she doesn't serve me cold beef, I'll offer up thanks to Buddha ...

A whiff of roast turkey crept in through the crack in the door, wonderfully appetising, and the aroma of brandy floated in too.

Ah, maybe today we'll get a little glass of something! Mr Ma swallowed a mouthful of saliva.

Ma Wei took the dog for a long walk round Regent's Park, and wasn't back till half past twelve. He led the dog into the house, then went upstairs to wash his hands, change his shoes and get ready for lunch.

'Ma Wei!' called Mr Ma. 'Come here!'

Ma Wei changed his shoes and went into the study.

'Ma Wei,' said Mr Ma, 'when do you think we'll be able to return to China?'

'You and your returning to China, Dad!' said Ma Wei, warming his hands by the fire.

There was nothing further that father and son could say on the subject.

Noticing the paper parcels on the table, Ma Wei went into his own room, fetched his presents and put them with the others.

'So you've bought them some presents, too?' asked Mr Ma.

'Of course; ladies have to have such things,' said Ma Wei, smiling.

'Ladies —' said Mr Ma, then cut himself short.

The bell rang downstairs. Ma Wei carried the presents, with Mr Ma following on behind.

The dining table had been set up in the drawing room and Mrs Wedderburn and daughter were already seated, both wearing new dresses, and with newly powdered faces. Napoleon was crouching on the little piano stool by the piano, a red velvet ribbon tied round his neck. On the piano stood two lighted red candles. The Peke was watching the candle flames leap up and down, unable to fathom the mystery of them. Mr Ma placed his packet of seven and sixpence at the little dog's feet.

'Sit down, you men!' said Mrs Wedderburn, smiling.

Ma Wei put all the presents in front of mother and daughter, then he and his father went to their seats.

On the table was a new tablecloth the colour of peach blossoms, and under the cups and plates were small tablemats, also new, in different colours. In the middle of the table was a vase of pink chrysanthemums, with a bunch of coloured paper streamers draped from the leaves of the flowers. On either side of the vase stood a tall-stemmed dish, bearing fruit, walnuts, hazelnuts and so on, and under each dish were a number of snowballs made of cotton wool.

At the four corners of the table lay red paper crackers with gold bands round them, and each person had a trinket in front of them: Mr Ma and son each a tiny doll, Mary a little ragdoll, and Mrs Wedderburn a bird. Next to each of these toys was another small cracker. Each person's serviette was rolled up inside a wine glass, and bore a crown of holly berries on its tip.

In front of Mrs Wedderburn lay the huge platter of roast turkey, and in front of Mary a dish of ham and fried sausages. Two bottles of port were standing on the table near Mr Ma, and the salad and boiled greens were placed by Ma Wei. The layout of the table gave everybody a task to do.

Mrs Wedderburn carved the turkey, Mary started slicing the ham, and Ma Wei waited to distribute the vegetables. Mr Ma felt like opening a bottle of wine, but wasn't bold enough to make the move. He tentatively went to open his presents, but since nobody else followed suit, he didn't feel he could very well start on them, either.

'Pour the wine, Mr Ma,' said Mrs Wedderburn.

Mr Ma opened a bottle, and filled everyone's glasses.

Mrs Wedderburn finished carving the turkey for them all, served it out, then gave each person a teaspoonful of bright-red jelly and a dessertspoonful of bread sauce. The turkey smelt most appetising to Mr Ma, but he was rather suspicious of the jelly. He cautioned himself: *Mustn't question what they give me, no matter what it may be.*

All raised their glasses, and touched glasses with each other in turn, then the ladies took a sip and the gentlemen took a sip. They tucked into the turkey, chatting as they ate. Mary was especially jolly, and the wine she was drinking made her cheeks redder and shinier than ever. When they'd finished the turkey, Mrs Wedderburn brought out the Christmas pudding. She poured a spoonful of brandy over it and set the brandy alight, so that flames shot out all around the pudding, and she left it to burn a while like that before serving it.

After the pudding, Mary passed the fruit dish round, asking what they'd like. Mr Ma chose a banana, Mrs Wedderburn took an apple, and Mary and Ma Wei ate nuts. Mary used the nutcracker to open hers, but Ma Wei threw his into his mouth and cracked them open with his teeth.

'Ooh, Mum! Look what good teeth he's got! He can bite the hazelnuts open.' Mary's eyes opened wide, full of admiration for the teeth of the Chinese.

'That's nothing. Look at me!' Mr Ma took a hazelnut too, and bit it open with a loud crack.

'Oh, you are naughty!' Now that she'd drunk a glass of wine, Mrs Wedderburn was feeling very merry and light-headed. She picked up a cotton-wool snowball and threw it at Mr Ma's head. Then Mary picked one up, and threw it at Ma Wei's face. Ma Wei caught the snowball, and with a flick of his wrist threw it at Mrs Wedderburn.

Mr Ma looked on dumbfounded, before eventually it dawned on him that the snowballs had actually been placed there so that they could all have the fun of throwing them at one another. Slowly he picked one up and threw it at Napoleon. Napoleon got hold of the snowball and chewed it, and a piece of red paper emerged.

'Go and get it, Mr Ma,' said Mrs Wedderburn, 'That's your hat!'

Mr Ma hastily snatched the red paper from the dog's jaws. Sure enough, it was a red paper hat.

'Put it on! Put it on!' shouted Mary.

Mr Ma put the hat on, and went off into a fit of giggles.

The others opened some of the snowballs and put their hats on as well. Mary still carried on pelting people with snowballs, until she'd covered Mr Ma with bits of cotton wool. Then Mrs Wedderburn told everybody to pull their crackers.

Bang! Bang! Bang! The explosions of the crackers frightened Napoleon so much that he took refuge under the table. In each cracker there was a small object. Mrs Wedderburn got two tiny whistles, which she stuck between her lips and blew. Ma Wei got a toffee. Mr Ma got another paper hat, which he placed on his head, on top of the other one, laughing away once more. Mary hadn't pulled hard enough, so she had to have another go with Mr Ma. He tightened his moustachioed lips and pulled the cracker with her. *Bang!* She got a half-size pencil.

'Do we look at the presents now?' asked Ma Wei.

'No, don't,' said Mrs Wedderburn. 'Take them into the study so everybody can compare and see who's got the best!'

'Wait a mo', Mum. Look at this!' As she spoke, Mary stretched out her left hand for her mother to see.

'Mary! You've gone and got engaged to Washington! Mary!'

Mrs Wedderburn took hold of her daughter's hand and stared at the gold ring on the plump finger. Then mother and daughter fell into each other's arms, murmuring away, and kissing for a solid three minutes. Ma Wei's face went pale. The elder Ma, in a daze, goggled at them kissing, at a loss as to what he should do.

Pulling himself together and forcing a smile, Ma Wei raised his glass of wine towards them, and signalled with his eyes to his father, who also raised his glass.

'Our congratulations, Miss Mary!' And Ma Wei took a sip of wine. But it was a long time before he managed to swallow it.

Mary looked at Mr Ma and looked at her mother, her blue eyes twinkling, radiating a sparkle of joy.

'Mum, I'm so happy!' said Mary, putting her head on her

mother's shoulder. 'I'm going to his home tomorrow for his family and friends to give us their formal congratulations. Oh, Mum, I'm so happy!'

Mrs Wedderburn gently patted her daughter's shoulder, tears flowing from her eyes.

'Mum, what's the matter? Are you crying, Mum?' Mary reached out an arm and put it round her mother's neck.

'I'm happy, Mary!' Mrs Wedderburn forced a smile. 'You take these presents to the study with the Mas, Mary, while I go and feed the dog. Be with you in a minute.'

'Come on, Ma Wei.' Mary picked up her and her mother's presents, and walked out of the room.

Ma Wei glanced at his father, gave a gloomy smile and absently picked up their presents and walked out.

Mr Ma blinked. He'd noticed something amiss with his son, but could think of no way to comfort him. Picking up his wine glass and pouring himself another glassful, he slowly sipped it beneath the mistletoe-hung light.

As Mrs Wedderburn came back into the room, he hastily put the glass down. She glanced at Mr Ma, glanced at the mistletoe, blushed, stepped back two paces, then suddenly stiffened her graceful neck, went even redder and rushed at him, clasped his face in her hands and kissed him smack on the lips. Mr Ma's face immediately went purple and his whole body quivered. He gave her a numb, gormless smile, and rushed upstairs.

Mrs Wedderburn waited a moment, then she, too, went upstairs.

That night when she went to bed, Mrs Wedderburn lay there clutching her husband's photograph and kissing it again and again, tears falling. 'I've done you wrong, darling. I couldn't help it. I was so lonely, and Mary'll be gone soon, and there'll be nobody to keep me company. Forgive me, darling. My love, I held out all these years, but I couldn't bear it any longer. I was lonely. On my own, and so miserable. Forgive me . . .'

And she went to sleep, hugging the photograph to her.

V

ON THE morning of Boxing Day, the ground was spread with a layer of white frost. The sun appeared, peeping from thin clouds, and the sunshine brought everybody out. Those who had eaten too much over Christmas, fathers, sons and brothers alike, all bare-legged, went off for a run in the countryside, a bit of cross-country being preferable to indigestion pills. Others took their wives and children to see their parents, the children all looking very odd and awkward in their new clothes. Some people had gone to bed very late the previous day, and were still lingering under their bedclothes at noon with nasty hangovers. Others rose very early so as to have lunch in good time and go to see a play or film, or a conjuring performance, or a music-hall show or a circus . . . Whatever their choice, they were simply determined to enjoy themselves.

Mrs Wedderburn and her daughter were up early, and just as they finished breakfast, Li Tzu-jung arrived.

His nose was frozen bright red, and the brim of his hat bore flakes of frost that had drifted down from the trees. There was some dirt on his overcoat, as he'd worn the new shoes Mr Ma had given him, and had slipped up as he was leaving his house. Luckily, tumbling head over heels was a common occurrence for him, and he'd not even bothered to dust himself off when he scrambled to his feet again. He'd come out so early partly because the watch that Ma Wei had given him was gaining more than twenty minutes a day. So now he carried both old and new watches on him, to compare their times. Anyway, time was a human construction, so why not let it go a bit faster? It could only make life seem busier and fuller. Don't imagine that by ignoring time and walking slowly, you'll avoid reaching life's end . . .

'Right, Ma, old mate, let's go,' said Li Tzu-jung, not yet even through the door.

'Come in and sit down for a while, old Li!' said Ma Wei at the door.

'I won't come in. If we're going to see a play, we'll have to go and buy the tickets early. If we don't manage to get a ticket, we can always go and see a circus, or watch a film. If we leave it too late, though, we won't get in anywhere. Let's go – hurry up.'

Ma Wei stepped back into the hallway, put his overcoat on, stuck his hat on his head and left the house.

'We'll go to Piccadilly and buy the tickets first,' said Li Tzu-jung.

'All right,' replied Ma Wei, but with a frowning brow and gloomy face.

'What's up now, old Ma?' asked Li Tzu-jung.

'Nothing's up. Ate too much yesterday.' Ma Wei thrust his hands in his overcoat pockets and marched straight on.

'I don't believe that,' said Li Tzu-jung, looking at Ma Wei's face.

Ma Wei gave a shake of his head, wishing Li Tzu-jung were elsewhere. Admirable, Li Tzu-jung, and affable . . . and sometimes most obnoxious!

Seeing that Ma Wei wasn't going to say anything, Li Tzu-jung felt a bit irritated. An affable young bloke, that Ma Wei, but sometimes so obnoxious. (Neither actually disliked the other, but their mutual affection made it sometimes seem that they did.)

'It's that Miss Wedderburn affair again, I suppose, eh?' Li Tzu-jung enunciated his words in a singularly unpleasant tone.

'None of your business!' Ma Wei's tone was even less pleasant.

'I'm making it my business!' said Li Tzu-jung, and gave a broad grin. Then as Ma Wei didn't utter a word, he continued. 'Ma, old mate, the shop's at long last looking up, and now you're off on that same old track again. Are you planning to throw out your career and other obligations, all your hopes and aspirations, just like that?'

'I know all that!' Ma Wei reddened, and he shot a sideways glare at Li Tzu-jung.

'She doesn't love you! What's the point of trying to squeeze blood from a stone?'

'I know that!'

'What *do* you know, might I ask?' Li Tzu-jung wasn't letting him get away with anything. Guessing Ma Wei's thoughts, he relentlessly pressed home his point. 'I'm just a silly young fellow, and all I'm capable of is silly things, but I could never sacrifice my vocation and career for a woman. Take a look at the facts; yes, look at the facts! Stare them in the face! If you don't keep at it with the shop, then you and your father have had it! Can't you see how obvious that is yet?'

'Yes, you *are* silly! You can't see how important love is.' Ma Wei looked up at the sky, where the sun was still visible through the clouds.

'You may be right, but catch me loving a girl who didn't love me!' Li Tzu-jung threw himself body and soul into that statement, lunging forwards violently, and, the soles of his new shoes being so stiff and slippery, he nearly went head over heels again.

'All right! That's enough. Don't talk about it any more.'

'What do you mean, enough? Since we left the house you've been as much fun as a wet blanket; you haven't said a decent word to me. I like that! Enough!'

'You make me sick, Li Tzu-jung!'

'And the same to you, Ma Wei!' Li Tzu-jung grinned.

'It's no good. I'll have to tell you.' There was a tiny smile on Ma Wei's face. 'It's like this, old Li: she's got engaged to someone else.'

'And where do you come into it then?'

'I've never been able to forget her; I can't. I've been trying these last few months. When I meet her, I deliberately look the other way. But it doesn't work . . . just doesn't work. She's always there, lurking at the back of my mind. I know all about my vocation and my duties. And I know she doesn't love me. But that doesn't mean I'm capable of forgetting her. Now she's engaged, I feel just about heartbroken. I know being heartbroken won't do me any good. Oh, I know that, but . . .' His eyes stared at the ground, and he gave a bitter laugh and stopped speaking.

Li Tzu-jung didn't say anything either.

They walked on for quite a way before Li Tzu-jung gave a smile and spoke up. 'Look here, old Ma, I appreciate how awful you must be feeling, and I know it's no good my trying to persuade you to see things differently. It's not that you haven't made the effort. You've tried to forget her, I know. But it's all been to no effect, and I can't do anything to help, either. How about moving, so you don't see her any more?'

'Yes, I'll have to have a word with my father about that.'

The two young men went round the Piccadilly theatres to try to buy some tickets. They went to quite a few but couldn't get a single ticket, as it was the first day's performances after Christmas and most shows were already sold out. So the two of them had a bite to eat in a restaurant, then hurried to Olympia to watch the circus.

Li Tzu-jung found everything entertaining – the monkeys riding horses, the lions jumping through hoops, the bears riding bicycles, the little donkeys dancing . . . all struck him as amusing. But seeing no trace of a smile on Ma Wei's face, he didn't feel comfortable laughing out loud, so kept his laughs in his belly.

After the circus, the two of them had a cup of tea before parting ways.

'Ma, my lad, you've got to pull up your socks and stick at it!' said Li Tzu-jung. 'Things are looking up, so what's the point of ruining everything by backsliding again? You've had one go at defeating the depression through hard work – why not give it another try? You haven't a hope now anyway – she's engaged. Anyway, thanks for today, old Ma. Be seeing you.'

'See you, old Li.'

When Ma Wei got home, Mrs Wedderburn was sitting talking with his father in the study.

'Hello, Ma Wei,' she said with a smile. 'What did you see? Was it good?'

'We went to watch the circus. It was very good,' said Ma Wei, sitting down.

'You know, we must go and see it, too. It's a really excellent circus this year.'

We? Ma Wei mused to himself. *No more 'Mr Ma'? Bit odd.*

'We'll go on Friday, so we can take Mary, shall we?' suggested Mr Ma with a smile.

There we go again: that same sort of 'we', Ma Wei noted.

'Dad, how about us moving somewhere else, eh?' asked Ma Wei.

'What for?'

'No special reason. Freshens you up, a change of scenery.'

Mr Ma put two more lumps of coal on the fire.

'If you don't want to, Dad, forget I ever mentioned it. Makes no great difference whether we move or not.'

'We're very comfortable here, I think, so what's the point of uprooting ourselves again for some wild whim? And we'd waste more money, too. Anyway, Mrs Wedderburn . . .' Instead of continuing, Mr Ma gave a couple of simulated coughs. Father and son gave up speaking. Downstairs, Mary began to sing. She was playing the piano very badly, but her voice was wonderfully sweet and clear. Ma Wei stood up, and paced to and fro a few times.

'Ma Wei,' said Mr Ma in a subdued voice, 'that ring your uncle left you . . . Will you let me keep it?' His hand was in his pocket, clutching the little brocade box.

'What if I said I would, Father?'

'Let me have it, won't you?'

'Uncle gave it to me as a memento of him, so I suppose I was meant to keep it. But anyhow, what's so special about a ring? What do want it for, Dad? You wouldn't wear it.'

'It's like this, Ma Wei.' Mr Ma's face slowly reddened a shade, and he stammered out his words. 'It's like this. You see, I need it. Yes, you see . . . it's Mrs Wedderburn. I couldn't help it . . . I've let you down. I'm sorry, I couldn't help it. She . . . You see . . .'

Ma Wei felt like saying a great deal, with the same words that Li Tzu-jung had been using to tell him off. Yes, he felt like giving his father a piece of his mind. But he couldn't. How could he have the cheek to tell his father off, in view of his own case?

Li Tzu-jung can say things like that, but I've no right to criticise anyone. Anyway, some good may come of it if Father marries Mrs Wedderburn. She knows how to cope, and she's more thrifty than young girls are. She's got a home and a family, and she might suddenly get a notion to put heart and soul into running the shop. But what about the future, when we go back to China?

At this point in his thinking, he found himself giving voice to his thoughts. 'Father, if you set up home here, will we still be going back to China some day?'

Mr Ma was stunned by Ma Wei's question. Good God! How on earth could he have failed to take that aspect into account? He was going to return to China, of that he was quite certain. But taking her with him? *Even if she agreed to go, how could I look after her? To be sure, if I were a man of wealth, it'd be easy to arrange. Buy a big mansion in Shanghai, and keep everything just as it is in England. But I'm not a wealthy man. How would she find it if I took her with me, with no society there for her, and no entertainment, and her not speaking the language, and maybe not able to stomach the food? It'd be too cruel! Going there would be the end of her, beyond any doubt.*

What if I didn't take her back to China but stayed here for good, and was buried in the same place as my brother? No, no. Never! I've just got to return to China. I can't spend my last years in this country, and die here! No good . . . It's no good, there's nothing I can do . . .

'Ma Wei, here, take the ring.'

His head hung low, Mr Ma handed the ring in its box to Ma Wei, then cupped his forehead in both hands, and uttered no sound.

Yes, the elder Ma really was in a fix, and with no one in whom to confide. What about Ma Wei? But how could a father discuss such things directly and openly with his son? What about the Reverend Ely? No, the reverend was in a huff with Mr Ma because he'd not been helping him read Chinese books; if the elder Ma went there, it'd be just asking to be snubbed.

There's nobody I can tell. Nobody I can talk to about it. He still lay awake at midnight, his thoughts taking him ever further from any solution to his problems. Yet it was no good not thinking, either. When at last he closed his eyes and fell properly asleep, who should he see in his dreams but his late wife. Women! They won't even behave themselves when they've passed away. Mr Ma was fairly wary of women generally, but being wary didn't help. Women are women, and even if all of them went to the Three Immortals convent and became nuns, this sort of trouble would still be inevitable. Women!

When he rose the next morning, his mind was hazy and confused, like the ragged black clouds in the sky. As father and son ate breakfast, Ma Wei didn't say a word, just sat there tight-lipped, chewing grimly away at his toast, bent on grinding his teeth to bits. Mr Ma glanced sideways, peering at him over the top of his spectacles, and felt an ache inside him. Quickly looking away, he absent-mindedly stretched out a hand and took a spoonful of salt, which he tipped into his cup of tea.

Mrs Wedderburn and her daughter were engaged in a discussion about the circus, and Mary's eyes were as blue and bright as rolling azure waters as she stared at her mother's pointed nose. She'd agreed to go, but when she heard that Mr Ma would be going with them, she tried to back out, first of all saying that Washington had made a date to take her to the pictures, then saying that someone had invited her out dancing. Ma Wei found all this rather unpleasant hearing, and, in a temper, pushed his saucer aside, stood up and marched out.

'Dear me, what's the matter with him?' said Mrs Wedderburn, and her mouth hung open, making her look like a little startled hen.

Mary shrugged her shoulders and grinned.

Mr Ma said nothing, just drank a mouthful of salted tea from his cup. When he'd finished his breakfast, he slipped out of the house, pipe in mouth. The vast majority of the shops in the main streets were still shut, and the town looked exceedingly desolate and forlorn. He hailed a taxi, and made for Alexander's house.

The front door of Alexander's house was dark red, much the same hue as Alexander's face. Mr Ma pressed the bell, and a woman of fiftyish came out. One of her eyes was blind and milky-white, and her nose was enormous, and enormously red, as if she'd had a couple of bottles of ale. Otherwise there was nothing remarkable about her.

Mr Ma didn't say anything, nor did the old woman. She gave a nod, and her blind eye stirred unseeingly, then she walked into the house, with Mr Ma tagging along behind. The two of them seemed to comprehend one another perfectly, needing no words to communicate.

Alexander's study was so big and spacious that you couldn't take it all in at one glance. In one wall burned a huge fire heaped with logs, its flames shooting up as if intent on scorching the whole world red-hot. The carpet on the floor was so thick that, with each step you took, you felt your foot might sink right through it. There was only one big table, and three or four chairs. The table's legs were thicker than an elephant's, while the chair backs were scarcely an inch lower than an emperor's throne. All sorts of things were hung on the walls: photographs, oil paintings, Chinese congratulatory birthday scrolls, a host of swords, and three big stag's heads, their antlers splaying out dangerously.

Alexander was standing in front of the fire, a fat cigar in his mouth, its ash already piling a little tumulus on the carpet.

'Ma, old chap! Hurry up and get yourself warm!' Alexander pulled over a chair for him, then said to the old lady, 'Mrs Harding! Be grateful if you'd fetch us a bottle of port – the 1910 stuff.' The old lady's unseeing eye twitched, and she turned and went out, like some mysterious ghost appearing and vanishing without trace.

'I say, Ma, old chap, did you have a good Christmas? Any booze? Bet the little widow wouldn't let you drink your fill, what!' Alexander slapped the elder Ma on the shoulder, and Ma almost staggered into the fire.

Pulling himself together, Mr Ma gave a few chuckles. Alexander went off into peals of laughter too, his guffaws shaking and shuddering the table no end, in spite of its elephantine legs.

'Ma, old chap, I've found you a spot of work. Earn you a bit of extra cash. Would you be willing?' asked Alexander.

'What might it be?' Mr Ma seemed to find the words 'extra cash' rather distasteful, and, although his face retained its smile, there appeared around his upper lip the shadow of a sneer.

'No need to go into the details just now. It's five pounds a go. Are you game?' asked Alexander, jabbing his cigar towards Mr Ma's nose.

The door opened and in came an old black cat, followed by Mrs Harding. She bore a small tray, upon which stood a bottle of port and two glasses. She put the tray on the table, poured them some wine, then walked out, treading on the black cat as she passed.

'Drink up, Ma!' said Alexander, raising his glass of wine. 'Genuine 1910 vintage, what! What d'you think, then? Will you do it? Five pounds a go.'

'What exactly is it, though?' asked Mr Ma, drinking a mouthful of wine.

'Filming. D'you savvy?'

'But what do I know about filming? Don't pull my leg,' said Mr Ma, staring at the red wine in his glass.

'It's easy! Dead easy!' Alexander sat down and placed his feet, like two small boats, in front of the fire. 'Well, I'll tell you. I'm giving a film company a hand now, writing scenarios. Set in the Orient, of course. Since I was out East for a good many years, I'm more of an expert than the rest of 'em. Let me tell you: if you've got a skerrick of know-how, you can earn yourself a pretty penny. No good knowing something if you don't turn it into cash . . . Where was I now?

'Well, now, they're in the middle of filming now. It's set in Shanghai. They've raked together a crowd of Chinamen from the East End. Flat-nosed, slit-eyed creatures the lot. Just for the crowd scenes, of course – for mobs and rioting, to make the film look like the genuine China. So the quality of their noses and eyes makes no odds. They're a flock of sheep as far as the director's concerned. Farm scenes need a flock of sheep, and filming Shanghai scenes, you need a flock of Chinamen, eh, what!

'Back to the subject again. They want a decent-looking old Chinaman to play the part of a rich Chinese merchant. Not much acting or expression needed. As long as the fellow's presentable-looking, and can stand there like a proper human being, that'll do. There are three scenes to perform, at a fiver each. How about it? No acting involved. You just stand wherever the director wants, and walk a few steps whenever he tells you. Easy, eh, what? Pick up fifteen pounds for doing damn all! Are you game?'

Alexander's voice was growing louder as he spoke, and after reeling off this speech without pause for breath, he drank his whole glass of wine noisily, the liquid gurgling down his throat.

While he listened to Alexander ranting away, Mr Ma was doing some mental calculations. *I have to marry her, so I've got to buy a wedding ring. If I take the money from the shop, that young fellow Li Tzu-jung's bound to kick up a stink even if Ma Wei doesn't voice any objections. But if I play this part of the rich merchant, there's nothing to it, and I'll earn a clear fifteen pounds. I can buy her a ring with that. Not bad at all! Of course, acting's not what you might call respectable, and I'd be letting myself down socially by rubbing shoulders with that bunch of East End creatures. Yes, I'd be demeaning my station in life! But . . .*

'Well, you'll do it, then?' said Alexander, like some bomb exploding under Mr Ma's ear. 'Have another glass?'

'Yes, I'll do it.' Rubbing his ear, Mr Ma nodded.

'Good man! That's settled then! In two days' time, we'll go and see the director together. Come on, have another glass.'

They finished the bottle between them.

'Mrs Harding! Harding!' Alexander shouted. 'Bring us another bottle.'

The old lady brought them another bottle of wine, and trod on the black cat once more. The cat rolled its eyes and glared at her, but made no sound.

Alexander pressed close to Mr Ma's ear. 'Stupid cat, that,' he confided, 'Can't yowl or miaow – he's still too drunk. Got sozzled with me last night. If he wasn't always drunk, he'd never stick it out here, bet your life! You see, cats are invisible to that one working eye of Mrs Harding's!' And he went off into guffaws.

Mr Ma, too, burst out laughing, and laughed away all the cares and troubles of these few days past.

VI

THE NEW Year was the last dying ripple of Christmas. People didn't celebrate it with any wild enthusiasm, and the shops were open as normal. Although 'Happy New Year!' was forever buzzing in one's ears, there was nowhere the slightest sign of happiness or newness. The weather was as miserable as ever, with spots of rain whispering eerily down through the fog and making people tuck in their heads like listless egrets. At midnight on the last night of the old year, all the bells and sirens in the city rang out in unison. Alone and bare-headed, Ma Wei stood in the black shadows of the street, and spilled a few tears in secret. Partly because he was homesick, and partly because other sorrows in his mind chose that moment to spring forth. Then he wiped away his tears, and gave a sigh.

Got to keep at it still! Tomorrow's the new year, so you'd better forget the past.

The next day he got up very early, and after breakfast decided to go for a walk, somewhere away from it all, so as to start the new year boldly. He told his father to go to the shop in the morning, as he wouldn't be able to get there till after twelve o'clock.

He went out and took a bus straight to Kew Gardens. Over an hour later, the bus arrived outside the gardens. There was no one about, and the gate stood forlornly silent and shut. Turning away, he walked onto the big bridge nearby, where he leant on the stone parapet and gazed at the River Thames.

The water flowed grey and murky, and the old trees along the banks were silent and mournful, standing sentinel to the rippling river. There were no more than one or two black birds on the trees, their heads tucked in, chattering away in a grumbly fashion. By the bank was moored a row of small boats, bobbing up and down, looking fed-up and fidgety with boredom.

Ma Wei stared dumbly at the waters, his thoughts drifting with the grey ripples ever further into the distance, and now completely lost from sight. Far away, grey clouds joined the river and the trees into one grey mist, vague and vast, like some other world, as grey, pale and wretched as this world, but very far off and less clear to the eye.

In the distance, a clock chimed ten, and Ma Wei, slowly and heavily, as if loath to leave the bridge, went back to the gardens. The gate was open now. He placed a penny on the small iron table. The gatekeeper looked at him, blinking sleepily, and Ma Wei said, 'Happy New Year!'

Apart from a few gardeners, there wasn't a soul to be seen in the gardens. Ma Wei stuck out his chest and took in a few deep breaths, as if the fresh air of Kew Gardens had been specially served up for him. Old trees, young trees, tall trees and small trees, all had bare twigs and were taking a long rest, with no blossoms for people to look at and no fruit for birds to eat, only their thin, bent twigs and branches painting patterns of nature on the air. Squat evergreen bushes crouched behind the big trees, green-leaved but with none of the proud dignity of the old bare-armed trees. The ivy twining through the withered willows was like a huge dormant snake, and only the tops of the trees displayed a few greyish-green seedpods. The glass greenhouse in the middle of the gardens was draped with a sheet of white frost. You could still see the greenery inside but Ma Wei didn't go in. In the flowerbeds lining the paths there grew not a single flower, and their soil had all been turned, forming a mass of triangular clods.

Seagulls and small wild ducks were squawking and clucking away on the river, a plaintive note to their calls. Most of the ducks squatted with their heads tucked in, occasionally rubbing their flat beaks against their wings, looking rather doltish.

The seagulls, however, were by no means as sedate, and flew up and down through the air, sketching broken silver lines across the grey sky. Some little black ducks stayed floating on the water, trailing a V-shaped wake behind their tails, never flying or mounting the banks but forever swimming, with their eyes darting alertly around. And sometimes, at the sight of their reflection in the water, they'd poke their head down into it, and fish around. Poor black ducks! Ma Wei rather admired the little creatures, though. The wild ducks were too listless, and the seagulls too giddy and frivolous. Only the little black ducks kept hoping.

The grass that covered the ground was much greener than in summer, although not so lush and sleek. Near the riverbank it emitted a scent into the damp air, a very pure, faint and most pleasant perfume. As Ma Wei strolled the bank, gazing at the upside-down reflections in the water, treading the soft grass and smelling its aroma, he felt very easy and relaxed; yet an indefinable melancholy kept winding through his thoughts. Some big seagulls on the river saw him, and stretched out their yellow-beaked heads, asking for food. He hadn't anything on him to give them, and the silly seagulls exchanged dull sidelong glances with each other, as if expressing their disappointment.

When he'd gone as far as he could go along the river, he caught sight of the tip of a pagoda over the tops of the pine trees. Seeing the old pines and the Chinese pagoda, he felt himself grow more cheerful, and stood there in a daze for ages, his thoughts taken back to the Orient by that pagoda spire.

All that time the only people he saw strolling by were one or two couples, passing like shadows between the groves of trees. He took his bearings and set off towards the little bamboo garden. There was no one there, and no sound except for the gentle stirring of the bamboo leaves, hung with pearls of water. He bent down to inspect the small notices stuck in the ground at the foot of the bamboo plants. Bamboo from Japan, from China and from all over the East was growing there together.

This empire-building isn't just stupid self-aggrandisement, thought Ma Wei to himself. *They don't just seize lands and destroy nations: they also make a proper business of bringing back things from other lands and studying them. Animals, plants, geography, language, customs . . . they study the lot. That's where the empire-builders' real might lies. It's not just that they get their way by brute military force – they've got plenty of knowledge too. Yes, knowledge and military strength. Maybe military strength can be dispensed with some day, but there'll always be a need for knowledge. They're a terrible lot, the English, but, at the same time, so admirable!*

The damp on the ground made his feet feel decidedly icy. He left the bamboo garden and went to the azalea mounds, two small hills of soil with a little gully between them and azaleas growing all over them. It was a bit warmer in the gully than elsewhere, and the dry leaves on the ground had the smell of herbs.

Must look so beautiful in spring when the azaleas come out. Red, white and pink . . . like . . . The thought suddenly struck him: *like Mary's cheeks!*

Thinking this gave him an unpleasant feeling all over, as though his heart were about to leap out of his mouth. Unconsciously, he raised his thumb to his lips, and bit the nail.

No good. It won't do!

The thought of her made him hate himself, and filled him with impatience and remorse.

Got to forget her. Mustn't copy my dad.

Feeling in his pocket, his hand touched the little ring. He placed it on the palm of his hand, stared vacantly at it, then threw it violently to the ground. It fell into a pile of brown leaves, and, through a gap its diamond shone and sparkled.

He stood there, frozen, for a long time. Then, hearing footsteps, he picked the ring up and put it back in his pocket. As the gully path was winding, he couldn't see the person coming towards him. He turned and walked the other way, not wishing to see anyone.

'Ma Wei! Ma Wei!' came a call from behind him.

Hearing someone call his name, at first he walked on a few steps, but then turned his head.

'Hello, Elder Sister Ely.'

'Hsin-hsi!' Miss Ely wished him a happy new year in Chinese, and, smiling, shook hands with him.

She'd filled out a bit. A fox fur round her neck helped her to seem plumper than usual. She wore a blue woollen suit, and a floppy, green velvet hat, its brim dipping gracefully. She looked most calm and serene, and as she stood there in that narrow gully, you couldn't have said which was the more tranquil and undisturbed, her or those placid azalea bushes.

'Elder Sister Ely,' said Ma Wei, 'what's brought you out here so early?'

'You have to come here early. Later on when there are more people, it's not so enjoyable. Did you have a good time over the new year, Ma Wei?' She wiped her nose with her tiny handkerchief, and, as she bunched her fingers, her gloves moved in an oddly pretty way.

'Yes. Did you go anywhere?' They walked along, side by side.

'No,' she replied as they came out of the gully. 'The weather's so cold you don't feel like going anywhere.'

Ma Wei said nothing. There was a frown on his forehead, and his big dark eyes were fixed on the grass.

'Ma Wei,' said Miss Ely, looking at his face, 'why is it you're never cheerful?'

Her voice was very gentle, and her eyes glowed with kindness, intelligence and fine beauty.

Ma Wei sighed, and glanced at her.

'Come on, tell me, Ma Wei. Tell me.' She spoke very earnestly, and with complete sincerity. Then she gave a slight smile, one as pure and good as the smiles of the angels in paradise.

'Where to start, Elder Sister?' Ma Wei forced a smile that was even glummer than a frown would have been. 'And anyway, there are lots of things I couldn't tell you, Elder Sister, you being a girl.'

She smiled again, feeling Ma Wei's words to be heartfelt but a bit childish. 'Come on, tell me. You needn't bother about my being a girl! Why should a girl be denied the right to hear anything allowed to men?' She smiled again, as if laughing at Ma Wei and all the world's worthless conventions.

'Let's find somewhere to sit down for a while, shall we?' he asked.

'If you're not too tired, I think we're best off walking. We'll get too cold if we sit. I already have a tiny chilblain on my little toe. Right then, proceed, Ma Wei.'

'They're all unsolvable problems,' he said slowly and dully, still reluctant to tell her.

'Let's hear them. Whether they can be solved is quite another matter.' She spoke very cheerily, and a little louder, too.

'Well, I'll give you the gist of it.' Ma Wei knew that he'd no choice but to spill the beans, so he resigned himself to giving her the basics. If he tried to tell her in detail, he'd never find the words to give full expression to his feelings. 'I love Mary. She doesn't love me, but I can't get her out of my mind. I've tried everything, and tried, tried, and tried again. But it doesn't work. It's no good my feeling bitter towards myself or towards her. I know all about my career and other obligations, but she . . . she's on my mind.

'That's the first problem. The second one's my father. For all I know, by now he's engaged to Mrs Wedderburn. You know, Elder Sister, how the average English person regards the Chinese as curs. If my father and Mrs Wedderburn get married, she can say goodbye to her friends and relatives. They won't have anything more to do with her. And that'll make her life a living hell. And if my father took her back to China, she'd go mad after three days. Our customs are so different and my father isn't wealthy, and the misery of it'd be too much for her. I can't say anything to them. They're in love, and they want to make one another happier – whether it'd turn out as happiness or misery's another matter – so I can't tell them I disagree, can I?

'Then there's our business, the shop. All the responsibility's on my shoulders now. I love studying, but I have to look after the shop and our trade. My father's totally hopeless as far as business is concerned, and if I don't keep an eye on things, you can guarantee the shop'll lose forty or fifty pounds a month. And if I *do* look after the shop, then I can forget all about devoting myself to my studies. And if it wasn't to study, what on earth did I come here for in the first place?

'You're an intelligent person, Elder Sister, and fond of us, so please try to think of some good suggestions, will you?'

There were two aged Masson pines ahead of them, with a few shabby pine cones hanging on their twigs. The grey clouds thinned, and sunbeams of a most delicate beauty turned the pine branches a faint golden yellow.

As Ma Wei finished speaking, he stared at the pine cones on the trees. Catherine pulled at the fox fur on her shoulders to loosen it, and in so doing a warm fragrance floated up from her bosom.

'Isn't Mary engaged to Washington now?' she asked slowly.

'Yes. How did you know that, Elder Sister?' He carried on staring at the pine cones.

'I know him.' Catherine's face grew set. After a long pause, she smiled again, but very unnaturally. 'If she already belongs to someone else, why keep on thinking about her, Ma Wei?'

'That's precisely what's not so easy to solve!' Ma Wei's tone was mildly mocking.

'No, it's not easy to solve. Not easy at all.'

It was as if she were talking to herself. She was nodding her head, sending the brim of her hat gently quivering up and down. 'Ah, love! Love's something nobody really understands.'

'Haven't you got any good suggestions, then, Elder Sister?' Ma Wei looked a bit impatient.

Catherine didn't seem to have heard him. 'Ah, love, love!' she murmured again.

'Elder Sister, are you free on Saturday?'

'Why?' She suddenly looked at him.

'I'd like to ask you out for a Chinese meal. Can you come, Elder Sister?'

'Yes. Thank you, Ma Wei. What time?'

'Would one o'clock suit you? I could meet you at the Top Graduate.'

'All right then. Look how pretty those pine cones on the trees are, Ma Wei: like little bells.'

Ma Wei didn't say anything, just looked up.

Neither said any more. They came out of the grove of pines, went round past the flowerbeds and found themselves back at the main gate. Both turned to look back at the gardens. In there all was still tranquillity, serene and beautiful. Both in an inexpressible turmoil of love and sorrow, they put all that behind them, and walked through the gate.

Hmm . . . Happy New Year?

VII

OF THE few Chinese restaurants in London, the Top Graduate is the most popular. It's roomy, the food's cheap, and at any time of night or day it gives the impression that all the great minds and worthy nobility of the world are gathered there. Not only do Siamese, Japanese and Indians frequent it for their meals, but even English people, impecunious artists, members of the Socialist Party – sporting red ties – and fat old ladies – in quest of the quaint – often go there for a cup of Lung Ching tea or a bowl of chop suey. The artists and Socialists go there to demonstrate their lack of nationalist sentiments, and the old ladies to collect material for their tea parties. Actually, none of them like Lung Ching tea or chop suey.

Chinese diners are few, though, partly because real Chinese food can't be had there, and partly because the waitresses don't welcome them very much. Naturally, no respectable girls work in Chinese restaurants. Decent girls aren't going to get involved with the Chinese, are they now? They all know that when you're around Chinese people, mortal danger threatens constantly. But beautiful girls of doubtful virtue, ignoring such considerations, can, by batting their eyelids at gullible Indians, earn two or three pounds in an evening. Or, by flirting with a Japanese, they may at least get a packet of boiled sweets. They make, however, no attempt to charm any Chinese man, having no time for them as customers. Everybody despises the Chinese, and fallen women are no exception to the rule. Even they have their freedom of choice and their pride, and you won't catch any of them going out of their way to attract the attentions of those subhuman Chinamen. Why, of course not!

The restaurant manager, Mr Fan, is popular with everyone. His eyes are half-hidden, as if he's never properly woken up, but there's always a smile on his face. The artists are very fond of him, because he invites them to paint whatever they wish on his walls: women with tiny bound feet, wizened old men smoking opium, and pigtailed yokels kowtowing to Buddha. The artists know as much of China as do English people in general, but are able to express that knowledge in painting.

The socialists are very fond of Manager Fan, because he likes to say, 'Me no likee capitalisma!' The fat old ladies love him because he's forever using 'me' instead of 'I', and sometimes, when the mood takes him, even 'I' instead of 'me', all of which the old ladies feel to possess considerable entertainment value. If the average English person detests the Chinese, the wealthy, men and women alike, regard the Chinese as objects of amusement. The Chinese use chopsticks instead of cutlery. The Chinese drink their soup *after* the main meal. The Chinese drink tea without milk or sugar. The Chinese eat meals without potatoes. In the eyes of ordinary people, like Mrs Wedderburn and her daughter, all such things are absolutely wrong and deplorable. But in the eyes of the wealthy, fat old ladies, all these things are whimsically irrational, comically laughable, extraordinarily funny . . . In short, quaint.

Manager Fan and Mr Ma were already the best of friends, like brothers to one another. Although Mr Ma thoroughly despised businessmen, he'd made an exception for Manager Fan; the man was impeccably hospitable, his little half-hidden eyes forever twinkling in a smile, and since he would often make something special for Mr Ma, the elder Ma would have found it awkward trying to avoid an acquaintance with him. Anyway, he was, to be sure, a businessman, but even among businessmen some good chaps are to be found, aren't there?

When Mr Ma came to the restaurant for a meal, he never took any notice of the students there, as they all looked so ill-bred.

There was no common ground for conversation. And if those students happened to be Chinese, Mr Ma would ignore them all the more. When that bunch of students returned to China, they'd all become government officials. Recalling his own lack of good fortune in the matter of a government career, Mr Ma would sometimes even glare at them through his big spectacles.

With the socialists, Mr Ma got on like a house on fire. Although he didn't read the newspapers, and was thus unaware of the nasty things said about the Chinese each day, he knew full well that English people's attitudes towards him weren't the most favourable. Even those fat old ladies, so fond of hearing about China, weren't slow to make catty remarks in his direction. But the socialists were always sticking up for the Chinese, and cursing their own government's policies of aggression. Although Mr Ma had no idea of the meaning of 'nation', he was very proud of being Chinese, and as the socialists were the only ones to praise the Chinese, Mr Ma, when they did so, would automatically brighten and invite them to a meal. After they'd eaten, the socialists would call him a true socialist, him being willing to sacrifice his money to provide them with a meal.

If the elder Ma told the average English person that the Chinese drink tea without milk, the most polite reply that he could hope for would be, 'What? Without milk! How can you bear it? Dreadful!', which would make him twitch his little moustache and fall silent.

But if he told the socialists that you shouldn't put milk in Chinese tea, they'd at once declare, 'There you are! The Chinese are the only ones who know the proper way to drink tea, aren't they! After all, it was the Chinese who gave the world tea, and they know how it should be drunk. But for them, it'd never have occurred to us to drink tea, or wear silk, or print things. Ooh yes, the Chinese are so civilised. You've got to hand it to Chinese civilisation. Beggars description, it does!'

Listening to such words, Mr Ma would feel tickled pink. And, fully convinced that the Chinese were indeed the most civilised people in the world, he'd invite the socialists for another meal on him.

By the time Ma Wei reached the Top Graduate, Mr Ma had polished off a plate of dumplings and gone home, Mrs Wedderburn having decreed that he should return early.

The kitchen of the Top Graduate is in the basement, with tea and food being carried up by a dumb waiter that's much the same as the well windlasses used in China. This machine is Manager Fan's invention. It's not only simple to operate but also sounds spectacular as it rises swishing and gurgling, bearing with it a whiff of commingled food smells.

The dining room's divided into two: an inner and an outer part. The outer is long and narrow, with pictures depicting the history of Chinese civilisation painted on its walls – the old men smoking opium, and the young girls with bound feet. Also inscribed on the walls are such lines of Chinese poetry as 'During the Festival of Pure Light the rain is coming down wildly'. The inner part of the dining room is broad and low-ceilinged, its walls hung with a few cigarette advertisements. The Chinese patrons always prefer the inner part, because to them it has the air of a private recess for the genteel. All the foreigners prefer sitting in the outer part, partly to look at the pictures on the walls, and partly to watch the dumb waiter going up and down.

The outer part being full up, Ma Wei went to the inner part of the restaurant, found a vacant table next to the window and sat down. There were two Chinese students already there, strangers to him. Half-consciously, he gave a slight nod in their direction, but they completely ignored him.

'Waiting for someone?' asked a young waitress indifferently, cocking her head to one side.

Ma Wei nodded.

The two Chinese students were discussing how to request the legation to make a protest against anti-Chinese films. From their conversation, Ma Wei was able to make out that one was called Mao, and the other was Ts'ao. He saw that the one called Mao had spectacles and almost no eyebrows, while the one called Ts'ao was lacking both spectacles and decent eyesight. He guessed that Mao was advocating they should force the legation to issue a stern protest, and, if the legation refused, to drag them all out onto the street, from the minister down to the secretaries, and beat them up. Ts'ao was saying that when a nation's weak, it's no use protesting, and when a nation's strong, there's no need to protest, as others don't say nasty things. As they spoke, their disagreement steadily increased, and their voices grew louder and louder. Mao was raring to take on old Ts'ao there and then, but since Ts'ao seemed unwilling to accept a thrashing, Mao didn't dare lift a finger against him.

Then they both stopped speaking, lowered their heads to their meals and chomped away with fierce intensity.

Miss Ely came in. 'Sorry, Ma Wei, I'm late.' She shook hands with him.

'No, no, you're not late,' said Ma Wei, and handed her the menu. She pulled off her coat and sat down with unaffected grace.

Ts'ao and Mao glanced at her, spoke a few words in Chinese, then started speaking in English.

She chose a dish of fried spring rolls, and Ma Wei ordered three vegetable dishes to go with it.

'Been feeling any better these last few days, Ma Wei?' Miss Ely gave a little smile.

'Much cheerier!' replied Ma Wei, smiling.

Ts'ao glanced maliciously towards Ma Wei, and Ma Wei felt a bit uneasy.

'Have you seen anything of Washington?' asked Miss Ely quietly, looking at the menu.

'No. He hasn't called round for Mary for a few days,' replied Ma Wei.

'Ah!' Miss Ely seemed rather relieved. She glanced at Ma Wei, but as their eyes met, she turned her gaze elsewhere.

The first dish to come was the spring rolls, and Ma Wei served her one with his chopsticks. She cut her spring roll in two with her fork and took a very delicate bite of it, her chin moving daintily, then slowly swallowed the morsel. She ate so sweetly, so serenely and leisurely, so perfectly. There was nothing resembling Mary's ways in her manner.

Ma Wei had just cut his spring roll with his chopsticks and was about to pop it into his mouth, when the fellow Mao remarked in English, 'Foreign prostitutes are only for sleeping with. If you have the money, by all means take them to bed, but restaurants and cafes are not the place for a rendezvous. I must confess, Ts'ao, old chap, I object to young whippersnappers trotting harlots around with them all day.'

Miss Ely's cheeks went as bright as a bottle of red ink, but she was still very cool and calm as she put her fork down and made to stand up.

'Don't!' Ma Wei's face had gone as white as a sheet, and he uttered that one word through trembling lips.

'Look here, Mao, old chap,' said the one with bad eyesight, 'What's got into you? Not all foreign women are prostitutes.' He was speaking in Chinese.

'All those I know are,' said Mao, still in English, 'and I don't like to see people prancing around with them in public places.' He glanced at Ma Wei once more. 'What a way to show off! Taking her out for a meal to prove you can afford it! I'm more choosy about my cash; I prefer to spend the night with'em.'

Miss Ely stood up. Ma Wei stood up as well, and barred her way. 'No, don't. I'll take care of him. Just see if I don't.'

Catherine said nothing, just stood there, trembling all over.

Ma Wei went across and challenged Mao. 'Who are you saying things about?' His eyes glared, shooting forth two pure white flames.

'I wasn't saying anything about anybody. Can't one have a conversation in a restaurant then?' Mr Mao, while not daring to answer directly, was unwilling to back down.

'No matter who it was you were talking about, I'm asking you to apologise. If you don't, you'll get a taste of this.' Ma Wei thumped his fist on the table.

Old Mao sprang back like a tiny grasshopper, jumping into a corner, and shaking his head for all he was worth.

Ma Wei stepped two paces forwards, glaring at Mao. Mr Mao's invisible eyebrows were drawn together in a sullen frown, and he kept on shaking his head.

'We can talk it over. Settle it with words. No need to lose your temper.' Ts'ao tried to stand in Ma Wei's way.

Ma Wei pushed him with the flat of his hand, and old Ts'ao sat down again. Glaring at Mao, Ma Wei demanded, 'Are you going to apologise?'

Mr Mao was still shaking his head – now mockingly, in a fine old regular rhythm.

With a scornful laugh, Ma Wei took aim at Mr Mao's face, and let fly with a right and left, landing two clouts between Mao's spectacles and upper lip. Shaken to the marrow and in pain, Mr Mao nonetheless felt thoroughly gratified, and gave up shaking his head.

Two of the waitresses came rushing towards them, giggling, but both turned pale as they saw what had happened. Diners from the outer part of the restaurant also flocked over to have a look, curious as to what was afoot. Manager Fan of the hidden eyes came up and placed a restraining hand on Ma Wei's shoulder.

Miss Ely glanced at Ma Wei, then, head low, walked out. He made no move to stop her. She'd just reached the small door in the partition between the two parts of the restaurant when one of those watching the fun called out, 'Kay? It's you! What are you doing here?'

'Ah, Paul,' said Catherine, head bowed. 'Let's go home together, shall we?' She wouldn't look at her brother.

'Wait a sec. We'll go when I've got things straight!'

With these words, Paul pushed his way through the crowd, shoving past Manager Fan. Beaming broadly, Manager Fan tumbled to the ground, very cleverly managing to knock his head on the leg of a table, thus raising a greeny-blue lump on his forehead.

'Ma Wei, what do you think you're up to?' asked Paul angrily, thrusting his hands in his blazer pockets. 'I'm warning you: don't think you're man enough to go around with our girls! If you try pulling any more fast ones, you'll be asking for a jolly good thrashing!'

Ma Wei said nothing, but his pale face slowly gained colour.

'You see, Ts'ao, old chap,' said Mr Mao in English. 'No good comes of going round with prostitutes in public, does it?'

Ma Wei clenched his teeth and sprang at Mao. Paul swung a punch at Ma Wei's chin. Ma Wei stepped back a good few paces, but avoided falling by supporting himself on a table. With the speed of a dragonfly, Mr Mao escaped through the crowd. Manager Fan was about to intervene with a soothing word, but hesitated, beamed broadly, felt the lump on his head with his fingers and thought better of advancing.

'Come on! There's another where that came from!' said Paul with a sneer.

Ma Wei rubbed his neck and glanced at Paul.

Some Chinese people wanted to come in and settle things peacefully, but the English people stopped them. 'Let's see them fight. Let them fight it out! Let's have fair play – let 'em fight it out fair and square.'

The handful of socialists among them had always rallied to the cause of peace, always proselytised for harmony. But, all said and done, they were Englishmen, and as soon as they heard the words 'fair fight', they cheered from the bottom of their hearts, and stood by to watch the pair battle it out.

Ma Wei drew in a deep breath, tore off his collar and bounced back at Paul. Paul went pale now. He blocked Ma Wei's right hand, and with his free fist pounded at Ma Wei's ribs, sending him back to where he'd come from. Without any pause for breath, Ma Wei pushed himself off from a table, and immediately lunged back. He made a feint towards Paul's chest, then, not allowing Paul time to recover, delivered a crashing right uppercut to Paul's chin. Paul staggered back a few steps, then clenched his teeth and tried to come back. But while Paul was still preoccupied with keeping his balance, Ma Wei punched him again. One hand clutching at a table, Paul slipped downwards. His legs did their best to bring him upright again, but no amount of trying could get him straight. Ma Wei looked at him. Paul stayed down. Ma Wei stepped forwards, helped him to his feet, then thrust out his right hand towards him.

'Shake!' he said.

Paul twisted his head away sharply, refusing Ma Wei's proffered hand. Ma Wei sat him roughly on a chair, picked up his own collar, and slowly walked out, blood dripping steadily from his mouth.

The socialists watched Ma Wei, not saying anything but feeling rather bitter towards him. Normally it's easy to advocate peace, but when you see a foreigner thrashing one of your fellow countrymen, it's somehow quite a different matter.

Mr Mao and Mr Ts'ao had long since departed. Ma Wei halted outside the restaurant, looking for Miss Ely, but she was nowhere to be seen. He fixed his collar back on, wiped the blood from his lips and burst into wry laughter.

VIII

'MUM,' SAID Mary. Tears glistened in her eyes, making them look like blue grapes with the dew of the morning upon them. 'I haven't seen him for days and days, and I've written to him, but he doesn't reply. I'll have to go and see him. I've got to find out. Oh, Mum, I hate him now!' She fell into her mother's arms and began to wail.

'Mary, Mary, dear. Don't cry,' said Mrs Wedderburn, patting Mary's forehead, tears in her own eyes too. 'Washington must be so busy he hasn't had time to come and see you. Sometimes you can't give both love and work your full attention. Just trust in him; don't misjudge him. He must be busy. You're used to going out on Saturdays, Mary, and it's just because there's nobody to take you out today that you're feeling so low. Just you wait. He's bound to come this evening. If he doesn't, I'll take you to the pictures, eh, darling?'

Mary lifted her head, put her arms round her mother's neck and gave her a kiss. Mrs Wedderburn smoothed back her daughter's hair. Mary sobbed, wiping her eyes with her tiny handkerchief all the while.

'So you think he's busy, do you, Mum? Do you really think he is? So busy he's not even got time to write a postcard? I don't believe it. I think he's gone and got another girlfriend, and forgotten me. Men are like that. I hate him!'

'Don't say such things, Mary. Love always has its ups and downs. Be patient – just have trust in him. He'll be yours in the end. Your father used to . . .' Mrs Wedderburn broke off, and gently shook her head.

'Mum, you're always on about patience and trust. Why's it always the women who have to be patient and trusting while men can do as they like?' said Mary, looking into her mother's face.

'Now then, you're engaged to him, aren't you?' asked Mrs Wedderburn sternly.

'But both sides have to keep their word on the engagement.' Mary was sitting on her mother's lap, and the tips of her toes were brushing to and fro against the carpet. 'If he's breaking it off, then why should I suffer on my own? Anyway, I never wanted to get engaged. It was him who begged me to, and now look —'

'Don't say such things, Mary!' said Mrs Wedderburn quickly. 'Human beings can't escape the laws of nature. Men go after women, and women can't leave men. Marriage is the result of love, but it's also the trial of love, the real beginning of love. Listen to what your mum's telling you, Mary. Be patient, and trust him. He won't leave you in the lurch. And anyhow, I'm sure he's been very busy these last few days.'

Mary stood up, placed herself in front of the mirror, looked at herself, then paced up and down the room. 'I'm perfectly all right and happy on my own, Mum. I can do without men!'

'You?' Mrs Wedderburn said the word very tartly.

'Or when a man's needed, I'll just go and find one. Can't escape the laws of nature, can we?' Mary spoke sarcastically.

'Mary!' Mrs Wedderburn gave her daughter a look, and stuck her pink nose high in the air.

Mary went silent, and carried on walking up and down. She was feeling a bit more cheerful. Although she didn't believe a word of what she'd just uttered, saying it was a good way of venting her depression. Yes, she'd just go and find a man!

Until the innate human desire for a family has been eradicated, marriage is indispensable. Regardless of what rites and form the wedding might take, marriage there must be. Human nature's inherently selfish, and its greatest indulgence is to build a little family. This part of human nature won't be easy to eradicate, however much people may advocate the abolition of marriage.

Mrs Wedderburn hadn't taken Mary's statement seriously either, and was now trying to work out some way of cheering her up. She knew it was no good leaving her be, with time on her hands. Today's young people must always have something to do, be it dancing, car-racing, watching a film or . . . or whatever, as long as they had something. After a great deal of thought, she decided that going to the pictures seemed the cheapest choice. But she couldn't go that afternoon, because she and Mr Ma had arranged to go to town together.

At this point in her thinking, her thoughts took another turn. How could she mention to Mary the matter of her own marriage! *Mary's so proud – how can I tell her I'm going to marry an old Chink?* From there, her thoughts turned to the larger problem: whether it was in fact worthwhile embarking on such a marriage. If she wanted to maintain her social station, she'd do better not to marry him. But what about her own happiness . . . ? Should she actually follow Mary's suggestion? When you feel lonely, just go and find a man? The consequences might be even worse than those provoked by marrying a Chinaman. Society, customs and relations between men and women can never really be free. And anyway, what room, what place was there for real freedom between men and women? Questions without answers.

She dabbed her little nose and glanced at Mary. Her daughter was still pacing up and down, so fiercely she'd made her face all red.

'Mrs Wedderburn,' called Mr Ma in a soft voice from outside the door.

'Come in,' said Mrs Wedderburn, very merrily.

Pipe in mouth, Mr Ma swaggered in. The collar he'd just bought, a size and a half too big, and resembling the outer rim of a flour sieve, was swivelling round his neck. His tie was new too, but tied in such a manner that it hung all askew.

'Come over here!' said Mrs Wedderburn, smiling.

She adjusted his tie for him. Mary cast a sidelong glance at them. 'Didn't we say we were going into town to do some shopping?' asked Mr Ma.

'Mary's a bit . . . unwell. I wouldn't feel easy leaving her here on her own,' said Mrs Wedderburn, then turned to Mary. 'Come with us, eh, Mary?'

'No. I'm staying at home, just in case Washington turns up.' Having managed to lift her depression a little, Mary still entertained hopes that Washington might come round.

'All right, then,' said Mrs Wedderburn, and went out to change her dress.

Then Ma Wei arrived home. His face was still deathly pale, and, because Paul had punched one of his teeth loose, his mouth was still dripping with blood. His stiff collar was all awry, and there were spots of blood on his tie. His hair was dishevelled and his breathing was laboured.

'Ma Wei!' Mr Ma's neck swivelled a big circle in his collar.

'Oh, Ma Wei!' Mary's eyes went red round the rims, and her lips began to quiver.

Ma Wei smiled proudly at them, plonked himself down on a chair and wiped his mouth with his sleeve.

'Ma Wei!' Mr Ma gazed at his son's face. 'What's been happening?'

'I've had a fight,' said Ma Wei, his eyes towards the carpet.

'With whom? With whom?' Mr Ma's face paled, and his scrappy moustache bristled.

'Paul.' Ma Wei grinned, and looked at his hands. 'I beat him!'

'Paul! You —'

Mr Ma and Mary spoke together, then, neither wanting to cut across the other, there was a pause before Mr Ma said, 'Really, Ma Wei! We mustn't offend people!'

Mr Ma was very much afraid of fighting, and even when drunk would never think of so much as throwing a wine cup at anyone's head. When Mrs Ma was alive, they'd sometimes had rows, it was true, but fighting with one's wife was quite a different matter. Anyway, there's generally no danger of wives managing to overcome their husbands in a fight! When Ma Wei was little, Mr Ma was always telling him not to get into fights, and if he came across a fight in town, to steer well clear of it. And now look what had happened – he'd been fighting with a foreign devil here in London, and, what was worse, with Paul, the Reverend Ely's son! Gazing dumbly at his son, Mr Ma almost fainted.

'Oh, Ma Wei!' screamed Mrs Wedderburn as she came in, the image of a tiny startled bird.

'He's had a fight with Paul, and beaten him. What can we do? What can we do?' Mr Ma bleated to Mrs Wedderburn.

'Oh, you naughty young scamp!' Mrs Wedderburn went over and looked at Ma Wei. Then she said to Mr Ma, 'Boys are always fighting with each other.'

She turned to her daughter. 'Mary! You go and get some clean water, and wash his mouth for him.' And turning to Mr Ma again, she said, 'Let's go then!'

The elder Ma shook his head.

Without a word, Mrs Wedderburn grabbed Mr Ma's arm, and walked out, dragging him out after her.

Mary brought a bowl of cold water, some mouthwash and some cotton wool. First she made Ma Wei rinse his mouth, then she gently wiped his lips with the cotton wool. Her long eyelashes flickered up and down right in front of his face, and her blue eyes filled with charity and compassion as she gave his lips a few wipes, put back her head to take a look, and wiped them again. Her hair brushed his cheek, and it was like electrified golden wire, making his face burn. He lowered his head, not daring to look at her any more, but he was still able to feel the heat of her body, smell its tender perfume, and he began to tremble all over.

'How did you get into the fight, Ma Wei?' asked Mary.

'I was having a meal with Miss Ely when Paul came in and punched me,' said Ma Wei, smiling.

'Oh!' As she looked at him, Mary felt a bit resentful of his actually having dared to fight Paul. But she rather admired him too – not only for having dared to fight, but for having won. Hero worship's an outstanding characteristic of Westerners: the winner of a fight can do no wrong. And as Mary looked at Ma Wei, she couldn't help finding him quite adorable. His collar was crooked, there were spots of blood on his tie and his hair was tousled, all of which tugged most powerfully at her heartstrings. It was all so extraordinary, so fine, so heroic, such a striking revelation of his masculinity, his strength, his courage, his brutishness and his real flesh-and-bloodedness, all of which served to inspire a girl's faith in a man, and to heighten her warmth of feeling towards him.

She carried on wiping his lips, but her mind was now filled with these sorts of thoughts. She wiped slower and slower, this way and that, sometimes wiping onto his cheeks, and sometimes wiping up to his ear. In her blue eyes, his yellow face took on a golden hue and a white halo radiated from his head. He was no longer the detestable yellow-faced Ma Wei. He was the embodiment of manhood. He was a hot-blooded hero, a knight.

As she slowly wiped his face with her right hand, she placed her left hand gently on his knee. Slowly, trembling, he placed his hand over hers. And his eyes shone as he looked at her smooth red cheeks.

'Mary . . . Mary, you know what?' Ma Wei pushed each word out with great difficulty. 'Did you know I love you?'

Mary suddenly withdrew her hand and straightened up. 'You? Me? Oh, impossible!' she said.

'Why? Because I'm Chinese? Love goes beyond frontiers or nationality. Are the Chinese so worthless they can't even be allowed any love, then?' said Ma Wei, slowly standing up and looking her in the face. 'I know you don't think much of the Chinese, and you always connect them in your mind with murder, poisoning and rape. But we've been living together for nearly a year now – can't you see I'm different from what you imagined? I know you get all your ideas about the Chinese from lying newspapers and rubbishy novels, but you don't really believe all they say, do you? I know you're engaged to Washington, and all I'm asking for is for you and me to be good friends. All I want you to know is that I love you. Loving someone doesn't mean you have to love them physically, and if you could just understand how much I love you, and be good friends with me, I'd be happy for the rest of my life. I envy Washington, but for you, I'd do my best to not be bitterly jealous of him. I . . .'

Ma Wei seemed unable to say another word, felt unable even to stand there any longer. His heart was almost leaping out of his chest, and his legs couldn't resist gravity any more. He plonked down onto his chair.

Mary slowly combed her hair with a small wooden brush, saying nothing for ages. Then she gave a small smile. 'Have you seen Washington at all these last few days, Ma Wei?'

'No. Miss Ely just asked me the same question. No, I haven't seen him.'

'Catherine? What's she doing asking about him? Does she know Washington?' Mary's eyes opened very wide and round, her face flushed and she stuffed the wooden brush into her pocket, then rubbed her hands together nervously.

'I don't know,' said Ma Wei, frowning. 'Sorry. Didn't mean to mention Catherine. I've no idea what their relationship is. Luckily though, a person's not limited to one friend, eh?' He gave a faint smile, teasing her.

Mary shot him a sudden glare, and, without a word, rushed out.

IX

MRS WEDDERBURN, head held stiffly erect, walked on ahead, while Mr Ma, head tucked in, trailed on behind. As they marched the highways and threaded the byways, she walked faster and faster, while he walked slower and slower. The more people about, the more nervous she became, and the less he was able to keep up with her. If you married an Englishman, you could at least walk hand in hand with him, but it would never have done to stroll around town holding hands with an old Chinaman. Inwardly, she was rather repenting of what she'd let herself in for.

Inwardly, Mr Ma was doing the same thing. If you walked around with a Chinese wife, you could leave her trailing at least forty or fifty feet behind you, but now here he was, left miles behind by a woman. She halted and waited for him, and he bent at the waist and strode towards her. She smiled, and he smiled, and then neither of them regretted anything.

They went into a jeweller's in Holborn. Mr Ma asked to look at some rings. The shop assistant brought over a box of brass rings, of the type little girls play with, all fourpence each. Mr Ma asked to see some more expensive ones. The shop assistant gave him a glance, and fetched a box of silver-plated rings, three shillings each. Mr Ma said that he wanted more expensive ones than that, and the shop assistant gave a very forced smile.

'The next price range is over a pound!'

Mrs Wedderburn tugged at Mr Ma, her face bright red. 'Let's go and buy one somewhere else,' she said.

Mr Ma nodded.

'I'm sorry, madam,' the shop assistant hastily apologised. 'My mistake. I thought this gentleman was Chinese. It never occurred to me that he might be Japanese. We have quite a number of Japanese customers. I'm so sorry. I'll go and fetch some good-quality rings.'

'This gentleman *is* Chinese!' Mrs Wedderburn retorted.

The assistant took a look at Mr Ma, then brought out another box of rings, all of which were gold.

'These are all over fifteen pounds. Have a look at them, please.' Then he gave a spiteful smile.

Mr Ma summoned up his mettle, pushed the box back and asked, 'Have you any over twenty pounds?'

The assistant's face blanched slightly, and he thought of telephoning the police, for a Chinaman with twenty pounds on him must be a robber. As he saw it, an ordinary Chinese fellow wouldn't have been able to scrape a pound together, let alone be bold enough to go buying rings. While he stood there wavering, undecided, Mrs Wedderburn once more grabbed hold of Mr Ma, and the two of them walked out of the shop together. The shop assistant put all the rings away, and quickly made a note of Mr Ma's looks, build and clothing, so that, should any burglary occur, he'd be able to give the particulars to the police.

Mrs Wedderburn was beside herself with anger, and once out of the shop, she marched Mr Ma off, saying as they went, 'We won't buy one! We just won't buy one!'

'Come, come, don't be annoyed,' said Mr Ma soothingly. 'It was only a little shop, with nothing much of value in it. Let's go and buy one somewhere else.'

'No, let's not buy one. Let's go home. I can't bear it.' And without warning she ran out into the main road next to a fast-moving bus, and flew on board like a little swallow. Mr Ma stamped his feet pointlessly a few times in the wake of the bus, and watched it speed away.

Foreign women! he grumbled to himself. *Such haughty natures!*

Mr Ma felt rather sad. His woman was wilful, his son was

uncouth, he himself had met with no success in his quest for a government career, and the traffic was racing round him like mad.

What can an old fellow like me do? Nothing at all – nothing at all. Just have to put up with it. Head bowed, he muttered away to himself. 'I won't go home just now. Ignore the lot of them! The more I indulge them, the worse their moods. No, that's right, I won't go home just now.'

He called a taxi, and went to the Reverend Ely's.

The door opened quickly to his knock. 'I know why you've come, Mr Ma,' said the Reverend Ely, shaking hands with Mr Ma. 'No need to apologise. Boys will be boys. Always fighting.'

All the way there in the taxi, Mr Ma had been weaving a tactful speech, preparing himself to make an abject apology, and when he heard the Reverend Ely's words, he felt rather put out, and responded with a wry smile.

The Reverend Ely looked a bit leaner in the face, as he'd been reading Chinese day and night, and although he'd torn two dictionaries to shreds with all the wear and tear, he was still unable to understand the books he was trying to read. His little brown eyes bore an expression of despair.

'I really don't know what to do, Reverend Ely,' said Mr Ma as he entered the drawing room. 'You see, Ma Wei's an only child, and it's very difficult to know how to deal with him. That he should . . . to Paul . . .'

'Sit down, Mr Ma,' said the Reverend Ely. 'No need to say anything more about the matter. The boys have had their fight, and that's the end of it. When Paul was at school he was forever fighting, and there was nothing I could do about it. Not that I'd have wished to. I say, did you get to church?'

Mr Ma blushed, unable to find an answer on the spur of the moment. After a long while, he said, 'I'll be going next week. Yes, next week.'

Although rather peeved, the Reverend Ely didn't pursue the matter any further. He pushed his spectacles up. 'Look here, Mr Ma,' he said, 'you really must give me some help. My Chinese still won't do, and without your help, I just —'

'I should be most happy to help you!' said Mr Ma very cheerfully. He thought to himself, *Ma Wei gave Paul a thrashing, so if I can help the Reverend Ely, that will square things both sides, leaving neither of us in the other's debt, won't it?*

'Mr Ma,' the Reverend Ely seemed to have divined the nature of Mr Ma's thoughts, 'your helping me and the fight with Paul are two quite separate matters, though. If they fight, that's their business. Nothing to do with us. If you're willing to help me, then I must do something for you. Time is money, and we can't waste another's time for nothing, eh?'

'Oh, no.' Mr Ma nodded. Actually he was saying to himself: *These foreign devils are bloody pig-headed, and no mistake. Always have to have things cut and dried – bloody awkward!*

The Reverend Ely's eyes twinkled in merriment. 'When are you free, Mr Ma? What can I help you with? We must decide today, so that we can get down to work straight away.'

'I'm not busy any day.' Mr Ma hated the word 'busy'.

The Reverend Ely was just about to speak, when in came Mrs Ely with her head of unruly kapok. The furrows on either side of her nose appeared particularly deep, and her eyelids especially puffy. She looked both dumbfounded and stern at the same time.

'Mr Ma, what on earth was Ma Wei doing?' she demanded sharply.

'Yes, I came here to —'

Giving Mr Ma no time to finish, she stiffened her neck, and asked once more, 'What on *earth* came over Ma Wei? I warn you, Mr Ma, just you dare allow your Chinese boys to rebel! Just let them dare try to fight us! Twenty years ago, you trembled at the very sight of an Englishman, and now you have the cheek to fight us. Just see what happens if you kill someone here. This isn't China, where you can slaughter and beat people at random. There are laws in England!'

Not uttering a sound, Mr Ma swallowed several mouthfuls of saliva.

The Reverend Ely opened his mouth, then shut it again. Mr Ma looked most deserving of pity, but Mrs Ely was fearsome.

Ma Wei hadn't tried to kill Paul. All he'd done was knock him down on the spur of the moment, and although Mrs Ely loved her son, she would never have lost her temper simply because her son had got a few bruises. No, she was infuriated because Ma Wei – a Chinese boy – had dared to fight Paul. The moment an English person opens their eyes, they see the whole world at their feet: Hong Kong, India, Egypt, Africa . . . all are their domains. They not only feel proud of themselves, but they also crave acknowledgement of their undoubted and manifold superiority. To Mrs Ely, the humiliation of Ma Wei's daring to fight Paul was unbearable. (Although Paul had suffered no real injury whatsoever.) No one could stand for that . . . except the Reverend Ely. And she felt mildly annoyed at her husband on that count.

'Mummy!' called Catherine, opening the door a tiny gap. 'Mummy!'

'What is it?' asked Mrs Ely, turning round like a howitzer training its barrel on a new target.

'Miss Wedderburn wants to have a few words with you.'

'Tell her to come in!' Mrs Ely shot forth another shell.

Catherine opened the door and in came Mary. Mrs Ely hastened over to her in two strides, and said, smiling, 'How are you, Mary?' She seemed to have completely forgotten about Mr Ma and her husband.

The Reverend Ely also hurried across. 'How are you, Mary?' he asked.

Mary didn't answer them. She was holding her hat in her hands, and fiddling with the decoration on the front of it. Her forehead was very red and her cheeks and lips white, while in each of her wide, staring eyes hung a few unshed tears. Her head jutted slightly forwards and her feet were scuffing at the floor, making it seem as though she were having trouble keeping upright.

'Sit down, Mary,' said Mrs Ely, still smiling.

The Reverend Ely moved a chair over and Mary flopped down, sitting all askew and not bothering to straighten her skirt, thus leaving the majority of her plump thighs uncovered. Mrs Ely pursed her lips severely.

Catherine's face was pale too, and very calm, but with a rather anxious look in her eyes. She glanced at her mother, and glanced at Mary. She saw Mr Ma, but didn't greet him.

'What *is* the matter, Mary?' Mrs Ely went up, and placed her hand on Mary's shoulder, in a great display of charitable kindness. Then she turned her head and glared at Mr Ma, with considerable ferocity.

'Ask your daughter. She knows!' Mary pointed at Catherine.

Mrs Ely turned around to look at Catherine, saying nothing, but conveying her question with her eyebrows.

'Mary says I've stolen her boyfriend, Washington,' said Miss Ely slowly.

'Who might Washington be?' Mrs Ely's head swivelled, describing a semicircle in the air.

'That's the young fellow who rides round on a motorbike. Bound to have a dangerous accident sooner or later,' Mr Ma told the Reverend Ely in a low voice.

'My fiancé!' said Mary, then bit her lower lip with her two front teeth.

'Why did you "steal" him? How have you stolen him?' Mrs Ely asked Catherine.

'What do you mean, "steal" him?' Catherine retorted, very steadily and firmly.

Mary cried, 'If you haven't taken him from me, why hasn't he come to call on me recently? You told me yourself just now that you often go out with him. Didn't you say that?'

'Yes, that's what I said. I didn't know he was your sweetheart. All I knew was that he was my friend. It's a common enough happening for friends to go out and amuse themselves together.' Miss Ely gave a tight smile.

Mrs Ely felt rather pained as she watched the two girls arguing. *She* was the one who made the decisions; she wasn't going to just stand by and listen to their nonsense! She drew herself up and said, 'Kay! So you do know this Washington then?'

'Yes, I know him, Mummy.'

Mrs Ely frowned.

'You've got to help me, Mrs Ely – you've got to save me!' said Mary, standing up. 'All my happiness depends on it! Tell Catherine to let him go. He's mine! He's mine!'

Mrs Ely gave a dry laugh. 'Come now, Mary. Do be careful of what you're saying. My daughter doesn't roam the streets stealing men! You are mistaken, my dear. If Catherine really had done as you imagine, I should know how to deal with her. As her mother, I should certainly know how to discipline her!'

She puffed out her cheeks, then said to Catherine, 'Go and make a pot of coffee, Kay. Mary, will you have a cup of coffee?'

Mary said nothing.

'Let's go home, shall we, Mary?' Into the silence stepped Mr Ma with his suggestion.

Mary nodded.

Mr Ma shook hands with the Reverend Ely, and, not daring to look at Mrs Ely, walked over and took Mary's hand. It was icy-cold.

Mary's and Catherine's eyes met. Catherine was still very calm and serene. She smiled at Mr Ma.

'Bye-bye, Mary,' she said to the girl. 'We're still friends, aren't we? Don't think wrongly of me.'

Mary shook her head, and raised her hand to stick her hat on her head.

'Just a moment, Mary. I'll call a taxi,' said Mr Ma.

X

AT BREAKFAST, everybody had grim, tight lips. Mr Ma felt that his son had done wrong. Ma Wei found the very sight of his father irritating. Neither dared openly criticise the other, so all they could do was sit there, face to face, looking glum. Mrs Wedderburn felt sorry for her daughter, but even sorrier for herself. Mary considered her mother quite laughable, but was in no mood for laughing. They, too, sat there face to face both looking grim.

Poor old Napoleon. Nobody took any notice of him. He'd tried licking Mary's luscious legs, but she pulled them away from him. He'd tried sniffing Mr Ma's big leather shoes, but he moved his feet away. Nobody wanted to play. Disheartened, he ran out into the backyard, pouted at the roses, and said to himself, *I wonder why all those funny humans are grumpy? Can't imagine! Dogs and humans both look ridiculous when they sulk.*

After breakfast, Mr Ma slowly made his way upstairs. He put his pipe in his mouth, but hadn't the heart to light it. Mary gave her mother a cold kiss and went off to work. Ma Wei donned his overcoat, and was about to go to the shop.

'Ma Wei!' Mrs Wedderburn called him to a halt. 'Come here!' Ma Wei followed her downstairs into the kitchen. There were unshed tears in Mrs Wedderburn's eyes as she said in a quiet voice, 'You'll have to move, Ma Wei.'

'Why, Mrs Wedderburn?' asked Ma Wei, forcing a smile.

Mrs Wedderburn gave a deep sigh.

'I can't tell you, Ma Wei. There's no reason. Just look for

somewhere, and arrange to move. I'm sorry. I'm very sorry.'

'Have we done something wrong?' asked Ma Wei.

'Oh, no, nothing at all. And it's just because there's been nothing wrong that I'm asking you to move.' Mrs Wedderburn gave what might have been a smile.

'Has my father —'

'You mustn't ask any more questions. Your father . . . your father . . . he . . . There's nothing wrong with him at all! And you're a good boy, too. I love you both . . . but we can't carry on like this . . . We can't carry on. Ma Wei, you go and tell your father. I can't say it to him.'

The tears flowed down either side of her nose, falling fast.

'All right, Mrs Wedderburn. I'll go and tell him.'

She nodded her head, and gently dabbed her eyes with her tiny handkerchief. Ma Wei walked out and headed upstairs.

'Dad, Mrs Wedderburn says we've got to move,' said Ma Wei, bursting into the study without warning, hoping to gauge his father's reaction.

'Ah,' said Mr Ma, giving him a look.

'We'll have to set about looking for rooms, won't we?' asked Ma Wei.

'Just wait. Just you wait till I give the word,' said Mr Ma, snatching his pipe from his mouth and jabbing it towards Ma Wei.

'Righto, Dad. I'm off to the shop. See you this evening.' And swiftly and lightly, Ma Wei ran downstairs.

Mr Ma gave thought carefully for more than half an hour, but no ideas came to him. Go downstairs and speak to her? He didn't dare. Move without speaking to her again? Couldn't very well do that. Get the Reverend Ely to have a word with her? No, he might refuse to intervene: foreign devils never like interfering in each others' affairs.

'This is precisely why arranged marriages are the best option,' he muttered to himself. 'Now if there'd been a marriage go-between organising things, it'd have been easy to come to terms, wouldn't it? Get the go-between to run from one party to the other, doing all the persuading, and then everything goes right. But now look how impossible it is to settle matters – I can't call on anyone else's services, nor go and have a word with her myself.'

Another half an hour's thinking produced no further ideas. So he tried to imagine Mrs Wedderburn's line of thinking.

Now why has she all of a sudden got cold feet? Just can't imagine. For the life of me, I just can't imagine. Does she think I'm too poor? I've got the shop, though. Perhaps she thinks I'm too old? She's not so young herself, though. Does she object to my being Chinese? Tcha! The Chinese are such civilised people! Does she think I'm ugly? Anyone with eyes in their head can see how refined and presentable I look. Immaculate, impeccable, a thoroughly fine chap. Not want me? A curious notion indeed!

His scrap of moustache bristled, and he was well on the way to losing his temper. *Why would I have anything to do with her now, in fact? That's quite a different matter! These little foreign women with their tiny noses and their cunning ways . . . Pah! Who'd be bothered getting tangled up with them? Yes, that's what we'll do – we'll move. Good Lord! Who gives a damn!*

Mr Ma was growing steadily more agitated, his lips and bit of moustache quivering in unison. Suddenly he stood up, and, pipe in mouth, marched downstairs.

I'll go and have a drink, he told himself. *Yes, I'll come home drunk before we're through! No one's going to stop me either by God!*

He gently patted his chest, then jabbed his thumb into the air in a gesture of confident resolution.

Hearing him come downstairs, Mrs Wedderburn purposely came out to see him. He brushed her with a sidelong glance, plonked his hat on his head, put on his coat, opened the door and went out. Once outside, he turned his head and said to the doorknocker, 'Good Lord!'

Alone in the hallway, Mrs Wedderburn began to cry.

Ma Wei was sitting in the little back room of the shop, looking at the postcards and catalogues for the spring sale that were all piled on the table. But he stared at them unseeingly, his mind in turmoil.

Things look so easy, but when you get closer you find they

aren't so simple any more. The matters on Ma Wei's mind could be counted on both hands, but having counted them, he found himself still confused and devoid of answers.

Move. Have it out frankly with my father. Even if it means fighting with him. Then start on a new footing, and really make a proper go of it. All very clear . . . especially when it's only in your mind. But just try doing it, and what happens? A fat lot of good! And should they in fact move or not? Ought he in fact to have it out with his father? And should he really try to forget Mary? Easy to talk! All men encounter similar difficulties, but great men are distinguished by their resolute nature. Ma Wei had the right ideas but lacked the determination.

He sat there, staring, his thoughts as sombre as the wretched London fog, his soul as glum as if it were enclosed in a tiny box, deprived of all light, and doomed to gradually die. Some of the love in his heart went out to Mary, some to his father, and some to Li Tzu-jung, all dispersing, bit by bit, leaving only his flesh and bones sitting there. Yes, a living hell! He hoped a customer might come in, but none did, not a single one. He hoped his father might come in, but he didn't. His father never came in early.

Li Tzu-jung turned up instead. He was like a ball of sunshine, illuminating Ma Wei's whole being.

'Ma, old lad! Why aren't you sending those postcards off?' said Li Tzu-jung, pointing to the pile on the table.

'No hurry, old Li. I'll send them off today without fail.' Ma Wei looked at Li Tzu-jung with a real smile lighting up his eyes. 'And what have you been up to these last few days?'

'Me? Toiling away!' As he said this, he took off his hat, rubbed the brim with his sleeve and placed the hat with great care on the table. 'I've some good news to tell you, old Ma.'

'About what?' asked Ma Wei.

'Me!' said Li Tzu-jung, pointing at his own nose and blushing slightly. 'Me. I've got engaged.'

'What? You? I don't believe it! I've never even seen you out with a girl,' said Ma Wei, putting his hand on Li Tzu-jung's shoulder.

'Don't believe me, eh? Well, I'm not having you on – it's true!

My mother arranged it for me.' Li Tzu-jung's face went red all over. 'The girl's twenty. A good cook. Can make her own clothes. And not bad-looking, either.'

'So you've never set eyes on her?' asked Ma Wei, his face growing stern.

'Oh yes, I've seen her. When we were kids, we used to play together every day,' said Li Tzu-jung complacently, raking his hair all over the place.

'Li, old fellow, you've got such a modern outlook. How can you go and do a thing like this? Think of your future happiness! Just think it over. You're so capable and knowledgeable, and what'll she be? A country bumpkin who can't read a word, no good for anything but cooking and sewing. Just imagine it, old Li!'

'She can read a few words!' Li Tzu-jung inadvertently admitted the truth of Ma Wei's words.

'A few!' said Ma Wei, frowning. 'I don't approve of your attitude at all, old Li. Mind you, I'm not suggesting we're too good for ordinary girls. All I'm saying's that you ought to be more concerned about your future happiness. Just think . . . she won't be able to help you. She can't read —'

'She can read a few words,' Li Tzu-jung corrected him obstinately.

'All right, so she can read a few words, but do you think that means she'll be able to help you in your vocation? Your way of thinking and your knowledge, and her way of thinking and being able to read a few words – they just don't go together.'

'You're right, old Ma,' said Li Tzu-jung after a moment. 'But you must listen to what I've got to say on the matter. I've got my own stupid reasons for things, haven't I?'

The young men sat facing one another.

'So you think my way of thinking's too old-fashioned, do you?' Li Tzu-jung asked.

'Either that, or too muddle-headed!' said Ma Wei, a smile glinting in his eyes.

'I'm not the slightest bit muddle-headed! I think marriage is necessary, because the relationship between men and women is one . . .' Li Tzu-jung scratched his head, unable to think of a suitable expression, looked at the ceiling and continued. 'But nowadays marriage is a very knotty problem. I know the proper way's love first, marriage after, but just open your eyes and take a look at Chinese women. Take a good look, and that'll cool you down. High school and university girls, oh yes, but have they really learnt anything practical from their education? Or, to put it another way, do they know how to wash clothes and cook?

'Then there's love. Love goes hand in hand with helping each other, with sympathy, with looking out for one another. I can't love a girl who can't help me or sympathise with me or look out for me. No matter how pretty she may be, nor how modern her outlook may be . . .'

'And do you think that cooking and washing are all that's required of a woman?'

'Not half I do, in modern China!' said Li Tzu-jung, looking at Ma Wei. 'In China now there are no opportunities for women to work outside the home, because millions of menfolk are out of a job. So better leave the jobs for the men, and let the women help the men by looking after things in the home. You won't get any improvements in society or quality of life till you've got happy and secure homes. A little knowledge is a dangerous thing, and that's just the trouble with our students nowadays. Learn a few things, and they casually forget reality. When they've skimmed through a couple of romance novels, they go around like crazy, advocating free love. And where does it lead? Always the same old thing: a man and a woman sleep together for a night, full stop. They don't give any thought to their obligations towards one another, so they've no chance of any real happiness. I wouldn't say I bear them any ill will for it, but myself, I'd rather marry a country bumpkin who can cook and do the washing than have an affair with a girl who's "acquired a little knowledge" and read one or two novels.'

'All right. Say no more, old Li,' said Ma Wei smiling. 'Go and have a chat with my father. He'd be only too glad to hear all that stuff, I can assure you. Needless to say, you haven't managed to convince me, and I can't make you understand me, either. So the best thing we can do is talk about something else, otherwise we'll find ourselves coming to blows . . .'

'I know you look down on me,' said Li Tzu-jung, 'and think I'm too common. You think I don't understand modern ways of viewing the world. I know, old Ma!'

'Apart from the fact that you're too down-to-earth, there's no reason for anybody to look down on you, old Li.'

'And apart from the fact that you're too head-in-the-clouds, there's no reason for anybody to look down on you, either, old Ma!'

The young men both burst out laughing.

'So now we understand each other, don't we?' asked Li Tzu-jung.

'Yes, as far as the facts are concerned. In our feelings we're miles away from each other, further than the earth from the sun.'

'But we've got to keep on trying to understand each other, eh?'

'Without a doubt.'

'Right then, congratulate me on my forthcoming marriage!'

Ma Wei stood up and shook hands with Li Tzu-jung, but said nothing.

'Look here, Ma, old lad, I didn't drop by to chat about the problem of marriage. Honestly I didn't. I'd completely forgotten the main purpose of my visit,' said Li Tzu-jung, looking suddenly repentant. 'I came to invite you out.'

'What? Are you inviting me out to dinner to celebrate your marriage?' asked Ma Wei.

'No, I'm not! Invite you out to dinner? You wait, and if ever you hear your old pal Li's become a millionaire, you can start hoping for a free meal off me!' Li Tzu-jung went off into peals of laughter, feeling uproariously witty.

'Now, it's like this: Lady Simon's throwing a party at her house this evening. Dinner, drink, dancing, music – the lot. She'll be forking out a good few hundred pounds on this one evening alone. I tell you, Ma, old mate, these wealthy foreigners certainly know how to chuck their money about! But what do you think this evening's party's for? It's an appeal for donations to build a hospital. And can you guess what sort of hospital? An *animal* hospital! They've got hospitals for the poor now, so what about the cats and dogs of the poor? What are they going to do when they get ill? That's how Lady Simon goes on at Lord Simon when she's got nothing better to do. And Lord Simon told her, well, make an appeal for donations to set up a hospital for animals. See? It's the man who's got the ideas again, eh, old Ma? Where'd I got to?' Li Tzu-jung slapped his forehead and had a think.

'Ah, yes. Lady Simon saw me yesterday, and asked me to find a Chinese fellow for her, to do a few tricks or sing a song. First she'd asked me if I could sing. "Lady Simon," I told her, "if you're not afraid of scaring all your guests away, I'm not afraid to sing." She had a laugh at that, and said she certainly wasn't going to have her guests frightened off. So then I thought of you. You can sing a couple of passages from K'un-ch'ü opera, can't you? If you helped her out by singing this evening, you can guarantee she'd be most grateful. In my experience, the English working class are a no-nonsense, sterling lot, and the English aristocracy's pretty magnanimous. It's just the middle-class English I've no love for. Right, are you coming? Free food and drink for an evening, and you get a look at upper-class English society at the same time. The guests'll all be wealthy folks. What d'you say?'

'I haven't got a dinner suit!' Ma Wei's reply implied that he'd like to go.

'Got any Chinese clothes?'

'I've got a lined silk jacket, and my father's got a satin suit for formal wear.'

'That's it! That'll do! Come to the house with the clothes. I'll be waiting for you in Lord Simon's study, and you can change there. Then I'll take you to Lady Simon. If you put on your Chinese clothes and sing some Chinese arias, she's bound to be thrilled. Let me tell you something: remember at the end of last year how Lord Simon bought an embroidered Chinese skirt from us? Well, Lady Simon's going to wear it tonight. And the other day I found her an old squirrel-fur mandarin robe in Piccadilly. So this evening she'll be dressed from head to toe in Chinese clothes. Foreigners do have a fondness for the exotic. And anyhow, Chinese clothes are beautiful, no denying. When I become president some day,

I'll issue an order forbidding the Chinese from wearing Western clothes. Are there any clothes in the world more grand and elegant, or more beautiful, than Chinese ones?'

'When Chinese wear Western dress, that's a fondness for the exotic, too!' objected Ma Wei.

'Yes, but a common, tasteless one. There's no aesthetic judgement coming into it.'

'A Western suit's light and convenient,' protested Ma Wei.

'It's just as convenient for work to wear a simple hsiao-kua jacket. And a silk smock or linen smock's lighter than anything. And it looks good!' countered Li Tzu-jung.

'You're a stick-in-the-mud diehard, old Li.'

'And you're a crazy reformist, old Ma.'

'Right. That's enough. Say no more – we're about to start a fight again!'

'See you this evening at the Simons' residence, at seven. No need to have any supper before you come: it's French cuisine tonight. See you tonight!' Li Tzu-jung picked up his hat. 'Get a move on sending off those postcards and catalogues, old Ma. If I see them piled here like this again, there'll be a fight and no mistake.'

'Shall I send one to the future Lady Li?' asked Ma Wei.

'Yes, you could do that. She can read a few words.'

'These are in English, old chap!'

Li Tzu-jung stuck his hat on, gave Ma Wei a punch and hurried out.

XI

THE WARM wind turned the fine silky threads of rain soft, leaving them flaccid and feeble, dawdling in the air, instead of coming straight down. In town, the flower-sellers had set out their daffodils and other spring flowers, adorning grey, dark London with colours of hope. The seasonal pantomimes and circuses of Christmas and the new year had all packed up, and people were analysing the forecasts for the football cup finals and the Oxford and Cambridge boat race. The Englishman's love of gambling and of sport is as deep-rooted as his beef-eating and cigarette-smoking.

Pearls of water hung from the aged trees in the parks and red buds were already peeping forth on their branches. At the roots of the trees, the moist earth softly breathed in the damp air, and one or two small narcissuses were poking through the soil, their heads clustered with white buds. The grass was much greener than in summer, and, as the wind blew across it, the blades of grass would gently sway, shaking off their drops of water. London is noisy, bustling and chaotic, but these parks are always calm and beautiful, providing a refuge where people can take a breath of fresh sweet-scented air.

Hands behind his back, Mr Ma strolled over the grass, with a very light step for fear of trampling the worms that lay hidden underfoot. He hadn't brought an umbrella, and the brim of his hat was covered with beads of water. His shoes got soaked through, but that didn't stop him walking. Far from being flustered, he was filled with determination. *Keep walking!* He walked and walked till he reached the road. On the far side of the street was another stretch of grass, and in the middle of the road stood a memorial to artillerymen who'd died in the war. Mr Ma seemed to remember the memorial, but couldn't quite recall where he was. He never remembered place names, and didn't like asking the way either. He thought of crossing the street to the park on the other side, but there was too much traffic. It made his eyes dizzy just to look at it. He scraped the mud off his shoes, and turned back again.

He found a bench, and sat down for a while. An old woman leading a long-faced, short-necked dog sat down on it too. He looked at her askance, half glared at her dog, stood up and stalked off across the grass.

What rotten luck! Bang in the middle of the morning I bump into a woman . . . And one trailing a mangy dog around with her too! He spat onto the grass.

After walking a while, he reached the road again. Another road, though, where there was quite bit of traffic but no memorial. *Now what street's this?* he asked himself. On the wall in the distance was a street-sign, but it was beneath him to go over and look at it. The elite are never seen hunting around for the names of places, are they? No! He thought of strolling around the park again, but by now his legs were aching, and the insides of his shoes felt icy-cold. It'd be no joking matter if he caught a cold. Better to go home.

Go home? What, go home without having solved a single one of the problems that he'd brought out with him that morning? But if he walked round the park for another three days, or three weeks, or even three years, would he be any the wiser? Not necessarily.

It was difficult – so very, very difficult. If from childhood one's never suffered any troubles or hardship, and never undergone any form of discipline, how can one have a ready solution to any problem that crops up?

Go back home. Yes, I'd better go back home. See her, and see how things go.

He hailed a taxi, and returned home.

Mrs Wedderburn was just tidying up the study when Mr Ma came in.

'Hello. What was it like out?' she asked.

'Oh, very nice. Very nice,' he replied. 'It was fascinating in the park. Tiny flowers no bigger than that.' He stuck out his little finger to illustrate the size. 'Just come up out of the soil, they had. Has Mary gone to work? Is she a bit more cheerful today?'

'Oh, she's on top of the world today,' Mrs Wedderburn replied, wiping the window and not looking at him. 'Her Aunt Doll's died, and left her a hundred pounds. Poor Dolly! The hundred pounds has sent Mary quite scatty. She wants to buy hats, a gramophone and a fur coat, and at the same time she plans on putting the money in the bank so as to earn the interest. But you can't earn interest if you've spent the money. Can't have your cake and eat it, can you? That girl! She can't make a decision to save herself!'

'Washington still hasn't been round?'

'No.' Mrs Wedderburn shook her head very slowly.

'Young people aren't reliable. Not reliable at all,' he said, sighing.

She turned and looked at him, a hint of a smile twinkling in her eyes.

Mr Ma continued, 'No, young folks aren't reliable. For the young, love's just the excitement of the moment. They don't give any thought as to how it'll continue, and how to build a home and family.' Never since his birth had Mr Ma uttered such fine words, and what's more, he spoke them very naturally and sincerely, shaking his head as he finished in a gesture of passionately felt regret. That slow stroll round the park hadn't been a waste of time; it had certainly given him some poetic inspiration. Then he looked at Mrs Wedderburn with a distinctly beseeching expression.

She caught the meaning behind his words, but said nothing, just turned back to wipe the windowpane.

He stepped forwards two paces boldly, saying to himself, *Now or never! Do or die!*

'Mrs Wedderburn,' he said, and no more than that. His voice expressed all that he wished to say. He stretched out a hand, with wildly trembling fingers.

'Mr Ma.' She turned around, resting her hands on the window-sill. 'Our affair's over. There's no need to mention it any more.'

'Just because of those few remarks of the shop assistant when we were going to buy a ring?' he asked.

'Oh, no. There are lots of reasons. That only sparked things off. When we came back, I had a careful think about things. There are lots of reasons, and there's not one that could make me dare carry on with it. I love you —'

'Love's enough! What does anything else matter?' he interrupted.

'Other people! Society! Society's so good at killing love. We English are equal as far as politics is concerned, but in social relations we're split into classes. And we're only free to marry folks of our own class. You can't talk about marriage unless you meet somebody of the same station in life, and with the same amount of money. That's the only sort of marriage with any chance of happiness.

'It's only in fairytales that princes marry village girls. It's nice reading about things like that, but they can't happen in real life. And if they did happen, the village girl wouldn't be happy. The people around her, their way of life, their manners and their speech would all be different. Everything'd be strange to her, so how could she be happy?'

She paused for breath, absent-mindedly wiping her dainty nose with her duster, then continued.

'As for you and me, there's no class between us, but we're different races. That means all sorts of nasty obstacles in our way. Race is even worse than class. I've thought about it carefully, and I don't think we'd better take the risk. You see, Mary's affair's as good as done for, and for her sake I just can't marry you. Some fine upstanding lad might fall in love with her, but if he heard she had a Chinese stepfather he'd run a mile. You can't get rid of people's prejudices.

'When you first came here, I thought you were some weird monster or hobgoblin, because everybody speaks so badly about the Chinese. Now I know you're not so bad at all, but other people don't know that, and after we married we'd still have to carry on living among them. Their ingrained fear and hatred would probably be the end of us before a couple of days were out.

'English men often have foreign wives. But it's quite a different kettle of fish for an English woman to marry a foreigner. You know, Mr Ma, the English are such a proud people, and they despise a woman who marries a foreigner. And they can't stand a foreigner who takes an English woman as his wife. I've often heard people say that Eastern women are guarded, kept in the home like a treasure, and their menfolk won't allow them to show themselves to outsiders, let alone marry anyone from another country. Well, it's the same with the English, and what they can't stand above all is having foreigners meddle with their womenfolk!

'Mr Ma, we can't fight racial prejudice, and it's not worth trying. You and I can be good friends forever, but we can't be anything more than that.'

Mr Ma went numb all over, and he couldn't get a word out. After a long silence, he said in a quiet voice, 'Can I carry on living here?'

'Of course you can! We're still good friends. I told Ma Wei to ask you to move on an impulse, a sudden feeling. If I'd really wanted you to move, I'd have been on your tail making sure you did it in a hurry, wouldn't I? Yes, you stay on here – of course you must!'

He said nothing, just sat down with head bent low.

'I'll go and get Napoleon to have a little play with you.' With that excuse, she left the room.

PART FIVE

I

IN THE middle of March, bright blue skies suddenly appeared over London. The trees, with no cloud or fog to obscure them, all at once seemed taller and leaner. The elm branches scattered reddish-yellow scales, and the willow trees, with miraculous speed, acquired a draping of delicate yellow. In bright fanfare, the weeds in the gardens thrust their tender shoots from the moist soil. People's faces, too, all bore some trace of a smile, and the chubby dogs bounded around joyfully in the streets, barking at the shadows cast by trees. The cars in town looked much more cheery and colourful, nipping around so neat and nimble in the sunshine, with a distinctly blue hue to the smoke that puffed from their exhausts. All the golden signs and various other adornments above the shops shone in splendour, dazzling the eyes and cheering the heart.

But despite the weather, there were no smiles on the faces of anyone in the Ely family as they held conference in the drawing room. Paul, pipe in mouth, was frowning. The Reverend Ely was resting his head against the back of his chair, and from time to time stealing a glance at Mrs Ely. Her hair had not a hint of springtime, hanging dry and parched round her head like a mass of dead tree-roots. She carried herself, as ever, very stiffly erect, and her eyes held a venomous gleam, while the ditches either side of her nose were as deep and dry as two frozen moats.

'We must go and bring Catherine back! I shall go and fetch her myself. Yes, I shall go in person!' said Mrs Ely through clenched teeth.

'I want nothing to do with her – so don't be in any hurry to fetch her back here, Mater!' said Paul, with a determined air.

'If we don't bring her back, and Mary sues Washington, it will be the end of us. Yes, the end! Let none of us entertain any doubts on that score! I shall not be able to continue with my church work, nor will you, Paul, be able to carry on at the bank. If she goes to court, we shall be utterly finished, ruined. None of us will be able to bear the publicity. There is nothing else for it – we must bring her back.' Mrs Ely spoke with great anguish and urgency, stressing her every word.

'If she's quite happy to run off with some fellow, there's nothing we can do to make her come back,' said Paul, an expression of fury on his face. 'If only I'd known what she was like! Selfish she is, wilful, thoroughly shameless! If I'd known!'

'You mustn't hate her so . . . It does no good. It's no use. It will break my heart if you hate her. Since her childhood, I have *never* for a single day neglected to instruct her in the Holy Bible. Never for a single day have I not watched her like a hawk – have I now? It's me, not you, who should feel bitter. But that would be no help. Hating her will not solve anything. Anyway, it is our duty to reform her through the power of love. She may have run away, but we still wish her here, as long as she consents to abandon evil and return to the true path, as long as she heeds the teachings of Christ, as long as she promises never again to entertain such misguided notions.

'I shall go and look for her, and, though I seek till the ends of the earth, I shall find her, and bring her back to us. I know that she cannot be happy now, so I shall find her, and restore her to her joyful self. I know that her happiness lies here with me, for it is my duty to ensure my daughter's happiness, no matter how terribly she lets me down.'

Mrs Ely reeled this all off in one breath, as if she'd made mental notes and was delivering a practised recitation. There was a certain dampness about her eyes, which seemed to be tears of a sort, but they were quite different from the tears of ordinary mortals.

'Oh, no, she's certain not to come back,' said Paul viciously. 'If she'd had any love for us, she would never have run off with that

Washington fellow. You do what you think, Mother. I'm going to ask the bank for a transfer to India, or Egypt, or Japan. Anywhere will do. I couldn't bear the sight of her again. If England ever goes to the dogs, it will be the fault of such selfish men and women! People who have no love for their family, no love for their country, nor any love for God!' he bellowed, and stood up and marched out.

The Great War in Europe had not only shaken the economic foundation of people's lives, but had also shaken people's ways of thinking. Many questioned the old ideas of morality and of the old concepts current in the world, and began to look at things in new ways. They sought in one go to throw off all the fetters of old powers and influences, and to create a new humanity that would live in peace, free from wars. Marriage, family, morals, religion and politics were all turned upside down by such new ways of thinking, and it looked almost as if they were about to be completely eradicated.

Some of the more broad-minded and generous-spirited people let themselves drift with the new tide, and through it attained new and substantial freedoms. Others, more set and narrow in their ways, reacted against the tide, meeting it, resisting it with all their might, and seeking to cling to the broken fragments of old things that floated on the waves. These two crowds of people surged to and fro, neither comprehending the other, neither concerned for the other, both mutually suspicious and resentful of each other. Between father and son, brother and sister, irremediable tragedies were enacted. The English are conservative, but even the English were tossed within this raging tide.

There was a difference of at least a hundred years between Catherine's outlook and that of Paul. She was for peace and freedom, against marriage and religion, and wanted nothing of narrow patriotism, nor an aristocratic form of representative government. As for Paul, he was for both war and patriotism, and for the status quo in marriage and religion. In Catherine's view, the recent war had been wholly evil, and everything that preceded it dreadful. In Paul's view, the last war had been a glorious one, and everything prior to it golden. Her outlook was the result of study, while his opinions were constructed on the basis of his nature and instinct.

She was a young person and so was he: two kinds of young people of the postwar period. Always with that smile of hers, she was questioning things, while he went around passing cut-and-dried judgements with his pipe in his mouth. She wanted to know and understand. He wanted conclusive results and effective action. She used her brain while he used his intuition. Neither of them understood the other, and he hated her, because he judged her on the basis of intuition, emotions and tradition.

Without a worry, she went to live with Washington, because they loved one another. Why should they buy a wedding ring for her? What need was there to go to church and stroke the bible? Why should she have to take his surname? To all these questions Catherine gave a smile.

Mary, much like Paul, would insist on a wedding ring, on going to church and on being called by her husband's surname. Her behaviour was that of a wild kitten, but her outlook was that of a dead cow. She liked to display her pale legs for men to see, but revealed them only from the knee downwards, and if a breeze whisked her skirt up a little, she would hastily pull it down, looking awkward and silly. Through her movements, her manner, her hats and her clothes, she lived to make men look at her. Beauty was her ultimate weapon, and she wielded it with the goal of grabbing a man and building a cosy home. Beyond that, nothing more! Yes, her aim in life went no further than that.

Mary didn't relish the idea of having children. That, to be sure, was in accord with one of the aspects of the new thinking, but in her case it was simply a matter of her own convenience. Having children might ruin her looks, and children meant a lot of tiresome bother. She objected to having children – but she'd never have admitted to agreeing with any of the new ideas about birth control.

Washington had compared Mary and Catherine, and decided to live with Catherine. He still loved Mary, and hadn't forgotten her, but his relationship with Catherine seemed even to surpass love. This thing that transcended love was a new, postwar discovery, and no one yet knew what it was. It was something that couldn't be pinned down by any definition – something tremendously free, exceptionally full of life. Mary could never comprehend it, nor would she be able to enjoy it, for her definition of 'love' confined itself to marriage, husband and wife, home. And this special some-thing wasn't restrained by the fetters of established conventionality.

Catherine and Washington wouldn't have felt ashamed to go hand in hand to see Mrs Ely, nor would they have been afraid of going to see Mary. What intimidated them was Mrs Ely's and Mary's lack of understanding. Neither he nor she was afraid of anyone, but they were rather reluctant to clash with the old ways of thinking; the matter was bigger than them. It was one of con-flicting tides of world opinion: not a problem of individuals but an historical change. They were both at one with their consciences, but people's consciences have different standards. That being the case, they knew the best thing they could do was just not show their faces, and avoid seeing Mrs Ely or Mary.

'Poor Paul! He so much wants to get on! I know what he must be going through,' muttered Mrs Ely to herself after Paul had gone.

The Reverend Ely glanced at her, realising that the time had now come for him to speak. He gave a couple of coughs, then said slowly and deliberately, 'Kay's not a bad girl. Don't think ill of her.'

'You always stick up for her. If you hadn't spoilt her, she would never have been capable of such scandalous deeds!' Mrs Ely shut the old clergyman up with one blast from her cannon.

The Reverend Ely felt decidedly resentful, but didn't dare lose his temper.

'I shall go and find her. With the words of Jesus Christ I shall persuade her to return!' Mrs Ely forced a smile as benevolent as the devil's grin.

'It's no good your going to look for her. She won't come back,' said the Reverend Ely quietly. 'If the two of them are happy to-gether, then she certainly won't come back. And if they're not happy, well, she's quite capable of earning her own living without us. I wish she would come back, since I love her so dearly.' The rims of his eyes moistened, and he continued. 'But I wouldn't force her to return. She has her own ideas and opinions. If she's able to put them into practice, it will bring her satisfaction and contentment, and I've no wish to snatch such happiness away from her. The present matter rests entirely with Mary. If Mary takes it to court, it will be the end of us. If not, all will be well. It rests with her, and her alone. You needn't go looking for Kay – I'll go and see her, and hear what she's got to say. Then I'll go and beseech Mary to grant us mercy.'

'*Beseech?* Mary? Beseech!' said Mrs Ely, pointing her finger at his nose. She'd never used the word 'beseech' in reference to her dealings with anyone except God.

'Yes, beseech her.' The Reverend Ely had become very forceful, too, and his voice, although quiet, was firm.

'Your daughter's run off, and you're going to *beseech* a little hussy like Mary! Think of your position, Reverend Ely!'

'My position! You and Paul might have some position, but not me. All *you* want to bring Kay back for is to save yourself from disgrace, with no consideration for her happiness. At the same time, you've not given the slightest thought to Mary's grief. I have nothing to lose. If Mary agrees to do as I ask, it will in effect be an act of self-sacrifice on her part, and she will be helping to fulfil Catherine's happiness. If she refuses to help, it is quite within her rights, and she is free to do so. I cannot force her. Poor Mary!'

Mrs Ely thought to grab something and throw it at her husband's head, but, suddenly mindful of God, she refrained. Shooting him a malevolent glare, she stalked out with her head of kapok quivering.

The Reverend Ely and Mrs Wedderburn sat face to face, while Mary, holding Napoleon, sat in front of the piano. In the light the Reverend Ely's face was deathly pale.

'Mary, Mary,' he said, 'Catherine has done wrong, and Washington has too. They have both done you an injustice. But things have gone so far that if you now take action against him, you will ruin not only him, but me too. You have a strong case in the eyes of the law, and if you seek damages, you can be sure of getting them. What with the damages and the cost of the proceedings, you would certainly send him bankrupt. And at the same time, the publicity would mean utter ruin for me and my family.

You have ample cause to sue, and all I can do is beseech you to show him a little lenience. Washington's no young rogue, nor is Catherine a malicious girl. They've simply been unfair in their conduct towards you. If you can find it in you to show them mercy, they will owe their life's happiness to your kindness.

'If you refuse to forgive them, I wouldn't for a moment call you too harsh, for you have every right. I'm merely begging you to show extraordinary compassion, and in so doing redeem my family and help the couple towards an unmarred happiness. In law they should be punished, but emotionally they may be forgiven. They have acted under the impulse of love. One can be sure that they didn't intend to belittle you or hurt you, Mary.

'Tell me, now: will you spare them or punish them? Tell me, Mary.'

The girl's teardrops fell onto Napoleon, and she made no reply.

'I think the proper thing would be to decide matters in court, wouldn't it, Reverend Ely?' said Mrs Wedderburn, her lips trembling.

The Reverend Ely said nothing, but clasped his forehead between his hands.

'No, Mum!' said Mary, rising very abruptly to her feet. 'I hate him! I hate him! I . . . I love him. I'm not going to punish him. I couldn't send him bankrupt. But you've got to make him come and tell me himself that it's over. I can't bear hearing things second-hand. Don't you bother yourself about it, Mum. And you needn't interfere either, Reverend Ely. I've got to see him – and I've got to see her too. Just to have a look at them . . . Ha ha! Ha!' Mary broke into manic laughter.

'Mary!' Mrs Wedderburn, flustered and alarmed, went over and put her arm round her daughter.

The Reverend Ely sat there dumbfounded.

'Ha ha! Ha ha!' Mary was still laughing hysterically, and her face was bright red. Then, after a few more laughs, she laid her head on the piano and began to cry.

Napoleon ran to the Reverend Ely, cocked his head on one side and looked quizzically at him.

II

EVERYWHERE WAS green in Welwyn Garden City, and during summer the scent of flowers was in every street. There was only one big shop in town, and it sold everything. The whole place used electricity, the use of coal being forbidden so as to keep the air pure. Only a few of the streets were thoroughfares for traffic, which made everything tranquil day and night.

The whole town was close to nature, but the maintenance of this closeness all depended on science. Electricity, the new forms of architecture and horticulture in the houses and gardens, and the layout of the streets – all were scientific. This use of science was a great improvement on nature. To make the new town so very natural, so very clean, so fine and beautiful, and so very hygienic, was something that could never have existed without scientific knowledge.

Intellectually, science is a quest for absolute truth, and in its practical applications it can provide a certain amount of happiness for humankind. Those who misuse science don't understand science, and attacking science because of the misuses to which it is put is likewise a misunderstanding of science. There are but two joys in human life: the quest for truth and the pleasures of the senses. Only science can cater for both.

The two young men had taken a bus out to Barnet, and from there walked to the new town. They followed the railway line, with pretty scenery all the way. The green grass-covered land bobbed up and down, and the woods were sparse one moment and dense the next. Private houses lay scattered all over the place, some hiding behind trees, some standing in isolation along the roadside. In the small gardens of some were a few white hens, while in others there hung white shirts, and everything had a distinctly cosy, homely air about it.

There were people out walking, both along the road and in the woods. Old ladies grasping umbrellas and wearing complicated hats were heading for church. Young boys and girls were strolling round side by side in the woods, and other youngsters rode off on bicycles into the more distant countryside. Middle-aged men in white jackets were taking their children into the grassy meadows to watch the cows, the pigs, the birds and so forth. Bands of children were playing football or tumbling around on the grass.

Most of the working-class men had small clay pipes in their mouths, and, newspapers in hand, were standing at the doors of their houses reading. Sometimes they too would pop into the meadows for a chat and a joke with the sheep and cows.

The English countryside's very pretty. Everywhere's green, and everything's so natural and unaffected – not to mention peaceful.

'Li, old fellow,' said Ma Wei, 'what's your view of Miss Ely's affair? I don't suppose you agree with her?'

Li Tzu-jung was absorbed in the contemplation of an evergreen tree covered in red berries, and he didn't seem to have heard what Ma Wei had said.

'Eh? What? Oh, Miss Ely? There's nothing about her I'd find fault with. Very beautiful, those red berries on that tree, don't you think?'

Ma Wei casually glanced at them. 'Oh yes, they are.' Then he asked, 'Don't you consider her conduct strange?'

'What's strange about it?' said Li Tzu-jung, smiling. 'That sort of thing often happens. I certainly wouldn't take the risk, though. With her, well, she's so capable. And she's got her wits about her, and knows what she's doing. She wants to live with a man, so she goes and does it. She's free to do it, and she can be a help to him. And if she decides she no longer wants to be with him, all they have to do is separate, and she can go her way and earn her own keep. You see, she writes pretty good English, can type and do shorthand, she's good at organising things, and she's not bad-looking, either. So what's she got to be afraid of?

'Anybody who tries living the new way has got to have something up here.' Li Tzu-jung tapped his head knowingly. 'They'd never survive without real skills; ranting wild slogans won't get them anywhere. Let me tell you, old Ma, the one thing I admire about foreigners is their ability to earn money! Take that old bird, Mrs Ely. She earns three or four hundred a year. Look at Mary. Like a little cloth doll, but she's got a gift for selling hats. Look at that rude old blunderbuss Alexander: he can write scenarios for a film company. And that fellow at the museum I met last week: a poet of sorts, and able to translate Chinese poems, so he makes money by doing it. I asked him, "Chinese poetry must be worthwhile, otherwise you wouldn't translate it, would you?" Guess what he said? "Chinese things are very fashionable nowadays, and you can make some easy cash translating a bit of Chinese poetry."

'Yes, they're real dab hands at making money, really terrific. And that's the only reason that their fine arts, music and literature can flourish as they do, because if money's in short supply you don't have time for the sort of mental luxury that creates the arts. Just ask yourself how much that roomful of antiques of Lord Simon's is worth! And he told me that when he dies, he's going to leave the lot to the British Museum. Does any Chinese person leave a roomful of antiques to a museum? When you can't even afford a doughnut, who's going to buy antiques? What a joke!

'It's only when you've got plenty of money that you're likely to start splashing it around. It's only when you've got plenty of money that you can promote the arts and charities. Money's not a bad thing if people use it for a noble cause. I hope I become a wealthy man, then I'll fork out my millions and set up a library, run a good newspaper, start up a museum, an art gallery, a new theatre . . . and so many other things. Yes, so many things – so many worthwhile things!'

Li Tzu-jung inhaled a breath of air. The air was wonderfully fragrant and sweet.

Ma Wei was still thinking about Miss Ely's affair, and had tuned out as Li Tzu-jung spoke. 'Poor Mary!' Ma Wei gave a sigh.

'You haven't heard a word of what I've been saying, have you, old Ma?' Li Tzu-jung was exasperated.

'Yes, I heard you. I heard it all.' Ma Wei smiled. 'But poor Mary.'

'Sod your Mary, and your Catherine! Poor? I'm the one to be pitied. Slaving away dawn till dusk, and still can't make my fortune,' bellowed Li Tzu-jung, flinging his arms and legs around in wild gestures, and scaring a flock of small birds out of the trees.

Ma Wei said nothing more, just walked on, marching forwards for all he was worth. His head was bowed, as if weighed down by an excess of thoughts.

Li Tzu-jung didn't utter a word either, but stretched his stocky legs, and began to keep pace with Ma Wei. The two of them walked three miles without a stop, puffing and panting from their exertions. Their faces were red all over, and their fingers began to swell. Neither was going to slow down for the other, and neither spoke. They just walked and walked, more and more energetically.

Ma Wei looked at Li Tzu-jung, and Li Tzu-jung threw out his chest. Both of them carried on walking.

'Poor Mary!' said Li Tzu-jung suddenly, imitating Ma Wei's tone of voice.

Ma Wei halted, and looked at him. 'You're deliberately making fun of me, old Li,' he said. 'What about Mary? And what's poor about her?'

'Well, you're always telling me I'm too down-to-earth,' said Li Tzu-jung, 'so I'll have to learn to be a bit more sentimental, won't I?'

They walked on more slowly.

'You don't understand me, Li, old fellow,' said Ma Wei, grasping Li Tzu-jung's arm. 'To tell the truth, I still can't stop thinking about Mary. There's just nothing I can do about it. Keeps me awake till midnight sometimes – honestly, it does. I think desperately about your advice, about how hopeless my father is, about my career, about studies and learning, but whatever I try to think about, I can't get her out of my mind. She's more beautiful than a fairy, and at the same time more dreadful than any demon!'

'Ma, my dear lad, you and me are like brothers to each other, so may I, once more, advise you, whatever you do, to cut out the crazy notions!' said Li Tzu-jung very sincerely. 'I think she'll sue Washington, and get at least five or six hundred pounds' damages. With that sum of money, when she gets all dolled up and has her photo in the papers, I guarantee that within three months she'll be married to some other bloke. Foreigners are scared stiff of the papers, but only too glad to have their name and photo appear in them. A bit of publicity goes a long way. Who knows who young Mary is now? Nobody! But once she hits the headlines, she's made. She'll get maybe several hundred letters a day proposing to her, and your prospects'll be absolutely nil. Forget it, old Ma!'

'No, you don't know Mary. She wouldn't do things like that,' said Ma Wei very emphatically.

'Just wait and see. She'd get rich and famous in one go, and she's no fool. Anyhow, the law's the law, and Washington'll be done for breach of promise.'

'So there's no hope for me?' Ma Wei sounded very dejected.

Li Tzu-jung shook his head.

'I'll have another try, and if she refuses me again, I'll give it up,' said Ma Wei.

'As you like,' said Li Tzu-jung in a disapproving tone.

'Tell you what, old Li, I'll have a word with her, and then I'll have everything out quite frankly with my father about the shop. If she turns me down, there's nothing I can do about it. But if my father won't listen to me, I'm out the door. If he refuses to bother about anything, and just keeps on wasting money, there's no point in any further discussion. I've got to study. I can't stick around in a shop all day. I've put up with it all these months, but the fact's lost on him. Unless I spell it out for him, he'll never understand my side of things. I've got to tell him.'

'Yes, it'd be a very good thing to tell him straight, without beating around the bush. But —' Li Tzu-jung was looking at the milestone by the roadside. 'Ha, we're nearly there. It's almost one o'clock. Where shall we go for a bite to eat? Bound to be no restaurants in the new town.'

'Never mind. There may be a pub at the station where we can get a glass of beer and a couple of sandwiches. That'll do,' said Ma Wei.

Not far from the station there was a slope with a fair number of pine trees on it. The two young men sat on the slope, and gazed over the new town. The houses, big and small, were all built at the foot of the slope, and beyond the houses lay a smooth, shiny highway, the main Cambridge road, along which cars sped to and fro, looking like tiny black shuttles. The sky was overcast but there wasn't any mist, and far away you could even see the old city of Welwyn, the spires of its churches towering up above the treetops like great bamboo shoots. Between the two cities lay an unbroken stretch of undulating green land, on which sheep and cows grazed in paddocks. As a flock of sheep began to run, it looked like one long drift of snow blown astir by the wind.

The two young men watched for a while, reluctant to move. Then the church clocks gently struck one o'clock.

After he got back from Welwyn Garden City, Ma Wei waited patiently for a time to chat with Mary, but the chance never arose.

One evening, Mrs Wedderburn had rather a headache, and went to bed early. Mr Ma had gone out after dinner, telling no one where he was going. Mary was sitting alone in the drawing room, holding Napoleon, and, with a gloomy face, telling the dog her troubles. Ma Wei gave a cough outside the door, then pushed the door open and went in.

'Hello, Ma Wei.'

'Ah, Mary, you didn't go out?' said Ma Wei, and came over to play with Napoleon.

'Ma Wei, would you help me?' asked Mary.

'How could I help you?' Ma Wei moved nearer to her.

'Tell me where Washington is, will you?' she said, with a forced smile.

'I don't know. Honest.'

'Never mind. If you don't know, it doesn't matter.' She pouted with disappointment.

'Mary,' he said, moving even closer. 'Mary, are you still in love with Washington? Couldn't you give someone who really loves you a break?'

'I hate him.' Mary drew herself back from Ma Wei. 'I hate you men.'

'There are some good men.' Ma Wei reddened a little, and his heart was pounding.

Mary giggled, most unnaturally. 'You go and buy a bottle of wine, Ma Wei, and we'll have a drink, eh? I'm awfully fed up. In fact, I'm nearly at my wit's end!'

'All right, I'll go and buy one. What do you want to drink?'

'Anything'll do, long as it's strong. I don't know anything about wines.'

Ma Wei nodded, put his hat on, and went out.

'Ma Wei, my cheeks are all red. They're ever so hot. You feel them.'

Ma Wei felt Mary's cheeks, and, sure enough, they were very hot.

'Let's feel yours.' Mary's eyes were extraordinarily bright and shiny, and her cheeks were red, like cherry-apple blossoms in the morning sun.

He clasped her hand, his whole body trembling, and a stream of heat flowing across his back. He picked up her hand, like some piece of cotton wool, and put it to his lips. The back of her hand rose lightly to meet his mouth . . . Still holding her hand, he put his other arm round her, and moved his lips to hers.

The heat of her cheeks and her shoulders enveloped him, and he lost all awareness of anything else, and could only hear the leaping of his heart. He put all the vigour of his being into the kiss, and she, too, embraced him so tightly it were as though they'd become one person. His lips, hot, forceful, pressed down, while hers, fragrantly tender, soft and smooth, pushed back. His feet and legs had lost all warmth.

Unconsciously, he bent forwards and brought his lips down yet firmer, burning with emotion. She, with eyes closed and face upturned, held her body close to his.

And then she opened her eyes, and gently pushed his face away with her hands. He stepped back, almost fainting.

She poured another glass of wine down her throat, drinking with great ferocity, licked her lips most fearsomely, then stood up and looked at Ma Wei.

'Ha ha! Why, it's you – little Ma Wei. I thought you were Washington. You'll do, though, Ma Wei. Give me another kiss. Here.' She put her head on one side, and proffered him her right cheek.

Ma Wei stepped back, dumbfounded. 'Are you drunk, Mary?' he asked, trembling.

'No, I'm not drunk. You must be, though!' She swayed across to him. 'Fancy you having the cheek to kiss me! You!'

'Mary!' He took her hand.

She let him hold it, bent her head and laughed like mad. She laughed and laughed, and then her voice changed, and she began to cry.

All this while, Napoleon had been looking at them, wondering what the dickens was going on. Suddenly he pricked up his little ears, and gave two barks. And Mr Ma opened the door and came in.

At the sight of their expressions, Mr Ma was flabbergasted, and lost himself in thought for a long moment, the outcome of which was that he lost his temper.

'Ma Wei! What on earth is going on!' asked Mr Ma in a tone of righteous indignation.

Ma Wei didn't reply.

Mary said nothing, just let Ma Wei help her downstairs.

Ma Wei felt a terrible ache of distress, as if he'd been stabbed, and was filled with remorse that he'd ever drunk wine with Mary. It pained him to think of the way she'd treated him, and his heart filled with bitterness as he realised she had no understanding of his love. Yet he recalled the fragrant hue of the few minutes past, those tender lips, and felt . . . terrible. Not bothering about his father, he went straight upstairs.

Mr Ma was in quite a state. Ever since Mrs Wedderburn had turned him down, he'd been boiling with wrath inside, but up till now he'd had nowhere to spill it. Now that this opportunity had presented itself, he was determined to pick a fight with Ma Wei.

He drank all the wine that they'd left, and, his rage thus fortified, went upstairs to see his son.

Ma Wei was quite safe, though, having locked his door. Mr Ma knocked, to no avail, and stamped his feet in vain, unable to get in.

'I shall see you tomorrow morning, Ma Wei. We must have a talk tomorrow! You have no business getting young ladies drunk, nor holding hands with them! Have you no shame? I shall see you tomorrow!'

Ma Wei uttered not a peep.

III

Mᴿ Mᴀ had a good and peaceful night's sleep, and slept all his anger away. The next morning, his stomach felt very empty, and all he could think of was breakfast, so he forgot all about his reckoning with Ma Wei.

After breakfast, he adjourned to the study to smoke his pipe, and it never occurred to him that Ma Wei would actually seek him out. But in came his son, frowning, his face set, with not the slightest sign of meekness in his eyes.

Mr Ma summoned back his anger of the previous evening. *I'd forgotten about it,* he told himself, *but he's got the nerve actually to come and see me! Right then, we'll have it out, you cocky young fellow!*

Looking at his father, Ma Wei could see nothing that failed to evoke his loathing, and Mr Ma, for his part, had decided that his son merited a minimum of three hundred strokes with the military rod. Neither had ever hated anyone so much before, but today it were as if some gust of evil cosmic energy, blown in from beyond the skies, was making them more and more furious as they looked at one another.

'Right, Dad,' said Ma Wei, speaking first, 'shall we talk things over then?'

'Very well!' Sucking on his pipe, Mr Ma squeezed out the words between his teeth.

'We'll discuss the business first, shall we?' asked Ma Wei.

'No, let's discuss the young ladies first, shall we?' Mr Ma gave his son a very acerbic look.

Ma Wei's face went pale, and he smiled sardonically. 'Yes,' he said, 'young ladies and not so young ladies . . . As far as women are concerned, Dad, neither of us have a leg to stand on.'

Mr Ma gave a couple of coughs, and said nothing. His face slowly reddened.

'Shall we discuss the business, then?' asked Ma Wei.

'Business – it's always business! Anyone would think that I had a head made for nothing but business!' said Mr Ma impatiently.

'Why shouldn't we mention business?' asked Ma Wei, glaring at his father. 'The shop's our livelihood, our bread and butter. We've got to thrash it out properly today – once and for all!'

'You, you young puppy! You dare to glare at me! You dare to tell me to my face what I should do! It's my shop – you needn't concern yourself. No need for you to trouble yourself about it!' Mr Ma was really worked up. He'd never allowed himself to fly off the handle at Ma Wei before.

'So, I'm not to trouble myself with it. Fine, then. We'll see who *does* trouble himself about it, then! And anyone who does is a bl—'

Not wanting to swear, Ma Wei pushed open the door and marched out.

Once outside the house, Ma Wei wondered where he should go. If he didn't go to the shop, he'd be wasting a day's trade. And to go to the shop would irritate him no end, after his father's words.

Suppressing his anger, he decided he'd have to go to the shop after all. All said and done, his father was still his father, and, anyhow, the business wasn't just his father's. If the shop collapsed, they'd both be doomed. Nothing else for it. Why did he have to have such a father?

London was a huge place, but Ma Wei felt very alone. There were seven million people in the city, but who among them was even aware of his existence? Who had any sympathy for him? His own father didn't understand him, had even cursed him. Mary rejected him, and he hadn't got any real friends who understood and appreciated his way of thinking. He felt terribly miserable and lonely, even though London was such a bustling, busy place. He had nowhere to go, even though there were four hundred cinemas in London, sixty-odd theatres, so many museums and art galleries, tens of thousands of shops and countless houses. He had nowhere to go. Everything looked so bleak and desolate. Everything he heard made him feel weepy. He'd lost the greatest treasure of humankind: love.

As he sat in the shop, listening to the noise of traffic in the streets and the sounds of the bells of St Paul's, he knew that he was still in the thriving, prosperous city of London, yet he felt as wretched as a solitary wanderer in the Gobi Desert, or a marooned sailor on a desert island, with only a flock of wild birds for company.

He tried to shake himself, to suppress his melancholy. *Go off, go dancing, go to the theatre, go and watch a game of football, go and see a film. Argh, I can't leave this shop! No one to give me a hand, and nobody could care less about me than my father! Make a complete break with him? Don't want that, though. Ignore him, but don't go dancing or out on the town either. Instead, just get down to your study and work, and try to reap some knowledge and experience from the misery of it all. Easier said than done. Emotions often get the better of intellect. When you're so worked up, you can't get stuck into your reading.*

If only Mary loved me, thought Ma Wei. *If I could just kiss her once a day, hold her hand every day, be with her and chat with her, nothing else would bother me. I'd get stuck into my work and studying, and share all my happiness with her. Perhaps my dad's thinking the same sort of thing, longing for Mrs Wedderburn. Well, sod him! Poor old Mary. She's longing for Washington just like I long for her. The things people do for love. There's never any system, never any certainty. The world's just one big net, trapping us all. Everybody wants to break out, trying to slip through it, but we all end up dying in the net. There's no way out. Human beings are feeble creatures, and our aspirations are useless!*

No, aspirations are mighty things, made of iron and steel. Anybody can be a hero if only he hacks through hardship and the silk strands of emotion with the steel blade of willpower. Ma Wei bunched his fist, and gave his chest a couple of thumps. *Get moving. Take action! Forward march! What's loneliness? A figment of your emotions!*

What's weakness? The lack of clear goals.

An old woman came in and asked Ma Wei whether he sold China tea. He forced a smile, and saw her out.

There's business for you! Can't blame my father for hating business. Do you sell tea? Bloody hell, no, we don't!

Li Tzu-jung's the only happy person I know, thought Ma Wei. *He looks at things as they are, just the tiny bits in front of his nose, and ignores everything else, and as a result he hasn't got a care or worry. He's like a lion that exerts itself as much to catch a deer as to catch a rabbit, and is equally pleased with either. As longs as it catches something, whether it's big or small doesn't matter.*

Li Tzu-jung's a giant character because he's able to create a world of his own. In that world there's only work, no ideals; only men and women, no love; only material things, no illusions; colours but no fine arts. He's happy, though, and anybody who can manage to be happy is a hero.

Ma Wei didn't see eye to eye with Li Tzu-jung, but he greatly admired and respected him. He wished he could be like him, but it was no good, he could never do it.

'Hello, Ma Wei!' shouted Alexander outside the window, his voice making the glass tremble. 'Where's you father?'

He opened the door, almost pushing it off its hinges, and came in. His nose was exceptionally red, and the smell of beer on his breath was like that from an open keg. He wore a new reddish-grey overcoat, and, as he stood there, he looked the image of a small mountain at sunset.

'My father's not here yet. Why?' Ma Wei shook Alexander's big hand. Alexander's thumb was every bit as big as Ma Wei's wrist.

'All right, then I'll give this to you, eh.' Alexander pulled out ten one-pound notes, and, as he handed them to Ma Wei, said, 'He told me to put some money on a couple of horses for him. One horse won, and the other lost. This is the balance of what I've still got to give him.'

'Does my father often bet?' asked Ma Wei.

'Need you ask? You Chinamen all love a flutter, what!' said Alexander. 'I say, Ma Wei, is your father really getting married to

Mrs Wedderburn? That day when he'd had a few, he told me he was going to go and buy the ring. Is it true?'

'No, couldn't possibly be. How could an English woman marry a Chinaman, what?' said Ma Wei, smiling sarcastically, with a bitter tone in his voice.

Alexander glanced at Ma Wei, and creased his big lips in a smile. 'Better for both of 'em if they don't get married. Better for both of 'em,' he said. 'Might I ask if your father told you whether he'd be going to the film studios today?'

'No. What would he be doing there?' asked Ma Wei.

'There you are, you see! The Chinese are always so secretive. Your father's agreed to help me make a film. Should be going there today. He mustn't forget.'

Ma Wei felt he hated his father more than ever.

'Is he at home?' asked Alexander.

'I don't know.' Ma Wei's reply was curt.

'See you soon, Ma Wei.' So saying, Alexander rolled his mountainous self out the door.

'Gambling, drinking, buying wedding rings and making films, and he didn't tell me a thing about any of it,' Ma Wei muttered to himself. 'All right, then! You needn't tell me. We'll see what we'll see when the time comes.'

IV

APRIL'S FINE rain, suddenly coming and going, washed the air clean and fresh. The tender leaves of the trees were still very small, but everywhere there was a hint of green. The shy spring sun ventured a few soft rays from the thin clouds, and the shadows of people and trees on the ground were very pale. The almond blossoms were the first to come out, pale pink and swaying in the breeze like bright-eyed little village girls dressed with simple charm.

The football and so forth had now come to an end, and people were beginning to discuss the spring season's horseracing. Sport is the most vital part of the English education, and is also an indispensable feature of English life in general. The Englishman derives from sport a great deal of discipline, obedience, patience, orderliness and team spirit.

Ma Wei had given up sport, and neither went rowing nor for any brisk walks. Day in day out, he sat at home or in the shop, brooding and feeling miserable. He saw nothing of Miss Ely, nor did Mary take much notice of him either. He was always carrying a book but couldn't keep at his studies, and the very sight of the gold lettering on the book cover would make him bitterly reproach himself. Li Tzu-jung didn't come often to the shop, either. And when he did, they struggled to make conversation.

Mr Ma was planning to sell the antique business and give the money to Manager Fan of the Top Graduate restaurant, to help him expand his restaurant's trade. In that way, Mr Ma would become a kind of shareholder and wouldn't need to bother about anything, just wait for his portion of the dividends. Ma Wei disagreed with the plan, and there were a good number of rows between father and son on that score.

Besides such actual troubles, Ma Wei also felt spiritually depressed. As springtime flourished, he grew ever more mentally and physically out of sorts, inexpressibly miserable. Such unhappiness is a heritage from primitive man, and at certain seasons it shoots forth its leaves and buds, just as the flowers do.

His overcoat felt too heavy now, so he wore a raincoat to the shop. When he reached St Paul's, he stood dumbly, gazing at the golden pinnacle of the bell tower. He loved looking at it.

'Ma, old mate!' Li Tzu-jung grabbed hold of him from behind. Ma Wei turned his head and looked round. Li Tzu-jung had a very flustered air, and his face was paler than usual.

'Ma, old mate,' Li Tzu-jung said again, 'don't go to the shop!'

'Why? What's up?' asked Ma Wei.

'You go home. Give me the keys to the shop.' Li Tzu-jung was speaking quickly and urgently.

'What's the matter?' asked Ma Wei.

'The workmen from the East End are going to smash your shop up. You hurry back home. I know how to handle them.' Li Tzu-jung stretched out his open hand, demanding the keys from Ma Wei.

'Fine!' Ma Wei suddenly perked up. 'I feel like a fight. Smash up the shop, eh? They'll have to take me on first!'

'No, old Ma – you go back home. Leave it all to me. I'm a good friend, aren't I? And you trust me, don't you?'

'Yes, I do. Like an elder brother. But I can't let you go there on your own. What if they attack you?'

'They won't. But if you're hanging around, it'll be all the more difficult to deal with them. You go – you go. Off you go, Ma Wei.' Li Tzu-jung was still holding out his hand for the keys.

Ma Wei shook his head. 'No,' he said between clenched teeth, 'I can't go, old Li. Couldn't think of letting you get hurt. It's our shop. I've got to take the responsibility. I'll give them a fight. Fed up with life, I am, and in the mood for a good old scrap . . .'

'Are you trying to send me spare, Ma Wei?' said Li Tzu-jung, spluttering frantically.

'Would you mind telling me just why they want to smash up our shop?' asked Ma Wei with a bitter smile.

'No time to explain. They've already started out from the East End,' said Li Tzu-jung, rubbing his hands together fretfully.

'I'm not scared. Come on, tell me,' said Ma Wei adamantly.

'No time. You clear off!'

'Right, if you won't tell me, then *you* clear off, old Li! And I'll have a go at them on my own.'

'I can't do that, old Ma! How could I leave you in the lurch like this? What sort of a creature do you take me for?' Li Tzu-jung spoke so earnestly that Ma Wei relented. In the space of this one exchange, Ma Wei realised that Li Tzu-jung wasn't just some ordinary fellow with a knack for business and earning money, but that he was a real, gutsy hero into the bargain. He felt as if he'd glimpsed Li Tzu-jung's very heart, which was as warm and honest as his words.

'Hey, old Li, how about we both go?'

'Well, you'll have to promise me one thing: whatever happens, you mustn't let them see you. Only move into action if you hear me call you to come out and fight. Otherwise, you're not to take a step outside the back room. Agree to those conditions?'

'All right. I'll take my orders from you. I don't know what to say, old Li. Just for our sake, you're —'

'Get a move on – cut the sentimental stuff. No time for that!' Li Tzu-jung dragged Ma Wei into the little street where the shop was. 'Open the door, and take down the shutters! Quick!'

'What? And get everything nice and ready for them to come and smash up the lot?' asked Ma Wei, with a look of indignation on his face.

'Forget the questions. You just do whatever I tell you. Switch the light on, but leave the back room light off. Right – you get in there, and you're not to come out unless you hear me call you. Sit by the telephone, and if you hear me clap my hands once, phone the police and tell them there's a robbery taking place here. No need to ring a number: just ask for the police station. Got that?'

Reeling all his instructions off in one breath, Li Tzu-jung frantically stowed a few of the more valuable things from the shop in the safe. Then he seated himself next to the display shelves without a sound, like some great general guarding a city.

Ma Wei sat in the back room, his heart thumping. Not that he was afraid of a fight, but he just didn't like waiting for it. He stealthily rose to his feet, and took a look at Li Tzu-jung. That made him feel calmer. Li Tzu-jung was sitting there absolutely motionless, as steady and sure as some old Buddhist monk in meditation. *With a friend like that,* thought Ma Wei, *there's nothing to be afraid of, is there?*

'Sit down, old Ma!' Li Tzu-jung issued a command. Ma Wei went back and sat down quite mechanically.

Four or five minutes later, a Chinese man with a flat cap appeared outside the window, peering in a sinister way into the shop. Li Tzu-jung stood up, and pretended to be tidying the goods on the shelves. Shortly afterwards, a good few flat-capped Chinese men came crowding up to the window, speaking and gesticulating wildly. Li Tzu-jung couldn't make out clearly what they were saying. All he could hear were the long drawn-out ends of their Cantonese sentences: '. . . ouuuu!', '. . . louuuu!', '. . . ouuuu!'

Crash! A chunk of brick knocked a big hole in the windowpane. Li Tzu-jung clapped his hands, and Ma Wei picked up the telephone. *Crash!* Another brick hurtled through.

Li Tzu-jung cast a glance back at Ma Wei, then slowly walked towards the door.

Crash! Two bricks came flying in together, bringing with them a host of glass splinters that made them look like two comets. One fell right at Li Tzu-jung's feet, and the other hurtled to the display shelves and smashed a vase.

Li Tzu-jung got to the door. The men outside were now trying to enter. As they attempted to barge their way in, Li Tzu-jung pushed back against the doorknob with great force. Then all of a sudden, he let go, and three or four of them came tumbling inside and landed in a heap.

With one leap, Li Tzu-jung jumped on top of the uppermost

man, straddling him, and treading with one foot on the neck of the man underneath.

'Ow!' 'Argh!' '. . . louu!' The men beneath him were shouting, making the weirdest noises. Sitting on them, he was pushing down as hard as he could while they were heaving upwards for all they were worth. He knew that he couldn't keep it up for much longer. He shouted to the men still outside the door.

'Chow, Hong, Lee Sam-hing! Pan Kow-lei! This is my shop! It's my shop! What are you up to?' He was shouting in Cantonese. He knew the men from his work as an interpreter. All the East End Chinese knew him too.

Hearing Li Tzu-jung call them by name, the men outside didn't push their way in, but instead just looked at one another, as if they didn't know what to do. Seeing that he'd shocked them into inaction, Li Tzu-jung jumped backwards off the pile of men, tumbling to the floor. As he scrambled to his feet, they did too, and Li Tzu-jung planted himself squarely in front of them, barring their way.

'Run! Run!' Li Tzu-jung yelled at them, waving his hands. 'The police'll be here any minute! Run!'

The men turned and shot a look towards the end of the street, where already a bunch of onlookers was gawping. But it was still early morning, and there weren't many people about. The Chinese men looked at each other once more, hesitant and wavering, and Li Tzu-jung let them have another. 'Run!'

One of them ran off, and the others, without a word, took to their heels too.

Just then, the police arrived at the end of the street, caught a couple of them and carted them off. But all the rest had managed to escape.

The lunchtime issues of the evening papers all bore the big headlines:
EAST END CHINESE RIOT AT ANTIQUES SHOP
EAST END CHINESE LAWLESS
STARTLING ROBBERY CASE
GOVERNMENT MUST TAKE STEPS TO CONTROL CHINESE

Photographs of the Mas' antiques shop, and of Ma Wei, appeared on the front page of the newspapers, and the *Evening Star* even printed under Ma Wei's photo the words 'Hero whose fighting fists routed the gangsters'. Crowd upon crowd of newspaper reporters turned up with their cameras to interrogate Ma Wei, and some of them even found their way to Gordon Street to interview Mr Ma. Their published reports of his words were 'Me no say. Me no speak', although Mr Ma had used no such language. When the newspapers report the English spoken by Chinese, they always use that kind of rubbishy nonsense style, otherwise readers wouldn't believe the articles. The English have no gift for languages, so they can never imagine that a foreigner might be able to speak good English.

The affair shook the whole city. Two extra squads of police were drafted to the East End to keep an eye on the movements of the Chinese. That same evening, a Member of Parliament questioned the home secretary as to why he didn't expel all the Chinese from the country.

From noon till the shop closed, there was a cluster of people outside the Mas' antiques shop, and within three hours Ma Wei sold more than fifty pounds' worth of goods.

Mr Ma was so frightened that he didn't dare set foot outside the house all day, and he waited eagerly for Ma Wei's return so that he could see whether in fact his son had been hurt in the fighting. At the same time he resolved to shut up shop, lest sooner or later his own head be knocked off by a flying brick.

There were two men standing outside the front door of Gordon Street all day. According to Mrs Wedderburn, they were plain-clothes detectives. Mr Ma grew more nervous and even stopped smoking, for fear the detectives might glimpse the sparks from the bowl of his pipe.

V

THE CHINESE workmen in London are divided into two factions. One of these is prepared to take any work that's offered, whether it's decent work or not. When the film company was looking around for cringing Chinamen, it went to this mob. The other group consists of hard workers, men of resolute and independent disposition, who, although illiterate, unable to speak English and possessing no trade skills, are truly patriotic, and would rather starve than do anything that might lose face for their country.

The men of both parties share a coarseness of manner, a limited knowledge and a miserable existence. Where they differ is that one party is solely interested in earning its daily bread, no matter how, while the other wants to earn its daily bread in a decent way. Neither party has any time for the other, and when their adherents meet they at once start fighting. When unpatriotic dolts meet patriotic dolts, there'll be fighting, no two ways about it. And as soon as they fight, they provide the foreigners with lots of funny stories, and nasty things get said about both patriotic and unpatriotic alike.

It's not their fault, though. The blame lies with the Chinese government for choosing to ignore these men. If a government affords no protection or assistance to its subjects, those subjects are easy targets, aren't they?

The Chinese students in England are also divided into two factions. One faction comes from China proper, while the other consists of the offspring of overseas Chinese. All love their mother country, China, while failing to comprehend the state in which that country is. The offspring of the overseas Chinese, having been born outside China, are ignorant of the state of affairs within the country. The students from China proper are forever trying to make foreigners understand China without having realised that while China's so feeble, there's no way foreigners will respect it or its people. Nations of the same stature are like brothers. But the little mouse needn't try getting chummy with the tiger.

It's become an established historical tradition to sneer at the Chinese in foreign films, plays and novels. On the Chinese stage, it's an established historical tradition that the actor playing Ts'ao Ts'ao, the warlord who lived in the second century AD, is always made up with lead-white face paint, which signifies treachery. Just as there could never be a Ts'ao Ts'ao with black make-up, the colour of integrity, there could never be a good Chinese person on the English stage. Such things aren't a matter of feeling, they're historical.

The English don't set out to belittle anyone, but seek to create a fine piece of literature. If a Chinese playwright had a black-faced Ts'ao Ts'ao in his play, everybody would ridicule him for his ignorance. If a foreigner wrote a play about the Chinese that didn't include murder and arson, people would naturally ridicule him in the same way. There's no hope for Ts'ao Ts'ao, and it's not likely that his face will change colour in the next few years. But there's still some hope for China. If only the Chinese can strengthen their nation, the foreigners will drop their pens and cease writing 'Chinese' plays. Humans abuse the weak and fear the strong.

The film that Alexander had persuaded Mr Ma to act in had been written by one of England's most celebrated literary figures. This gentleman was perfectly aware that the Chinese are a civilised people, but to suit others' attitudes and for the sake of art, he nonetheless depicted the Chinese as cruel and sinister. Had he not done so, he would have found it impossible to earn people's praise and approbation.

The film was set in Shanghai, and Alexander had provided all the detail for the sets. One street represented the foreign concessions, and another represented the Chinese part of the city. The former was clean, beautiful and orderly, and the latter was filthy, chaotic, and thoroughly dark and dismal.

As to the story, it concerned a Chinese girl's falling in love with an Englishman. Her father wants to kill her as punishment, but, for some odd reason, the old Chinaman takes poison himself. Upon his death, his friends and relatives seek to avenge him. They bury the girl alive, and after the burial, go off and seek out the young Englishman. He and some British soldiers get stuck into them, and beat them until they beg for mercy on bended knees. The workmen from the East End played the crowd of Chinese who got thrashed. Mr Ma played a rich Chinese merchant with a little pigtail, who, while the fight was in progress, stood by watching the fun and excitement.

When the Chinese students in London heard about the film, they were up in arms, held conference after conference, and requested the legation to make a protest. The legation duly protested, and the following day the film's screenwriter said some very nasty things about the Chinese legation in the newspapers. Saying such things about another nation's legation should in fact call for a stern response, but since China would never dare start a war, why respond?

Seeing that the sole effect of the legation's protest had been to elicit abuse, the students held another conference to discuss what was to be done. The chairman of the conference was the Mr Mao who'd been given a punching in the Top Graduate. It was Mr Mao's opinion that a protest was of no use, and the only thing to do was stop any Chinese person from acting in the film. The students elected Mr Mao their representative to go to the East End and communicate their decision. The workmen – those of the unpatriotic faction – had already signed a contract with the film company, and there was no means of going back on the agreement, so Mr Mao incited the doltishly patriotic workmen to declare war on those who were going to act in the film.

Mr Ma was, of course, not one of them, and what's more, he ran a shop and was well provided for, yet was still prepared to do such a shameful thing. For this the workmen held him in particular loathing, and everyone advocated smashing up his shop and wiping the floor with him. The students put forward the idea, and the foolish workmen agreed to go and carry it out. Which was how the Mas' shop got some bricks as customers.

Li Tzu-jung got wind of the matter in advance but didn't want to go and tell Ma Wei. He knew full well that Mr Ma was acting in the film not for a few pounds, but because Alexander had asked him to and he couldn't refuse; the Chinese are so concerned with face. (He'd no idea that Mr Ma had wanted the money to buy a wedding ring.) He knew full well that if he told Ma Wei, it would inevitably stir up a dispute between father and son. And he knew full well that if he went and had a word with the workmen, he could end up with a black eye for his troubles. Nor would it have been any use going and having a word with the students, since they were only concerned with patriotism, and took no account of realities. So he'd said nothing.

When the matter had nearly come to a head, an idea occurred to him: tell Mr Ma and son not to show their faces, while he himself went to deal with the workmen. In that way, danger would be avoided. It would give the workmen the chance to smash some glass and vent their temper, and of course the insurance company would pay for all the damage. At the same time, it would make the Mas' antiques shop famous, which would be very promising for future sales prospects. The main thing in business nowadays is publicity, and such an exciting incident would render Mr Ma and son celebrities. It would be a kind of free advertisement. As for the workmen, Li Tzu-jung had no wish to land them in prison, or make them suffer in any way. Their conduct was misguided, but the outlook behind it was reasonable. That was why he'd waited before asking Ma Wei to telephone the police, giving the workmen enough time to smash the window and make a quick escape.

It had never occurred to him that the police might catch two of the men.

It had never occurred to him that Mr Ma might be so scared that he would decide to sell the shop.

It had never occurred to him that the students' association might pass a resolution that would make trouble for Ma Wei.

It had never occurred to him that the workmen, in revenge for the arrest of two of their number, might want to knock off Mr Ma.

Nor had it occurred to him that, the film's release being imminent, the newspapers might deliberately play up the dire warning its story embodied, and use the incident to make all sorts of sneering innuendos concerning the legation's protest.

After the incident, he purposely kept out of the way to ensure that it was Ma Wei's photo they printed in the newspapers, which he thought would be a kind of advertisement. But who would have guessed it? When the Chinese in London saw the photograph, they all ground their teeth and cursed Ma Wei.

The ways of this world are complex, and nobody can think of everything, can they? But Li Tzu-jung, having been a self-confident person, now felt tremendously bitter and angry at himself.

Ma Wei understood Li Tzu-jung, and was resolved to carry on with the business no matter who reviled him, and no matter how much they wanted to beat him up. The opportunity was here now, and, come what may, he had to try making a go of things. He'd had no idea of what his father had been up to, and the arrest of the workmen was no fault of his, anyway. He had nothing on his conscience and wanted to forge ahead and get things moving. That was the only way he could do right by Li Tzu-jung.

It didn't occur to him that his father might be so pathetic and devoid of courage as to insist on selling the shop. What, sell the shop? But if he wanted to sell it, no one could stop him. The shop was his.

Mr Ma, unable to understand why anyone should wish to beat him up, spent every day with his scrap of moustache scrumpled up tightly, sighing away at the wickedness of the world. It made no sense to him that Ma Wei had actually acquired a new enthusiasm for the shop and was really getting down to business, and he could only conclude that Li Tzu-jung must have hypnotised Ma Wei. Worried about his son's safety, he felt, at the same time, extremely resentful towards Li Tzu-jung. He was puzzled as to why Mrs Wedderburn had congratulated him and told him that things looked bright for the shop's trade from now on.

So the bloody shop's been smashed in, he said to himself, *and yet things look bright for it? I don't know what goes on in these foreigners' minds!*

Alexander came to visit once, and he, too, said the same thing: 'Ma, old chap, you're made! The insurance company'll compensate you for the stuff that was smashed. Your shop's famous now. Hurry and get some goods in. Don't let the opportunity slip, what!'

Mr Ma just couldn't understand it at all.

In the evening, he stealthily went to see Manager Fan of the Top Graduate, firstly to discuss the sale of the antiques shop, and secondly to beg Manager Fan to try to make peace with the East End workmen for him. He would gladly give ten pounds apiece to the two workmen who'd been arrested. Manager Fan agreed to help him, and to top it off cooked him a dish of stuffed dumplings, and opened a bottle of grape wine for him. After a glassful of wine and two well-filled dumplings, Mr Ma let fall a tear of happiness.

On arriving home that night, he saw Ma Wei in cheerful conversation with Mrs Wedderburn and daughter, and felt rather jealous. The two ladies were treating Ma Wei like some hero, and suddenly looked down their noses at Mr Ma. He felt quite resentful towards them, especially Mrs Wedderburn. He sorely regretted he couldn't drag her over and give her a couple of kicks, but he very much doubted whether he'd in fact get the better of her if it came to a fight. Foreign women are strong. What was even more infuriating was that Napoleon had stopped greeting him these last few days; Mr Ma hadn't dared go out in the daytime lately, so hadn't been able to take the Peke for a stroll. At the very sight of him, Napoleon had started to give a sneer.

There was nothing else for it but to go to bed, and bemoan his troubles to his late wife in his dreams . . . But he never saw her in his dreams.

VI

MA WEI stood on the pavement at Marble Arch. The sun had long since set, and the people in the park had all gone. Before him he saw three shadows: a hopeless father, a faithful and sincere Li Tzu-jung, and a lovable Mary. He and his father couldn't get along, and Mary refused his love. All he could do was let Li Tzu-jung down. It was time to clear off and leave the lot of them.

It was still dark in the room as he stood silently by Li Tzu-jung's bed. The sound of Li Tzu-jung's breathing was very even, and he slept like an innocent child. Ma Wei stood there some time, then quietly called, 'Tzu-jung!'

Li Tzu-jung didn't wake up. A warm tear from Ma Wei's eye fell onto Li Tzu-jung's bedclothes.

'See you again sometime, Tzu-jung.'

How wretched and gloomy London was now that its people were all deep in sleep. The gas lamps still burned, shining with a lonely light, a deathly-pale glimmer. London seemed ghostly, with only those few lamps keeping their silent vigil. Watching; watching what? There wasn't anything to see. London was dead, and didn't even have a soul.

In another hour or two, London would spring to life once more. But Ma Wei didn't wait to see it.

'See you again sometime, London!'

'See you again!' a voice seemed to answer.

But whose?

NOTES

Pinyin transliterations of Chinese names and expressions have been bracketed next to their Wade-Giles equivalents where the latter has fallen out of use.

TEXT
PAGE

4   *revival of the Liberal Party*: The Liberal Party was the second largest political party in the UK in the nineteenth century but by the early twentieth century, they had lost much of their support as many voters went over to the Labour Party. The last majority Liberal government was elected in 1906.

13   *Fu-hsi*: First mythical Emperor of China who reigned over four thousand years ago. According to legend, he taught the people how to write, hunt and fish, and is said to have discovered the *I Ching*.

13   *President Yüan Shih-k'ai*: Yüan Shih-k'ai (Yuan Shikai) was the second president of the Republic of China. He proclaimed himself Emperor of China on 12 December 1915 but due to widespread opposition was forced to step down three months later on 22 March 1916.

22   *Methodist Congregational Mission*: Mission of the American Methodist Episcopal Church.

22   *Sun Yat-sen*: First president of the Republic of China.

22 *Three Principles of the People*: A philosophical doctrine developed by Sun Yat-sen that became an underlying tenet of the Kuomintang Party. The three principles are Nationalism, Democracy and the Livelihood of the People.

22 *National government*: The original National government, led by Sun Yat-sen based in Canton, was the southern rival to that of the northern Peiyang government during China's Warlord Era. After the death of Sun Yat-sen in 1925, the National government, under the leadership of Chiang Kai-shek, went on to nominally reunify China in 1928.

24 *Buddhist rituals of the reception, third requiem and the release of the flame-mouth, and the burial*: Buddhist funereal rites common to northern China consist of: reception, on the day of death, when the deceased is cleaned and dressed for the afterlife; third requiem, on the third day following reception, involving a series of rituals and celebrations to ensure the deceased a peaceful ascent to heaven, and release of the flame-mouth when the possessions of the departed are burned for use in the afterlife. The family of the deceased will also hold a simple feast to thank relatives and friends who have participated. Finally, burial marks the transport and interment of the body, which is usually accompanied by a procession with music or drums.

24 *'long three'*: A piece in Chinese dominoes making up two sets of three whereby the indentations are arranged in a diagonal line across the domino piece.

25 *Four Books*: The four philosophical primers: *Great Learning* by Tseng-tzu (Zeng Zi), *Doctrine of the Mean* by Tzu-ssu (Zi Si), *Analects* by Confucius, and *Mencius*, a collection of writings about the philosopher, Mencius, whose exact authorship is unclear.

25 *Liu-li-ch'ang*: Liu-li-ch'ang (Liulichang) is a quarter of old Peking that specialised in the trade of traditional Chinese crafts and antiques. The area has, in modern times, become a popular tourist destination.

25   *Ch'ien-men Gate:* The southern-most gate of Peking's historic city wall, Ch'ien-men (Qianmen) Gate was the main entrance to the city in former times.

25   *Shao-hsing wine:* A popular variety of fermented rice wine originating from modern-day Shao-hsing (Shaoxing), Chekiang province (Zhejiang), in eastern China.

25   *fried triangles:* A traditional Peking street food consisting of a fried triangle-shaped pastry wrapper filled with meat and vegetables.

29   *Ch'ing dynasty:* The last imperial dynasty of China, now referred to as the Qing dynasty, lasted from 1644 to 1912.

29   *circuit intendant:* An official rank in the imperial civil service, a circuit intendant was the head of a circuit, consisting of two or more territorial departments. A circuit intendant is one rank lower than what is now equivalent to a provincial mayor in the Communist government.

32   *Museum:* A station on the London Underground Central Line opened in 1900. It was closed in 1933 and a replacement station was opened at neighbouring Holborn.

40   *Confessions of an English Opium-Eater:* Thomas Penson De Quincey's autobiographical account of his experiences with opium, first published in 1821.

43   'The Moon Fairy Flees to the Moon': A saying derived from a popular legend about a woman who joins the ranks of the immortals and makes her home on the moon after her lover dies.

44   *Szechwan-silk:* Szechwan (Sichuan) province in southern China is known for its silk production.

45   *Great Beauty Restaurant:* A historic eatery established in 1808 in the Ch'ien-men Gate area of old Peking that originally specialised in Tz'u-chou (Suzhou) cuisine, but eventually grew to include dishes from both North and South China. See note to *Tz'u-chou* below for further explanation on Tz'u-chou.

45   *K'un-ch'ü opera:* One of the oldest forms of Chinese opera, it is considered the progenitor of Peking opera, from which the latter grew out of in the eighteenth century. K'un-ch'ü

(Kunqu) incorporates a mixture of drama, opera, ballet and poetry recital. See note to *Peking opera* for further explanation of Peking opera.

45   *Extending Virtue Theatre*: A Ming dynasty theatre located off Tashalai'erh (Dashilar) Street nearby Ch'ien-men Gate.

46   *Sincere Department Store*: Formerly one of the 'four great department stores' of Shanghai, the Sincere Department Store was opened in October 1917 on Nanking (Nanjing) Road in central Shanghai.

49   *Hsiang P'ien*: A popular variety of jasmine tea prized for its aromatic and fragrant taste, originating from Szechwan province.

52   *Yüeh Lao*: A mythical Chinese deity synonymous with marriage and love who appears at night to unite all predestined couples with a strand of silk.

57   *Four Archway Gates*: The name of a traditional architectural structure consisting of a series of four, three-arch gateways.

57   *po-po cakes*: A traditional northern-Chinese cake made from wheat or maize flour.

67   *kowtows*: A traditional bow of respect performed in a kneeling position, by the touching of the head to the floor, usually in sets of three.

85   *Shantung*: A coastal province in eastern China.

89   *Taoist philosopher*: is one of three primary schools of philosophy and religious tradition in China (the others being Confucianism and Buddhism) whose key text is the *Tao Te Ching*, attributed to Lao Tzu. Practitioners of Taoism underline the importance of living in harmony with Tao ('the way') and focus on meta-ethical issues and practices such as finding the path to ecstasy and immortality.

89   *Chuang Tzu*: An influential Taoist philosopher who lived in the fourth century BCE

90   *Man Friday*: The name of Robinson Crusoe's dependable sidekick from Daniel Defoe's *Robinson Crusoe*.

103   *Chiang-ning silk*: A tough, satin-like silk originating from Nanking (Nanjing).

107 *Kapok:* An organic cotton-like substance commonly used as stuffing.

107 *Tientsin:* After the Second Opium War, the Treaty of Tientsin was ratified by the Emperor of China in 1860, effectively opening up the city to foreign trade. Tientsin became a treaty port and a sizeable expatriate community established itself.

107 *Fukien lacquer:* Lacquerware originating from Fukien (Fujian) province in south-east China that was popular as a gift among royalty and foreign guests.

110 *old Chang:* Chang Tso-lin was the leader of the Feng-t'ien faction during China's Warlord Era. He became supreme ruler of Manchuria in 1920, and in 1926 managed to capture Peking and effectively declared himself leader of the republic a year later.

115 *Shanghai horseraces:* The original Shanghai Race Club was founded by the British in 1862 occupying what is now the People's Park and People's Square in central Shanghai. The spring and autumn race days were marked occasions in the annual sporting calendar, and gambling on the horses became a huge pastime for both the local and foreign communities.

147 *sempre legato:* Italian musical notation meaning to play continuously and smoothly.

108 *fortissimo:* Italian musical notation meaning to play loudly.

160 *The History of Mr Polly:* A comic novel written by H. G. Wells and published in 1910. Lao She has credited H. G. Wells as a source of inspiration for his writing.

162 *Gamages:* A popular department store located at Holborn Circus that opened in 1878 and closed in 1972.

163 *three immortals:* A popular name given to any dish based on three complementary ingredients of which shrimp is often a component.

166 *Mongol and Manchu books:* Mongolian and Manchurian traditions were effectively supplanted by local Han culture towards the end of the Ch'ing dynasty and were often regarded as lesser cultures.

167 *Field Marshal Chang*: See earlier note to *old Chang*.

167 *Field Marshal Kuo*: A commander under Chang Tso-lin, Field Marshal Kuo Sung-ling unsuccessfully led a three-month rebellion against his commanding officer in 1925.

168 *Twelve Heads*: A Ch'ing dynasty Manchu-to-Han pronunciation and transliteration guide that was used as a teaching aid for children.

168 *Chu-ke Liang*: A famous military strategist from the Three Kingdoms period synonymous with intelligence and strategic guile, who features in much Chinese literature and drama.

172 *I-hsing pot*: A type of traditional teapot used to brew tea. The teapot is made from I-hsing clay originating from Chiang-su (Jiangsu) province.

172 *Tz'u-chou*: A city close to Shanghai in Chiang-su province famed for its intricate private gardens and canals. Suzhou, as it is now called, has a rich cultural history and is known for its traditional crafts and industry.

172 *Ming*: The Ming dynasty was the last dynasty ruled by the ethnically Han Chinese, lasting from 1368 to 1644 BCE. Arts and crafts, particularly porcelain and lacquerware, flourished, and by the sixteenth century, an exclusive export market catering for European tastes had developed.

178 Asia *magazine*: A popular American magazine in the twenties and thirties that featured journalism about Asia and its people. Pearl S. Buck was an editor and eventual co-owner.

181 *Bernard Shaw*: George Bernard Shaw was a prolific Irish playwright and literary critic who wrote more than fifty plays. He continued to write through his nineties, leaving a final and unfinished play, *Why She Would Not*, upon his death at age ninety-four.

182 *London Missionary Society*: A non-denominational missionary society formed by Anglicans and nonconformists in 1795 whose presence expanded globally into a network of largely autonomous congregations.

188 *Peking opera*: An extremely popular operatic form in the Ch'ing dynasty that grew out of K'un-ch'ü opera in the eighteenth

century. Peking opera is characterised by a mixture of music, song, mime, dance and acrobatics.

188   *Hsi-p'i:* One of two principle melodies in Peking opera (the other being Erh-huang), generally characterised by a quick and lively tempo.

193   *School of Oriental Studies:* The University of London School of Oriental Studies, now known as the University of London School of Oriental and African Studies (SOAS).

200   *catty:* A catty is a Chinese unit of mass approximately equal to 500 grams.

217   *Grand Marshal of the Army:* Officially, the Grand Marshal of the Army and Navy was the highest military rank of the early Republic of China. Sun Yat-sen, Yüan Shih-k'ai and Chang Tso-lin were all grand marshals.

230   *Olympia:* An exhibition centre in West Kensington, London, first erected in 1886 as the National Agricultural Hall.

233   *Three Immortals convent:* A nunnery established since 1151 in the Buddhist monastery area of Pa-ta ch'u, to the north-west of old Peking.

245   *Lung Ching tea:* A popular variety of green tea from Hangchow (Hangzhou), China that was named an imperial tea by Emperor Kang-hsi in the Ch'ing dynasty.

245   *chop suey:* A dish invented in America by Chinese immigrants consisting of meat and eggs, stir-fried with sliced vegetables.

248   *windlasses:* A leveraging pulley system allowing the vertical transport of heavy objects, such as to bring water up from a well.

248   *'During the Festival of Pure Light, the rain is coming down wildly':* A famous line from the poem 'Ch'ing Ming' by the Tang dynasty poet, Tu Mu. Ch'ing Ming Festival is celebrated on the 104th day after the winter solstice, usually early April, to honour and tend to one's ancestral graves.

276   *hsiao-kua:* A traditional tight-fitting shirt

286   *if she goes to court:* See note to *breach of promise* below.

292   *Welwyn Garden City:* Founded in 1920, Welwyn Garden City was the second of England's Garden Cities, which were

originally designed as self-contained communities surrounded by green belts with equal proportions of residence, industry and agriculture

296   *breach of promise:* Informally known as 'heart balm', a man's promise of engagement to marry was considered a legally binding contract up to the early twentieth century. If he were to renege, he would be subject to litigation.

297   *the old city of Welwyn:* Welwyn lies over a kilometre to the north of Welwyn Garden City and is more commonly referred to as old Welwyn.

311   *Evening Star:* A local paper based in Ipswich, England began in 1885 as the *Star of the East*.

313   *Ts'ao Ts'ao:* A warlord, military genius and poet of the Three Kingdoms Period, he was frequently depicted as a cunning and deceitful man in classical opera, a persona that was popularised in the *Romance of the Three Kingdoms*.